Mixing Methods in Psychology

The acceptance of qualitative research methods in psychology has led to a split between qualitative and quantitative methods and has raised questions about how best to assess the validity of research practice. While the two approaches have traditionally been seen as competing paradigms, more recently, researchers have begun to argue that the divide is artificial.

Mixing Methods in Psychology looks in detail at the problems involved in attempting to reconcile qualitative and quantitative methods both within and across subjects. All angles of the debate are discussed, covering areas as diverse as health, education, social, clinical and economic psychology. The contributors, who are some of the leading figures in the field, present theoretical and methodological guidance as well as practical examples of how quantitative and qualitative methods can be fruitfully combined. By aiming to bridge the gap between the two methods, this book reveals how each can inform the other to produce more accurate theories and models of human behaviour.

This ground-breaking text will be essential reading for students and researchers wishing to combine methods, or for anyone who simply wants to gain a more thorough understanding of the debate.

Zazie Todd is a Lecturer in Psychology at the University of Leeds.
Brigitte Nerlich is a Senior Research Officer at the University of Nottingham.
Suzanne McKeown is a Sexual Health Promotion Specialist for the National Assembly for Wales.
David D. Clarke is head of the School of Psychology at the University of Nottingham.

Mixing Methods in Psychology

The integration of qualitative and quantitative methods in theory and practice

Edited by Zazie Todd, Brigitte Nerlich, Suzanne McKeown and David D. Clarke

Ψ Psychology Press
Taylor & Francis Group

HOVE AND NEW YORK

First published 2004
by Psychology Press
27 Church Road, Hove, East Sussex BN3 2FA

Simultaneously published in the USA and Canada
by Psychology Press
29 West 35th Street, New York, NY 10001

Psychology Press is a part of the Taylor & Francis Group

Typeset in Times by RefineCatch Ltd, Bungay, Suffolk
Printed and bound in Great Britain by Biddles Ltd, King's Lynn
Paperback cover design by Sandra Heath

This publication has been produced with paper manufactured to strict
environmental standards and with pulp derived from sustainable
forests.

British Library Cataloguing in Publication Data
A catalogue record for this book is available from the British Library

Library of Congress Cataloging in Publication Data
Mixing methods in psychology: the integration of qualitative and
quantitative methods in theory and practice / edited by Zazie Todd . . .
[et al.].
  p. cm.
Includes bibliographical references and index.
  ISBN 0-415-18649-8 (hbk.) – ISBN 0-415-18650-1 (pbk.)
  1. Psychology–Research–Methodology. I. Todd, Zazie.
BF76.5.M59 2004
150′.7′2–dc22   2003016650

ISBN 0-415-18649-8 (hbk)
ISBN 0-415-18650-1 (pbk)

Contents

Illustrations

Figures

Tables

Contributors

Sue Chilton is a Senior Lecturer in Economics and founder member of the Economics of Safety, Health, Environment and Risk (ESHER) Research group in the University of Newcastle upon Tyne Business School. She has published a wide range of articles on individual decision making under risk and uncertainty, the valuation of the environment, health and safety and on the use of qualitative research methods in economics. Current research interests include the integration of economic decision-making experiments and field surveys to gain insights into preferences over the environment and individual and societal welfare.

David Clarke is Professor of Psychology, and Head of The School of Psychology, at The University of Nottingham, England. He is Director of the "Action Analysis Group", and Co-Director of the "Accident Research Unit" within the School. He read Medical Sciences and Psychology at Cambridge, before doing a DPhil in Psychology at Oxford, and later a PhD in Social and Political Sciences at Cambridge. He is a Chartered Psychologist, a Fellow of the British Psychological Society, and the author of about 90 papers, chapters and books. His main research interest is sequence analysis and its application to various problems including behaviour in safety-critical situations, accidents, and violent crime. He is currently developing various extensions of sequence analysis methodology, including qualitative forecasting techniques, and "structured judgement" methods for real-time behavioural analysis.

Michael Cole is University Professor of Communication, Psychology and Human Development at the University of California. His research interests focus on the role of culture in human development.

Judith Covey is a Lecturer in Applied Psychology at University of Durham. Her main research interest is in the development and evaluation of methods for eliciting people's preferences.

David Crystal is an Associate Professor at Georgetown University. For the past 14 years he has studied cultural and developmental influences on children's reactions to human differences. His most recent research has focused on the physiological and psychological correlates of race-based playmate preferences in preschool children. Currently, he is investigating social reasoning about exclusion among children and adolescents.

Rom Harré began his academic career in mathematics, later turning to philosophy and psychology. He is Emeritus Fellow of Linacre College, Oxford and currently teaching at Georgetown and American Universities in Washington DC. His most recent publication is *Cognitive Science: A Philosophical Introduction* (Sage, 2002).

Karen Henwood is a Senior Lecturer in Clinical and Health Psychology, University of East Anglia, United Kingdom. She has undertaken research projects on gender and family relationships, masculinity and the body, and the meanings and non-economic values people attach to their natural environment. With Nick Pidgeon she has explored the role of qualitative methods in psychology and the social sciences. Her published work has appeared in journals such as *British Journal of Psychology*, *Feminism and Psychology*, *Theory and Psychology*, *Journal of Environmental Psychology*, and *Social Science and Medicine*. She has recently completed an ESRC funded project exploring the extent and potentials for development of qualitative research resources in UK social science.

Lorraine Hopkins pursued postgraduate studies in Economic Psychology at Exeter University and the University of Wales, Bangor where she was also research assistant to Professor Nick Pidgeon for a project funded by the Health and Safety Executive. Part of a multidisciplinary team of economists and psychologists, using both qualitative and quantitative methods, they investigated risk-taking behaviour in various contexts of safety. She has recently moved from the academic study of multidisciplinary approaches towards its application, partnering the creative and often assumed distinct, world of the arts with that of business. She continues to lecture part time at the University of Wales, Bangor in psychology, philosophy and qualitative methods.

Michael Jones-Lee is Professor of Economics and Co-Director of the Centre for the Analysis of Safety Policy and Attitudes to Risk (CASPAR) at the University of Newcastle upon Tyne. He has a longstanding interest in the economics of safety and has published widely on the subject. He has also acted as a consultant to a number of government departments and related agencies in the UK and abroad.

Margarita Lobeck was born in Dresden, East Germany, but has been living in the UK for the past five years. She has travelled extensively, being fascinated by different cultures. Living in Britain has made her become more aware of the fine balance of integration versus preservation of identity (she has still got her lederhosen in the cupboard, brought out on special occasions!). Margarita studied Dance Movement Therapy at Roehampton

Institute, London, has worked as an Assistant Psychologist for people suffering from eating disorders, and is currently training to be a Clinical Psychologist.

Graham Loomes is Professor of Economic Behaviour and Decision Theory. His research is focused on the analysis of preferences and decision making at University of East Anglia, with particular applications to health, safety and environmental issues. This involves the use of experimental techniques to aid the development of theory and methodology, and the conduct of surveys and field studies to apply the principles and methods to practical policy issues such as the monetary value to be attached to health and safety benefits.

Suzanne McKeown was a member of the Qualitative Methods Group while studying for a PhD at the Department of Psychology at Nottingham University. She has since worked as a senior reseach officer at Health Promotion Wales and now works at developing policy and strategy as the sexual health adviser for the Health Promotion Division at the National Assembly for Wales. Her particular interest is in the use of mixing qualitative and quantitative methods in evaluation of health promotion interventions.

Andy Miller is Educational Psychology Group Director and Special Professor of Educational Psychology at the University of Nottingham. He has also worked as a primary school teacher and an educational psychologist, specialising in this latter role in work with teachers, pupils and parents around the issue of difficult behaviour in schools.

Brigitte Nerlich is a Senior Research Officer at the Institute for the Study of Genetics, Biorisks and Society (IGBiS) at the University of Nottingham. Her most recent research focuses on the cultural and political contexts in which metaphors are used in the public and scientific debates about cloning, genetically modified food, the human genome project, designer babies, and foot and mouth disease.

Paula Nicolson is Professor in Health Psychology at the University of Sheffield and has been conducting qualitative research for over 20 years. She is a firm believer in mixing methods and that quantitative and qualitative data complement each other. She has conducted surveys, in-depth interviews, focus groups and used psychometric tests to explore the substantive areas of her research interests. These are gender, sexuality and reproductive health, and family relationships including violence, abuse and neglect.

Nick Pidgeon is Professor of Environmental Sciences and Director of the Centre for Environmental Risk, School of Environmental Sciences, University of East Anglia. He has published and edited a wide range of articles on the human and organisational causes of technical accidents, safety culture, perception and communication of risk, and on the use of qualitative research methods in psychology. Co-author of *Man-Made*

Disasters, 2nd ed., Butterworth Heinemann 1997 (with Barry Turner), and *Social Amplification of Risk*, Cambridge University Press 2003 (with Paul Slovic and Roger Kasperson).

Angela Robinson, Department of Economics, University of Newcastle Upon Tyne.

Anne Spencer, Department of Economics, Queen Mary and Westfield College, London.

Rex Stainton Rogers taught social-developmental psychology at the University of Reading. Sadly, he died in February of 1999 whilst at the peak of his career. Rex was a powerful and inspirational presence to all who knew him well. He was the key figure in developing Q methodology as a critical social psychological method. He enjoyed working collaboratively and his best known publications include: *Textuality and Tectonics: troubling social and psychological science* (Open University Press, 1994), which he wrote collectively (and, thanks to him and Wendy, in the most pleasurable of circumstances) with Chris Eccleston, Kate Gleeson, Nick Lee, Wendy Stainton Rogers, Paul Stenner and Marcia Worrell under the pseudonym of Beryl C. Curt; *Social Psychology: a critical agenda* (Polity Press, 1995) which he wrote with Paul Stenner, Kate Gleeson and Wendy Stainton Rogers; and *Stories of Childhood: shifting agendas of child concern* (Harvester Wheatsheaf, 1992) which was coauthored by Wendy Stainton Rogers. Apart from his intellectual work, Rex will also be remembered for his laughter, his love and his talent for opening up possibilities in the face of self-serving orthodoxy.

Paul Stenner lectures in the Department of Psychology, University College London. He did his doctoral work on the topic of the social constitution of emotion in general, and jealousy in particular, with Rex Stainton Rogers (and Christie Davies) at Reading University. From 1991 he lectured in social psychology at the University of East London before moving to the University of Bath to teach Science, Culture and Communication at Masters level. At UCL he teaches social psychology and specialises in critical and discursive approaches to the relationships between affect, ethics and identity, and in the history and philosophy of psychology. He can be contacted at p.stenner@ucl.ac.uk/020 7679 5391.

Zazie Todd is Lecturer in Social Psychology at the University of Leeds. She has taught qualitative (and, occasionally, quantitative) methods to a variety of groups, from clinical psychology trainees and educational psychologists to assorted health professionals. Her research on the psychology of metaphor, and on ludic reading, has adopted a mixed method approach.

Katie Vann has degrees in Philosophy, Interdisciplinary Social Science, and Communication Studies. She is currently a Postdoctoral Fellow at the Royal Netherlands Academy of Arts and Science.

Part I

Theoretical and historiographical foundations

1 Introduction

Zazie Todd, Brigitte Nerlich, and Suzanne McKeown

Synopsis and rationale

Qualitative methods has been a growth area in psychology in recent years. The many books introducing psychologists to qualitative research methods include Banister, Burman, Parker, Taylor, and Tindal's (1994) *Qualitative Methods in Psychology: A Research Guide* and Richardson's (1996b) edited BPS *Handbook of Qualitative Research Methods for Psychology and the Social Sciences*. At the same time, the debate over qualitative methods has continued to rage in the pages of *The Psychologist*.

In most cases, qualitative methods are seen as an alternative and competing paradigm to quantitative methods. The differences between the two approaches are illustrated by Bryman (1988), with quantitative research tending to use hard, reliable data, and to have a view of the social world as external to the observer, in contrast to qualitative methods which use rich data and see the social world as being constructed by the observer. Hammersley (1996) distinguishes two approaches to the qualitative–quantitative divide, neither of which he sees as an accurate conceptualisation: the idea of them as competing paradigms breaks down under closer scrutiny since neither position is always identified by a particular epistemological viewpoint or a particular kind of data; the alternative approach, that of a "methodological eclecticism" which sees the methods as equal but suitable for different purposes, can lead us to ignore some of the philosophical and theoretical issues which are nevertheless relevant to discussions of method.

There have been few books that attempt to bridge the gulf between the newer qualitative methods and the older, but still dominant, quantitative methods used in psychology and the social sciences. In this volume, we explore some of the issues around the qualitative–quantitative divide in psychology, looking at both the theoretical and practical considerations of a mixed-method approach.

Theoretical background: the split between quantitative and qualitative methods in psychology

To study the human being in all its aspects, psychologists make use of a range of methods. However, since the inception of psychology as a "science" in the nineteenth century, *quantitative* methods have been the favourite choice. They have even become, as Danziger calls it in analogy to Kant's categorical imperative, the "methodological imperative" (cf. Danziger, 1985). Since the end of the nineteenth century these methods have been increasingly refined by more and more complex types of statistics, and they have been adapted to computer technology.

However, since the 1960s some psychologists, especially those dealing with social phenomena, have become dissatisfied and disillusioned with the products of this purely quantitative approach to human nature, and have opted for a more *naturalistic, contextual* and *holistic understanding* of human beings in society. The methods they favour have come to be known as qualitative methods. They range from *ethnographic* fieldwork, especially participant observation or direct social observation in the context of *everyday life*, to structured and unstructured interviews, surveys, documentary historical research, and most prominently in recent years, various types of discourse and conversation analysis, personal construct work, action research, grounded theory, and feminist methodology (cf. Banister et al., 1994: 2). These methods focus on the *interpretative* (or *hermeneutic*) understanding of the *meaning* of human actions and institutions as against the purely quantitative measurement of human behaviour and cognition, its experimental study and the statistical generalisations drawn from it.

Quantitative and qualitative methods could "just" be possible *choices*, chosen to tackle certain psychological problems; instead they have become rather entrenched ideological or epistemological positions, also called *paradigms*. From the standpoint of those who choose quantitative methods, which are themselves modelled on and compatible with methods used in the natural sciences, using qualitative methods means debasing psychology as a "science". From the standpoint of those using predominantly qualitative methods, modelled on and compatible with methods used in the humanities, those who adhere to the quantitative "camp" devaluate the human being which should be at the centre of psychology as a discipline.

As Bryman writes, qualitative researchers prefer "an approach to the study of the social world which seeks to describe and analyse the culture and behaviour of humans and their groups from the point of view of those being studied" (Bryman, 1988: 46). They see this as quite different from the perspective of the natural scientist probing, for instance, a piece of rock (to take a rather crude example). In qualitative psychology researchers adopt the point of view of the subjects being studied, something that is impossible to do in the natural sciences. They also acknowledge their own central position in the construction of knowledge and are aware that "the knower is part of the matrix of what is known" (DuBois, 1983: 11 quoted in Banister et al., 1994: 151). This means that qualitative research has a reflexive quality (cf. Woolgar, 1988). This reflexivity bridges the gap between subject (investigator) and object (the investigated) (Banister et al., 1994: 2), a gap that had been opened up by quantitative research in order to be able to study persons in the ways rocks are studied. Quantitative psychology tried to study "subjects" as "objects", overlooking the intrinsic reflexivity involved. In focusing not on *measuring* but on *understanding* people's or subjects' behaviour, qualitative psychologists claim to produce what they believe psychology should produce: a better understanding of human thinking and acting which could lead to human beings being able to understand themselves better and to improve their thinking and acting.

However, this goal is not yet generally accepted by psychologists, who remain entrenched in their respective positions. Whereas qualitative researchers accuse quantitative ones of positivism, reductionism, determinism, and objectivism, quantitative researchers accuse qualitative ones of fuzziness and subjectivity. To summarise the opposing views very succinctly: we have a reliance on *measurement* vs. *meaning*, and on *lived experience* (*Erlebnis*) vs. *impersonal experiment*. In general, quantitative approaches are regarded as *mainstream* psychology, qualitative ones as an *alternative* approach.

It could be argued that ideally psychologists should all live happily in the paradise of "methodological pluralism" (cf. Sechrest & Sidani, 1995: 77). However, as things stand, the reasons why people choose to use quantitative or qualitative methods are not always such practical or pragmatic arguments. The reasons why psychologists choose quantitative or qualitative methods depend on a certain hierarchy of options. There are *epistemological* reasons (one could also say *ideological* ones), depending on the framework for the "acquisition of knowledge" in which the researchers work – this is mainly a choice between experimental psychology and any type of alternative psychology. The choice of method also depends on the *paradigm* the researchers work in, which is itself determined by the epistemology. These high-level choices then determine the choice of the *research programme,* and finally the choice of the *theory* the researchers want to test with the adequate *method*. One could call all these the *legitimate* reasons that can be used to justify the choice of a method. However, there are also less legitimate motives for choosing a method, and these are *political* reasons. A method is chosen that fits in with the most profitable research programme and with the most dominant paradigm and epistemology. The ultimate reason here is not the advancement of knowledge, but the advancement in the psychological establishment. And finally, methods are also chosen for their *cost-effectiveness*. Qualitative methods are usually more time-consuming and therefore more expensive, whereas certain quantitative methods are quickly and relatively cheaply implemented. They are therefore chosen even by qualitative researchers so as to give the research into a certain topic a quick-start, to be followed up by more intensive qualitative research if the results achieved through quantitative research warrant such an expense.

In this book we want to overcome the *political* barrier erected by some psychologists, be they from the qualitative or quantitative camp. To break this barrier we shall provide examples of psychologists who have successfully climbed over this political wall, explored the fields that lie on both sides, and made some breakthroughs that join them. In the following section some misconceptions about the qualitative/quantitative divide will be dispelled.

The differences between empirical, experimental, quantitative, and qualitative psychology

One should be careful not to confuse three different methodological strands in mainstream psychology, throw them all into one pot and cover them firmly with the lid marked: positivism and reductionism. These three strands are: (1) *empirical* psychology; (2) *experimental* psychology; and (3) *quantitative* psychology. Their roots are very different.

Empirical psychology has the longest tradition of the three, being "done" at least since Antiquity and systematised by nineteenth-century post-Lockean and post-Kantian empiricist philosophers and psychologists. In a sense, both quantitative *and* qualitative methods are empirical, that is, dependent on observation, the only difference is how these observations are made and how they are interpreted (cf. Sechrest & Sidani, 1995: 78).

Experimental psychology is of somewhat newer date. As Woodworth has pointed out in the "Preface" to his classical introduction to experimental psychology, a "few scattering titles date from the earlier centuries and from the first half of the nineteenth", but "the upswing began about 1850 and still continues". Writing in the 1930s, he regards "the recent period" as "outstanding in quality as well as quantity of original research". The pioneers of experimental psychology were Helmholtz, Weber and Fechner in Germany, Galton in England and Binet in France (cf. Woodworth, 1938: iii). The person who institutionalised psychology as an experimental laboratory science was Wundt. From then onwards there was a shift away from the single author writing monographs about "the soul", towards a team of authors writing articles based on experiments and publishing them in journals. That is, one can observe a shift from the single author to the aggregate author.

Quantitative psychology, linked to experimental psychology as new method to older paradigm, is of more recent origin still. Whereas the impetus for the establishment of experimental psychology came from advances in physiology, biology and physics, the use of predominantly quantitative methods was triggered by advances in mathematics and statistics, and the promises held by psychometrics.

What distinguished quantitative or statistical experimental psychology from the older forms of experimental psychology, was the focus away from the individual and towards the aggregate, this time not on the level of the authors of books or articles but at the level of the "subjects" studied. There was a shift away from using single subjects in experiments (who, in early experimental psychology, could still be the psychologists involved in the experiments themselves), towards a pool of subjects. The applicability of these aggregate results to individual cases then became a problem, that still plagues psychology today. As Danziger has pointed out:

> psychology was left with two very different frameworks for justifying its knowledge claims, the one based on an individual attribution of psycho-logical data, the other necessarily relying on statistical norms. Both types of knowledge claim rested on the demonstration of certain regu-larities that could be interpreted as having psychological significance. But the nature of the regularities was fundamentally different in the two cases. In the case of the traditional paradigm for experimental psychology, as established by Wundt, the regularities demonstrated had an immediate causal significance. [. . .] The knowledge one obtained referred directly to particular psychophysical systems. But where the established regularities were attributed to groups of individuals, the system to which one's data referred was no particular psychophysical system but a statistical system constituted by the attributes of a constructed collective subject.
>
> (Danziger, 1990: 77–78)

This means that *experimental* psychology, heralded by Wundt's setting up a first laboratory in 1879, was not always *quantitative* (cf. Shadish, 1995). The method still most commonly used was introspection and the results reached by introspection were not necessarily quantifiable. The famous social psy-chologist McDougall pointed out for instance that Titchener's manual *Experimental Psychology* was divided into two parts, dealing with "qualitative experiments" and "quantitative experiments" (McDougall, 1901: 538). But under the influence of physiology and psychophysics, quantitative methods came to be used more and more often, especially in Germany and England, either in tandem with introspection as in Wundt's laboratory, or exclusively so as in Ebbinghaus's and Galton's research. In France the quantification of experimental psychology went at a somewhat slower pace, and psychologists still used "experimental" as synonymous with empirical (experiential) and used methods like hypnotism and the observation of pathological cases ("nature's experiments") which were not quantitative (Carroy & Plas, 1996: 77–78). In 1898 Binet pointed out in an article on measurement in psychology that not everything could be measured, especially higher mental functions (Binet, 1898). In the eyes of French psychologists experimental quantitative psychology in Germany, which focused on the measurement of reaction times, was both a method and a "doctrinal position" (Carroy & Plas, 1996: 75), a doctrinal position that went on to be successfully exported all over the world and has dominated psychology up to the present.

Qualitative psychology, or psychology based on qualitative methods is rooted in the work of Dilthey, who was the first to attack German quantitative experimental psychology at the end of the nineteenth century and who proposed an entirely new (hermeneutic) method for the understanding of human minds and action (see Chapter 2), in phenomenology, ethnography, in various types of sociology (symbolic interactionism, microsociology and so on), but also in psychological works by Piaget and Vygotsky.

Mead, Piaget and Vygotsky can be regarded as pioneers of what later came to be know as "social constructionism" and "social constructivism", where the individual is seen as actively constructing knowledge, self, understanding, and in the final instance reality and truth in social interaction with others, especially in talk (studied through such qualitative methods as conversation analysis and discourse analysis). From the point of view of social constructionists as researchers it is therefore also claimed that science creates knowledge and truth rather than discovering knowledge (as claimed by "quantitative" researchers). Not only are multiple realities constructed in social interaction between people, social interaction between researchers constructs multiple accounts of these realities. Although accused of relativism, social constructionism also brought about a healthy scepticism with regard to claims made by "scientists". It had a major impact on social psychology (see, for example, Potter, 1996) and on cultural psychology. Michael Cole, for example, looked at cultural traditions and norms amongst the Kpelle tribe in Liberia as constructs that serve as "functional cognitive systems" (Cole & Scribner, 1974: 194). He argued that the constructs are defined through the activities and characteristics of a particular social group with specific objectives and needs.

The relationship between qualitative psychology, empirical, experimental and quantitative psychology is a complex one. Qualitative psychology can be said to be empirical because it is based on systematic observation; but it does not base its observations on experimentally controlled conditions and variables. Qualitative psychology is empirical, but is not experimental. However, whereas experiments are rejected by qualitative researchers, qualitative researchers do not altogether dismiss either the use of quantitative *data* or the summarising of results in quantitative form. What they object to is the averaging out of individual and cultural differences by the use of statistics, and the belief that measurement can create understanding. Quantitative (experimental) researchers by contrast reject qualitative data or data achieved by qualitative methods as a matter of course. However, in the present climate it will be a while yet until we can say that "qualitative methods are here to stay, and psychology is much better for it" (as Shadish said about evaluation in an article on the "Philosophy of Science and the Quantitative–Qualitative Debates", 1995a: 63).

Practical background: integrating quantitative and qualitative methods in psychology

It is curious that despite the growth of qualitative methods in psychology, used side by side with quantitative methods, very little consideration has been given to their combination. As shown above, there are a number of reasons why this is so. However psychologists have much to gain from exploiting both methods together and we turn now to ten reasons for mixing qualitative and quantitative methods. Some of these apply directly at the practical level of single research projects using both types of method; others apply at a higher level from which researchers can benefit from being trained in both camps.

1. Triangulation

"Triangulation" (Denzin, 1989) is frequently mentioned in the literature as a reason for mixing methods. There are actually several different forms of triangulation, only one of which involves using multiple methods, the others being multiple datasets, multiple investigators, and the use of multiple theories. The term arises from surveying, where drawing a line from one point does not give a precise location; a line is also needed from another landmark, and the point of intersection is the location, thus giving rise to a triangle between the actual location and the two landmarks. By analogy, triangulation in research takes advantage of using two methods (or datasets, or investigators, or theories) to get a more accurate picture of what is going on. If two methods are used which have different strengths and weaknesses, but which yield similar results, it increases our confidence that those results are a true representation of what's going on, as opposed to a fluke due to flaws in the method used. Of course this only applies where the methods complement one another: there is no point using triangulation with two methods which have the same liabilities (Brewer & Hunter, 1989).

The idea that combining methods leads to greater validity of the findings has been criticised as naive (Bryman, 1988) and clearly it is also not compatible with a social constructionist view that there is no one "correct" version of reality, only different competing versions (if there is no correct version then clearly multiple methods won't help to find it!). It is also the case that because different methods (whether qualitative or quantitative) are often suited to asking slightly different questions, it can be difficult to use them to study exactly the same research question. All these issues will, of course, be addressed at later stages in this book.

2. "Pick-me-up"

This may not be the best justification for mixing methods, but where a study that was designed to stand on its own yields results which are not entirely convincing, a small-scale study from the "opposing" (qualitative/quantitative) camp can act as a "pick-me-up" and "rescue" it. For example, if a questionnaire produces statistically significant results which are not what was expected, and are theoretically difficult to explain, the results could be seen as aberrant in some way or due to a type I error. A set of interviews could help to produce a theoretically plausible explanation and make sense of the data – and, of course, they could also confirm the suggestion of aberrance and lead you to consign the questionnaire to the wastebin!

3. As a prelude or pilot

The idea of using one type of study as a prelude to the other is not new – qualitative research has been seen by many quantitative researchers as "only" suitable for a pilot study. While we would of course argue that qualitative work can stand on its own, it nevertheless can be extremely useful when used as a pilot. A typical example would be to use interviews when designing a questionnaire, partly to assess the pilot set of questions that have been created and partly to see whether participants in the interview come up with any suggestions for topics which have been ignored in creating the pilot questions. The use of one method as a pilot for another can lead to improvements in the design of the study.

4. To explore different levels of the same phenomenon

As previously stated, using different methods to tackle the same precise question can be difficult. However, one advantage stemming from this is that different methods can be used in order to study different levels of the same phenomenon and to explore the micro/macro distinction (Brannen, 1992). Different methods may be more suited to looking at different levels of the same problem, and only through a mixed-methods approach can these different levels become enmeshed.

5. To repopulate psychology

Billig (1994) has argued against the "depopulation" of psychology, by which people become subjects and experimenters all but disappear from the pages of scientific reports. Yet qualitative researchers have pointed to the importance of the relationship between researcher and researched, which as Billig says is also important in quantitative research. As Ussher (1994) points out, this depopulation also leads to psychology's ignoring issues like gender and race. Ussher argues that these issues must be examined before the repopulation of psychology can succeed. Psychology as a whole has much to gain both from paying attention to the subjective (rather than dismissing it) and from considering issues such as reflexivity in qualitative and quantitative work. Mixed-method research requires psychologists to consider these issues in the design and analysis of studies, as well as to take a deeper look at the theories framing (or arising from) the work.

6. *Better communication across and within disciplines*

The divide between qualitative and quantitative researchers has led to a split in psychology, between those who prefer one approach and those who prefer the other, often with little communication or understanding about what goes on on the other side of the divide. This divide can also be seen between related disciplines, as colleagues in other areas set psychology up as a subject to be mocked for failing to take account of methodological advances in their area. Fractionation along this methodological divide is damaging to psychology, as researchers need to be able to read and understand across disciplines. Even psychologists from different areas within disciplines don't "speak" to each other as work carried out on the other side of the divide is ignored as irrelevant, subjective, or decontextualised. While there will always be grumbles between disciplines, being open to a wider range of methodologies will improve links as researchers will be able to read and understand work in related disciplines, instead of being thrown by unfamiliar ways of carrying out research. Work in other areas often has a direct bearing on psychological theories (e.g. anthropological work on metaphor which links directly with psychological theories about the "poetics of mind" (Gibbs, 1994)). Since many psychologists have only been trained in quantitative methods, if they gained a better understanding of qualitative methods it could lead to more productive research programs.

7. *Improved links between academics, practitioners and "consumers" of psychology*

As well as improving communication within and between discipline boundaries, mixed method research can improve the links between academic psychologists, practitioners, and those who consume psychology in some way whether as individuals (seeing clinical psychologists, following the advice of sports psychologists) or groups (trying to use psychology to improve advertising campaigns or to devise intervention polices in schools, etc.). In part this is because different methods will bring researchers into contact with different sectors of the (research and general) community and thus simply increase the number of contacts. In part also, because results from one kind of study may be more easy to present to a wider audience, mixed-method researchers can use one methodology to help explain further the results of the other parts of the research (as tables of numbers often seem less than exciting, carefully chosen quotes from interviews can help fire the imagination and illustrate the numbers, for example). In addition, ideas from action research in which the community is directly involved in the research (Stringer, 1996) could be used to increase involvement in the research process. This would also fit with moves to improve the links between theoretical and applied psychology as put forward by Gale (1997). Clearly this falls under our category of wider reasons for mixing methods. However it also shows how lessons from one side of the divide, which are often taken to be irrelevant to the other, if used to structure the research process, could have far-reaching consequences, and help, to some extent, to put the heart back into psychology – to remind it of its purpose and increase the involvement of those who use the results. Researchers trained in both qualitative and quantitative approaches are clearly those best placed to put into practice lessons from both fields.

8. Better exploitation of methods

Recent approaches have shown that methods which are typically seen as falling to one or other side of the divide, can in fact be more fully utilised as a mixed method approach. Examples are Smith's (1995) work with repertory grids or Stainton-Rogers and Stenner's use of Q-sort (see Chapter 6). It's also often forgotten that quantitative approaches can still lead to qualitative data or solutions, as for example in work using chaos theory where the data are originally quantitative but can lead to a qualitative description or "finger-print" for each variable (e.g. Totterdell, Briner, Parkinson, & Reynolds, 1996).

9. In defence against a hostile audience

Use of a mixed-method approach can make the results more presentable to a hostile audience, e.g. using quantitative work to back up qualitative work. This can be useful where there are concerns about e.g. getting a qualitative PhD proposal past a quantitative panel, or getting results of largely qualitative work published in a more traditionally quantitative journal. With the increasing interest in qualitative work in psychology, this is probably going to become less of a problem.

10. Improvements in theory

Using a mixed-method approach forces researchers to consider difficult issues to do with both the depth and breadth of their studies, and at all stages of the research process. As Brannen (1992: 32–33) says "in particular it can help to clarify the formulation of the research problem and the most appropriate ways in which problems or aspects of problems may be theorised or studied. With a single method the researcher is not forced to consider these issues in quite the same way. With multiple methods the researcher has to confront the tensions between different theoretical perspectives while at the same time considering the relationship between the data sets produced by the different methods".

Why don't people mix methods more?

There are a number of reasons why there haven't been more mixed-method studies in psychology. In part it has been due to the difficulties of finding people who are equally well-versed in both methodologies, a situation which is changing as more psychologists undergo training in qualitative research methods. It is also due to the different theoretical stances of the two approaches, which often mean that those who use one type of method do not consider the other to be worthwhile or complementary; however as we try to show throughout this book, the divide is more imagined than real. There are of course a number of problems researchers will find in carrying out mixed-method research, which operate at both a theoretical and a practical level. In advocating a mixed-method approach, we do not wish to underestimate the importance of these factors; rather, we hope that by exploring them, we can begin to move towards a "methodologically aware eclecticism" (Hammersley, 1996) that will inform psychology for the twenty-first century. In the chapters that follow, the qualitative–quantitative divide is considered from a range of perspectives, which we hope will provide answers to some of the questions facing researchers, and assist psychologists in carrying out mixed-method research.

We begin with a consideration of the different approaches taken to method during the history of psychology. In Chapter 2, Nerlich demonstrates that arguments over methods in psychology are nothing new. She describes the debate over rational versus empirical approaches which led Kant to propose an anthropological psychology. This, and the beginnings of physiological approaches to psychology, led to the Methodenstreit in German psychology. In her consideration of this period in psychology's history, Nerlich raises issues that resonate with methodological debates today. In Chapter 3, Henwood considers questions of validity, and whether psychologists should take a modern or post-modern approach. A survey of clinical psychologists' views of teaching on qualitative methods revealed four different approaches, which reflected evaluative judgements about the nature of qualitative research. Developing the discussion further with reflections on different approaches to issues of the quality of qualitative research, she presents a strong case for reinventing validity.

Part II of the book proceeds to consider three approaches to thoroughly "mixed" research. In Chapter 4, Harré and Crystal consider two axes of the methodological debate: that between causal versus discursive (or semantic) approaches to psychology, and that between intensive and extensive designs. They argue that statistical approaches can be useful when combined with a semantic interpretation of the results, and present two studies that show that utilising statistical and discursive approaches together provides a very useful tool for psychology. In Chapter 5, Clarke also puts forward the case for a hybrid qualitative–quantitative psychology, or what he terms "natural psychology". Clarke argues persuasively that psychologists should study topics that are of relevance to lay people, and that pre-conceived views of method have often prevented psychologists from studying these very topics. He gives examples of the use of structured judgement methods to benefit from the rigour of quantitative approaches without losing the benefits of working with interpretations which are so important in qualitative approaches. The last chapter in this section, by Stenner and Stainton Rogers, also looks at the role of statistical techniques in qualitative research. They present an account of Q methodology, a hybrid approach that represents what they term "quali-quantology". Using the example of a Q study of emotions, they successively demonstrate the challenges that this approach gives to both qualitative, and quantitative, researchers.

In Part III, we consider specific examples of the interaction between qualitative and quantitative approaches. In Chapter 7, Chilton, Covey, Hopkins, Jones-Lee, Loomes, Pidgeon, Robinson and Spencer consider the use of the contingent valuation paradigm within an interdisciplinary study of the value of life in the context of road-safety policy. They argue that incorporating a qualitative approach within what has traditionally been a quantitative paradigm has led to better theoretical understandings of the data. Qualitative techniques were used both prior to the quantitative part of the study, and afterwards as a way of improving the interpretation of the results. It is also the case that quantitative methods can be used within a more qualitative study, and in Chapter 8, Vann and Cole look at the role of statistics in cultural psychology. They consider two studies that combined qualitative and quantitative research within an interpretive paradigm. In both studies, simulation tasks were used as a tool for investigating cognitive life. In Chapter 9, Todd and Lobeck discuss the results of an attempted triangulation in a study of attitudes and second language acquisition. They consider issues of interpretation around the use of both quantitative (questionnaire) and qualitative (focus group) data within the same study, particularly when the results appear to differ!

The combination of methods does not just occur within research studies, but across sequences of studies, and in Part IV we return to the disciplinary developments that can arise from mixed-methods approaches. In Chapter 10, Miller considers the study of difficult behaviour in schools. After setting the background to this research, he describes the sequential use of quantitative, then qualitative, studies, to develop a model of difficult behaviour. An evaluation of each of the two studies, and of the researcher–practitioner partnership, leads to suggestions for future developments in educational psychology. In Chapter 11, Nicolson looks at clinical research on postnatal depression. Research in this area was traditionally quantitative, but a number of qualitative studies have emerged either as challenges to the dominant approach, or as complementary. She considers the value of feminist qualitative research within a field dominated by randomised controlled trials. In the final chapter, Todd and Nerlich look at issues arising from the book, and make a number of suggestions for future developments in mixed-method research. In particular, they argue that a pragmatic approach to the adoption of method, together with a consideration of the theoretical issues and problems that such approaches throw up, can only be beneficial to the discipline of psychology.

References

Banister, P., Burman, E., Parker, I., Taylor M., & Tindal, C. (1994). *Qualitative methods in psychology: A research guide*. Buckingham: Open University Press.

Billig, M. (1994). Repopulating the depopulated pages of social psychology. *Theory and Psychology*, *4*(3), 307–335.

Binet, A. (1898). La mesure en psychologie individuelle. *Revue Philosophique, XLVI*, 113–123.

Bogdan, R., & Taylor, S. J. (1975). *Introduction to qualitative research methods: A phenomenological approach to the social sciences*. New York: Wiley.

Brannen, J. (Ed.) (1992). *Mixing methods: Qualitative and quantitative research*. Aldershot: Avebury.

Brewer, J., & Hunter, A. (1989). *Multimethod research: A synthesis of styles*. Newbury Park, CA: Sage Publications.

Bryman, Alan (1988). *Quantity and quality in social research*. London: Unwin Hyman.

Carroy, J., & Plas, R. (1996). The origins of French experimental psychology: Experiment and experimentalism. *History of the Human Sciences*, *9*(1), 73–84.

Cole, M., & Scribner, S. (1974). *Culture and thought: A psychological introduction*. New York: Wiley.

Danziger, K. (1985). The methodological imperative in psychology. *Philosophy of the Social Sciences*, *15*, 1–13.

Danziger, K. (1990). *Constructing the subject. Historical origins of psychological research*. Cambridge: Cambridge University Press.

Denzin, N. K. (1989). *The research act: A theoretical introduction to sociological methods* (3rd ed.). New Jersey: Prentice Hall.

Denzin, N. K., & Lincoln, Y. S. (1994). *Handbook of qualitative research*. London: Sage.

Dubois, B. (1983). Passionate Scholarship: notes on values knowing and method in feminist social science. In G. Bowles & R. Duelli-Klein (Eds.) *Theories of Women's Studies* (pp. 105–116). London: Routledge and Kegan Paul.

Gale, T. (1997). The reconstruction of British psychology. *Psychologist*, *10*(1), 11–15.

Gibbs, R. W. Jr (1994). *The poetics of mind*. Cambridge: Cambridge University Press.

Glassner, B., & Moreno, J. D. (Eds.) 1989. *The qualitative–quantitative distinction in the social sciences*. Boston/Dordrecht: Kluwer.

Hammersley, M. (1996). The relationship between qualitative and quantitative research: Paradigm loyalty versus methodological eclecticism. In J. T. E. Richardson (Ed.), *Handbook of qualitative research methods for psychology and the social sciences*. Leicester: BPS Books.

Henwood, K. L., & Nicolson, P. (Eds.) (1992). Qualitative research and psychological theorising. (Special Issue). *The Psychologist*, *83*, 97–111. (Reprinted in M. Hammersley (Ed.) (1993). *Social research: Philosophy, politics and practice*. London: Sage).

Kelle, U. (1995). *Computer-aided qualitative data analysis. Theory, methods and practice*. London: Sage.

McDougall, W. (1901). Book notice of Edward Bradford Titchener's *Experimental psychology: A manual for laboratory practice* [1900], for *Mind, N.S.*, 538–541.

Potter, Jonathan (1996). *Representing reality: Discourse, rhetoric and social construction*. London: Sage.

Reichardt, C. S., & Cook, T. D. (1979). Beyond qualitative versus quantitative methods. In T. D. Cook, & C. S. Richard (Eds.), *Qualitative and quantitative methods in evaluation research* (pp. 7–32). Newbury Park, CA.: Sage Publications.

Reichardt, C. S., & Rallis, S. F. (Eds.) (1994a). *The qualitative–quantitative debate: New perspectives*. San Francisco: Jossey-Bass.

Reichardt, C. S., & Rallis, S. F. (1994b). Qualitative and quantitative inquiries are not incompatible: A call for a new partnership. In C. S. Reichardt & S. F. Rallis (Eds.), *The qualitative–quantitative debate: New perspectives* (pp. 85–91). San Francisco: Jossey-Bass.

Richardson, John T. E. (1996a). Introduction. In T. E. Richardson (Ed.), *Handbook of qualitative research methods for psychology and the social sciences* (pp. 3–10). Leicester: BPS Books.

Richardson, John T. E. (Ed.) (1996b). *Handbook of qualitative research methods for psychology and the social sciences*. Leicester: BPS Books.

Sechrest, L., & Sidani, S. (1995). Quantitative and qualitative methods: Is there an alternative? *Evaluation and Program Planning, 18*(1), 77–87.

Shadish, W. R. (1995a). Philosophy of science and the quantitative–qualitative debates. *Evaluation and Program Planning, 18*(1), 63–75.

Shadish, W. R. (Ed.) (1995b). Special issue on The quantitative–qualitative debates: 'DeKuhnifying' the conceptual context. *Evaluation and Program Planning, 18*(1).

Silverman, D. (1993). *Interpreting qualitative data: Methods for analysing talk, text and interaction*. London: Sage.

Smith, J. A. (1995). Repertory grids: an interactive, case-study perspective. In J. A. Smith, R. Harré, & L. Van Langenhove (1995). *Rethinking methods in psychology*. London: Sage.

Stringer, E. T. (1996). *Action research: A handbook for practitioners*. Newbury Park, CA: Sage.

Totterdell, P., Briner, R. B., Parkinson, B., & Reynolds, S. (1996). Fingerprinting time-series – dynamic patterns in self-report and performance-measures uncovered by a graphical nonlinear method. *British Journal of Psychology, 87*(1), 43–60.

Ussher, J. M. (1994). Sexing the phallocentric pages of psychology – repopulation is not enough. *Theory and Psychology, 4*(3), 345–352.

Weitzman, E. A. (1995). *Computer programs for qualitative data analysis. A software sourcebook*. London: Sage.

Woodworth, R. S. (1938). *Experimental psychology* (3rd ed.). London: Methuen.

Woolgar, S. (Ed.) (1988). *Knowledge and reflexivity*. London: Sage.

2 Coming full (hermeneutic) circle

The controversy about psychological methods

Brigitte Nerlich

> In one form or another, the debate about quantitative and qualitative research has been taking place since at least the mid-nineteenth century. At that time there was much argument about the scientific status of history and the social sciences, with quantification often being seen as one of the key features of natural science.
>
> (Hammersley, 1992: 39)

> Positivists examine their procedures and conclusions carefully in an attempt to make them as valid as possible, humanists do likewise, but whereas the methodological lynch pin of positivist validity is the experiment or other type of controlled observation, that of the humanists is the hermeneutic circle, a process of repeated interpretation and checking until the details of the events and their overall interpretation are fully consonant.
>
> (Gabriel, 1980: 52)

1. Introduction

In our introduction to this book various terms have been used to highlight the differences between quantitative and qualitative methods. These terms can also be employed to provide clues that enable use to write the history of these two types of methods, a history that could shed light on present day difficulties in combining quantitative and qualitative methods. The key terms are *naturalistic, holistic, contextual, interpretative, hermeneutic, reflexive* vs. *measurement* and *experiment*.

Terms like *naturalistic* and *contextual* point to the *ethnographic* roots of present day qualitative methods (see Viddich & Lyman, 1994). One of the first to advocate an ethnographic approach to the study of culture and language was Bronislaw Malinowski, who held the first chair in social anthropology at the London School of Economics (see Nerlich & Clarke, 1996, chapter 11, section 2). His central goal was to study language and culture from the point of view of the natives or, as Malinowski called them in a letter to his friend Alan Gardiner: Niggers (see Malinowski, 1918: 2). One can see that "his plea for the social anthropologist to come down from the verandah and mix with the natives" (Bryman, 1988: 45) does not necessarily entail respect for the natives! A quite separate development in ethnography started with the work of Franz Boas, the founder of American cultural anthropology (see Toren, 1996: 102). Later on the advocates of an ethnography of speaking and ethnomethodology (Garfinkel, 1967) borrowed ideas from both British and American ethnolinguistics. This chapter will not deal with the ethnographical roots of qualitative methods, but focus instead on the origins of qualitative methods in psychology and the controversy surrounding their use in socio-psychological traditions.

Terms like *holistic* and *meaning* point in the direction of three socio-psychological traditions, which, as we shall see, have a common source: Wilhelm Dilthey's work. First, there is *symbolic interactionism* with George Herbert Mead as the figurehead and Herbert Blumer as a populariser. Second, there is the *case-study* approach favoured by the Chicago School of sociology and social psychology. And third, there is the *phenomenology* of Alfred Schütz which also has its roots in the work of Edmund Husserl, an advocate of a "phenomenological psychology" (see Husserl, 1925/1977),[1] as well as in Max Weber's concept of *Verstehen* (see Ritzer, 1996: 222). Going beyond Husserl and Dilthey, Schütz wanted to study the mundane everyday world of social interactions (*Lebenswelt*), especially the phenomenon of *intersubjectivity*. In this chapter our focus will be on Mead.[2]

The starting point for all three currents of thought (symbolic interactionism, Chicago sociology, phenomenological sociology) was Dilthey's plea for a descriptive and analytical (*beschreibende und zergliedernde*) psychology which he opposed to what he called an explanatory (*erklärende*) psychology. He made this plea in 1894 when psychology was just turning "scientific" on a grand scale, with the application of quantitative methods, the setting up of laboratories in which experiments could be made systematically, and when statistics first made an impact on psychology. Dilthey saw all this as endangering the real purpose of psychology, that of understanding human nature in the context of human life. He called the sciences that enable us to understand social and historical reality *Geisteswissenschaften* (human studies), and he believed that these sciences (such as psychology, history, economics, philology, literary criticism, comparative religion, and jurisprudence) are quite different from the *Naturwissenschaften* (natural sciences). Unlike the natural sciences, they require an effort of sympathetic understanding (*Verstehen*) on the part of the researcher, something that psychologists, wanting to turn psychology into a natural science, consciously overlooked.

Dilthey wrote his "Ideas for a descriptive and analytic psychology" for the *Sitzungsberichte der Akademie der Wissenschaften zu Berlin* (see Dilthey, 1894/1977) and sent a prepublication copy to the eminent psychologist and colleague Hermann Ebbinghaus for comments. However, instead of writing back to Dilthey, Ebbinghaus wrote a damming review of Dilthey's piece and published it in his own *Zeitschrift für Psychologie und Physiologie der Sinnesorgane* under the title "On explanatory and descriptive psychology" (see Ebbinghaus, 1896). Dilthey became the advocate of a psychology as part of the *Geisteswissenschaften*, Ebbinghaus became an advocate of a psychology as part of the *Naturwissenschaften*.

This was the beginning of what came to be known as the *Methodenstreit* in German psychology. This controversy concerned essentially the use of quantitative and qualitative methods in psychology and related fields and therefore has echoes in the present debate about the suitability of these methods for psychology. Just as today, some psychologists registered a "crisis" in psychology, aggravated by the rise of behaviourism in the United States in the 1920s, which some of them tried to diffuse by reconsidering the aims and objectives, the methods and techniques that psychology should pursue and that psychologists should use (see Bühler, 1927; Parker, 1989; Politzer, 1928/1994; Vygotsky, 1926, in: Van der Veer, & Valsinger, 1991).

2. The history of psychology leading up to the *Methodenstreit*

At the turn of the nineteenth to the twentieth century a series of intellectual debates raged in Germany. What has become known as the *Methodenstreit* in Germany first opened in the 1880s between two economists, Gustav Schmoller and Carl Menger, who debated whether the social sciences were exact or historical; deductive or inductive; abstract or empirical. In 1883 Menger published his *Untersuchungen über die Methode der Sozialwissenschaften und der Politischen Ökonomie insbesondere* in which he defeated the historical school (see Manicas, 1987: 124ff):

> At the poles in this debate were those (the positivists) who thought that history was composed of general (*nomothetic*) laws and those (the subjectivists) who reduced history to idiosyncratic (*idiographic*) actions and events. The positivists thought that history could be like a natural science; the subjectivists saw the two as radically different. For example, a nomothetic thinker would generalise about social revolutions, whereas an idiographic analyst would focus on the specific events leading up to the American Revolution.
>
> (Ritzer, 1996: 220–221)

As we shall see, this *Methodenstreit* did not only affect economy and history, but also sociology and psychology. Before studying the *Methodenstreit* and its repercussions, I shall provide a brief overview of its origins in the history of psychology leading up to the psychology of the nineteenth century, which Woodward and Ash call "the problematic science" (1982). Why was it problematic then and why is it problematic now?

2.1 Psychology and the natural sciences

Psychology's problematic status in general and the qualitative–quantitative divide in particular have their origins in psychologists' continued efforts to imitate the successes achieved by the natural sciences, by physics and astronomy in the seventeenth century and by chemistry, biology and physiology in the nineteenth century. In the seventeenth century psychology (or mental philosophy) desperately tried to match the advances made in the natural sciences under Kepler, Galileo, and Descartes, and to detach psychology from its philosophical and metaphysical roots. As Husserl has pointed out in the introduction to his phenomenological psychology, a "passionate endeavor to carry out just such a methodical reform in psychology, to reshape it also as a science which explains its subject matter exactly, on the basis of elementary laws, arose immediately" (Husserl, 1925/1977: 10). Most of these efforts failed however until the nineteenth century, when psychology received a new impetus from the progress made in biology and physiology. Psychologists now saw a real opportunity to shed all philosophical baggage and to establish a new psychology on scientific methods. As William James wrote: "Psychology, indeed, is to-day hardly more than what physics was before Galileo, what chemistry was before Lavoisier", but he hoped that there was enough material to "be so organized even now as to become worthy of the name of natural science at no very distant day" (James, 1892/1983: 270).

2.2 *Psychology and philosophy*

However, it was not as easy as expected to wrench psychology free from philosophy, as physiological psychology could not deal with all psychological problems, especially those higher psychological functions, like thinking, memorising and reasoning. Physiology provided the methods for studying perception and sensation, but the old method of introspection was still seen as the only possible one for studying thought processes. Let us now look at psychologists' successive attempts at matching the advancements made in the natural sciences.

Everybody knows that, as with all Western sciences of man and nature the foundations for psychology were laid in antiquity. However, to understand the German *Methodenstreit*, it suffices that we reach back to Locke, Hume, Leibniz, Wolff and, most importantly, Kant.

John Locke's *Essay Concerning Human Understanding* (1690) laid the foundations for an empiricist psychology, then still a philosophy of the mind or the soul. Radicalising Locke's thoughts, David Hume wished to introduce into philosophical analysis those experimental methods by which Isaac Newton had achieved such spectacular results in the explanation of natural phenomena. As an empiricist, Hume attempted to show how human knowledge arises from sense experience and from logical, associative, relations between ideas. Gottfried Wilhelm Leibniz in turn radicalised Locke's distinction between sensation and reflection by introducing a "crucial distinction between sensibility and understanding, that is, between the 'material' sensations received from the world and the 'formal' classification of these sensations by the mind" (Leary, 1982: 18–19), or between sensation and apperception. Christian August Wolff then divided psychology into two parts in the 1730s: *empirical* psychology, "as the science of what experience teaches us about the soul", "an inductive science that leads to empirical generalisations about the soul and its achievements" and *rational* psychology, the "science of all that is possible to the human soul (as opposed to all that has actually happened to it)", which is "a branch of metaphysics, a demonstrative science that provides necessarily true statements regarding the nature and essence of the soul" (Leary, 1982: 19).

This inaugurated two traditions in German psychology, *rational* and *empirical* psychology, a distinction that Dilthey did not fail to mention in his *Ideas* of 1894. An example of rational psychology was Alexander Gottlieb Baumgarten's treatise *Metaphysica* of 1739, which Immanuel Kant used to teach from. An example of the very rich tradition of empirical psychology or *Erfahrungsseelenlehre* was Johann Nicolas Teten's *Philosophische Versuche über menschliche Natur und ihre Entwicklung* (Philosophical Essays on Human Nature and its Development) of 1777, which Kant knew well. Tetens must be remembered for his defence of a faculty psychology, of which Kant's philosophy bears the traces. Kant's three "critiques", those of pure, practical, and aesthetic reason, are based on the distinction between three psychological faculties: cognition, desire, and feeling. Other examples of German empirical psychology are studied in Lia Formigari's book *La sémiotique empiriste face au kantisme* (1994, chap. 4).

Both empirical and rational psychology failed to find Kant's approval. With his critique of their "problematic character" (Leary, 1982: 21) Kant "laid the foundation for later developments in the broad field of inquiry that had already been labelled 'psychology' "(p. 18). Kant argued that psychology could not become a truly *rational* science, as it could not use mathematics, and that it could not become an *empirical* science because it could not use experiments, as it cannot control its phenomena. It could therefore remain either "merely" empirical, that is a mere collection of data, or be based on a different methodology altogether. The method Kant favoured was an *anthropological* or, as one could say, ethnographical one (see Kant, 1798/1974). He argued that it "could become more useful to humanity if it would forsake its traditional introspective method and begin to make systematic observations of men and women 'in the world' as they behave and interrelate with their fellow citizens" (Leary, 1982: 23). In Kant's view these observations could ultimately be distilled into "laws of experience", "that would assist men and women in the course of their lives", and could help them to make "better choices about their own best course of action" (p. 24).

However, as has become abundantly clear in the most recent past, psychology tried instead to become what Kant had deemed impossible, that is, *rational* (mathematical) and *empirical*, forsaking the *anthropological* direction that Kant had indicated. This approach has only recently been rediscovered in qualitative psychology. However, as we shall see, Dilthey, whose decisive attack on experimental psychology led to a crisis in psychology as early as the 1920s, continued to argue for a psychology based on anthropological principles. Dilthey might have read Kant's *Anthropology*, but his immediate source was the poet-philosopher Novalis (Friedrich von Hardenberg, 1772–1801), who, shortly before his death, had pleaded for the establishment of a *reale Psychologie* or *Anthropologie*, which would replace the mechanical, analytical and abstract psychology of his time and instead study "man purely as a whole, as a system" (see Hodges, 1952: 8).

To understand the *Methodenstreit* further, we also have to look at those opponents of Kant, such as Johann Georg Hamann and Johann Gottfried von Herder, who accused him of purifying reason to a degree that he left out what was most important in their eyes, namely language, culture, and history. They both published metacritiques of the *Critique of Pure Reason* in which they discussed the function of language in human reasoning and thus inaugurated a type of analytical philosophy, a philosophy of language that foreshadows twentieth-century analytical philosophy (see Cloeren, 1988). Herder also promoted the notion of history as the art of cultural understanding, stressing the importance of cultural and linguistic diversity. Herder's work itself can be seen as picking up ideas from Giambattista Vico (1668–1744), which had been forgotten during the enlightenment, a period when all sciences were enraptured by the progress achieved in the natural sciences. As Gordon Scott has pointed out, Vico was one of the first to make a distinction between the methods of the *historical* and the methods of the *natural* sciences. In Vico's view:

> Only God knows history in its totality, because he made the world, but the specific events of history can be understood by the human intellect [. . .] because they are made by human actions. The historian shares the quality of humanity with those men, great and small, whose actions create the phenomena of history. This enables him to enter *inside* the historical process, thus achieving a subjective understanding of it that is more profound than the objective knowledge attainable by the natural scientist, who is compelled to remain *outside* the phenomena he studies. [. . .] by this reasoning Vico made the bold claim that one can discover laws of social development that are more certain even than the laws of physics. In calling his book *New Science* (1725) he meant to contend that the science of history furnishes the most precise and most irrefutable form of human knowledge. Historians, and other social scientists, have no need to consider themselves inferior to natural scientists, or to try to mimic their methodology, for a categorically different, and superior, methodology is available to them.
>
> (Scott, 1991: 405)

This view was shared by Herder and the whole of the Romantic movement in Germany, but also by Dilthey "who in his argument with the early experimentalists such as Ebbinghaus, maintained that the human sciences would be mistaken to pursue causal explanation at the expense of establishing under-standing (*Verstehen* or 'meaning')" (Pidgeon, 1996: 76). Following Herder's lead, Dilthey's research programme was not to write another "critique of *pure* reason", but a "critique of *historical* reason", and his plea for a non-experimental psychology was part of it.

2.3 Psychology between philosophy and physiology

We have seen that the roots for thinking that psychology should be based on qualitative (anthropological, cultural-contextual, hermeneutic) methods can be traced back to Kant as well as his Romantic opponents. Now, somewhat ironically perhaps, the arguments used by those championing a quantitative and empirical approach to psychology are rooted in various types of psychology developed by Kant's followers during the nineteenth century, when psychology also came under the influence of biology and physiology. Another boost for the use of empirical and quantitative methods came from a general shift in the social sciences towards more positivist and empiricist methodologies as advocated for example by the English empiricists, by the French father of "sociology", Auguste Comte, and the French physician and physiologist Claude Bernard. Let us first look at Kant's various followers.

Kant's philosophy of the active spirit was further developed by Johann Gottlieb Fichte who advocated "an idealistic view of consciousness and an ever-active, striving ego, which is ultimately manifested as will" (Leary, 1982: 31). This view of consciousness and the will left its traces in two new psychologies – the associationist psychology of representations as developed by Friedrich Herbart, as well as in Hermann von Helmholtz's theory of the active role of the mind in perception (ibid.). Herbart wished to base his psychology on mathematical laws and was deeply influenced by the advances in chemistry and physics, whereas Helmholtz was influenced by advances in physiology and optics.

Another follower of Kant was Friedrich Wilhelm Joseph (von) Schelling who developed a new philosophy of identity, arguing that mind and body are two aspects of the same reality. This was the basis for what came to be known as *psychophysics* with Gustav Theodor Fechner as one of the most important representatives, and "the person most often credited with bringing actual measurement into the realm of psychology" (Leary, 1982: 32). Fechner sought to define the quantitative relationship between degrees of physical stimula-tion and the resulting sensation (1859). By associating sensations with numer-ical values, he hoped to make psychology a truly objective science. The concept of the psycho-physical parallelism or the parallelism between brains and minds, and the controversy surrounding the relation between the two "halves", is still with us today.

Georg Wilhelm Friedrich Hegel in turn regarded psychology as part of his philosophy of mind. His concept of the "objective spirit" inspired many, such as Dilthey, Bühler and Wundt who wanted to study social phenomena, such as language, law and myth, as collective phenomena which are not the result of singular, subjective acts of individual minds but influence individual minds in a pervasive way. These collective entities could be studied by what Dilthey called *Geisteswissenschaften* and what neo-Kantians, such as Wilhelm Windelband and Heinrich Rickert called *Kulturwissenschaften*. Unlike his younger colleagues, Wundt accepted the distinction between cultural studies and natural sciences. He therefore studied social phenomena in his *Völkerpsychologie* (1900/1922), whereas he based his individual psychology on the experimental method and came to be known as one of the founding fathers of *experimental* psychology.

> Clearly, he [Wundt] agreed with Hegel when he claimed that the higher mental processes, involving the truly human, symbolic aspects of experience, can only be understood within a social context, using a non-experimental methodology. In reaching this conclusion, Wundt lent his considerable authority to a distinction developed by the neo-Kantians of the later part of the nineteenth century, namely, the distinction between psychology as a natural science (or *Naturwissenschaft*) and psychology as a social science (or *Geisteswissenschaft*).
>
> (Leary, 1982: 33)

Wundt therefore never regarded psychology as an autonomous discipline. In spite of the fact that he set up the first psychological laboratory in Leipzig in 1879 and advocated experimental methods, he always saw psychology as part of philosophy. Had Dilthey sent his *Ideas* for a descriptive and hermeneutic psychology to Wundt and not to Ebbinghaus, he might have had a better reception!

This more philosophical approach to psychology, epitomised by the title that Wundt chose for his new psychological journal, namely *Philosophische Studien* (first issue 1881), was however gradually undermined by a new *physiological* perspective. The first attempts at a new physiological psychology were published by Helmholtz (under whom Wundt had worked as an assistant earlier in his career) in the context of his work on perception. Wundt himself published a book on the foundations of physiological psychology as early as 1874. Physiological psychology became *the* new psychology, and was celebrated as such at the first international congress of psychology, the "Congrès international de psychologie physiologique", held in Paris on 10 August 1889 (see Carroy & Plas, 1996: 74). The enthusiasm for physiological psychology reached its climax during the 1870s and 1880s and culminated in Germany in the launch of a new psychological journal that challenged Wundt's monopoly. It was entitled *Zeitschrift für Psychologie und Physiologie der Sinnesorgane* (first issue 1890) and was edited by Ebbinghaus and the physicist-physiologist Arthur König.

> The new psychology borrowed much from sensory physiology during the crucial years of its institutional entrenchment between 1870 and 1895. It

borrowed from physiology the experimental methods necessary to support a research program and flesh out the techniques of psychophysics,
the body of facts and expertise necessary to sustain its teaching and
licensing activities, much of the prestige of that well-established and
powerful German science, and the methodological program necessary
to differentiate itself and raise itself above its parent discipline of
philosophy and the older psychological tradition rooted in it.

(Turner, 1982: 151)

Whereas physiology can be credited with bringing experimental methods to
the fore in the development of psychology, psychophysics can be credited
with bringing quantification into psychology.

Despite the later, interminable debates over just what psycho-physics
meant and measured, it seemed to create almost overnight a body of compel-
ling, practicable, uniquely psychological experimental techniques that promised quantitative results as 'hard' and as reproducible as anything biophysics
could offer.

3. Psychology between explanation and understanding: the Methodenstreit

Unlike Wundt, Ebbinghaus embraced a radically empirical and experimental
psychology wholeheartedly. He went beyond Wundt in claiming that the
experimental approach could be fruitfully applied to various fields of psychological research, which had been considered inaccessible to the experimental
method, namely memory, thinking, and learning. He also abandoned the
method of introspection, up to then still favoured by psychologists like
Wundt, and replaced it by the use of mathematics and statistics.

This radically experimental and quantitative psychology advocated by
Ebbinghaus had its roots in Fechner's experimental work on sensation and
perception which Ebbinghaus admired greatly. In 1885 Ebbinghaus published
his most famous text: *Über das Gedächtnis: Untersuchungen zur Experimentel-
len Psychologie, (Memory: A contribution to Experimental Psychology*,
Ebbinghaus, 1913/1964). This text became famous because of two important
methodological innovations: (1) Ebbinghaus discovered the *forgetting curve*,
the rate at which items are forgotten, and showed that the amount learned is
linearly related to learning time. That is, "Ebbinghaus took the fact of ease of
relearning something once known [. . .] and made it part of science by developing the quantitative saving score, in which the saving in relearning is scored
as a per cent of the time (or trials) required in original learning" (Hilgard,
1964: viii, in Ebbinghaus, 1964). (2) He invented the use of the *nonsense syllable*
(a consonant-vowel-consonant triplet that is pronounceable but is not a real
word, such as *zat, wob*, etc.), in order to minimise the effect of meaning on
memory. His thorough experiments, using himself as the only experimental
subject, established a highly influential methodology in memory research.

Five years after *Memory* Ebbinghaus created the journal of psychology and the physiology of sensory organs mentioned earlier. This date (1890) marks the beginning of a deterioration in Ebbinghaus's relations with colleagues at the university of Berlin, notably Dilthey, who were not yet ready for the radical reorientation of psychology that he longed for. When, in 1893, Ebbinghaus was not appointed to a vacant chair of philosophy, he decided to leave Berlin for the smaller university of Breslau. So it was that when Dilthey sent him his *Ideas* in 1894, Ebbinghaus could quarrel with him from a safe distance (see Nicolas, 1994).

What was the debate all about? It concerned the question as to whether the subject matter of psychology could be investigated sufficiently using experimental methods alone or whether the understanding of meaning was a necessary precondition; in short: whether psychology belonged to the natural or the human sciences. In his *Ideas*, Dilthey maintained that those arguing for psychology as a natural science could only deal with elementary sense experience, but not with the full-blooded psychological *Erlebnis*, or lived experience. He claimed that psychological experiences of this sort could not be *explained* by the normal psychological methods, that is, by subsuming their parts or elements under a hypothetical chain of causal connections. According to Dilthey they can only be *understood* (and then described and analysed) in their already given totality – what Dilthey called the "psychic nexus". "The fundamental task of description in the human studies lies in articulating an indeterminate nexus rather than in synthetically combining elements" (Makkreel, 1977: 7). So, whereas Ebbinghaus wanted to study psychological phenomena by putting elements together according to a hypothetical (causal) link, Dilthey wanted to describe (*beschreiben*) and take apart (*zergliedern*) the totality of a given experience. Ebbinghaus wanted to explain, Dilthey to understand.

Dilthey agreed with Vico in saying that whereas we can only "explain nature, we understand psychic life" (Dilthey, 1977: 27). We can understand it because it is of our own making, whereas nature is not.

> As a consequence there exists a system of nature for the physical and natural sciences only thanks to inferential arguments which supplement the data of experience by means of a combination of hypotheses. In the human studies, to the contrary, the nexus of psychic life constitutes originally a primitive and fundamental datum.
>
> (Dilthey, 1977: 27)

The same goes for society as a whole. Here again one can distinguish between nature which is alien to us, and society which is our own creation, our world (see Dilthey GS, I: 36–37; quoted in Makkreel, 1977: 57). Nature we explain from without, society and psychological phenomena we understand from within. However, how does this understanding work? One of the main criticisms that Ebbinghaus voiced can be expressed in modern terms as: this type of understanding cannot be operationalised. But let us see what Dilthey has to say. The predominant method in psychology had been introspection, and in his *Ideas* Dilthey still believed that introspection could be the basis of understanding psychological phenomena. However, he gradually came to lose faith in introspection. "He found that our experience of ourselves, no matter how self-evident (*selbstverständlich*) does not constitute self-understanding (*Selbstverständnis*)" (Makkreel, 1977: 12). He therefore came to regard self-understanding as built on similar foundations to the understanding of *others*, namely as being based on understanding other people's *expressions*. Our *inner* experience is only accessible via the understanding of an *outer* expression of it. Whereas in the *Ideas* Dilthey thought that inner lived experience could be described and analysed as such, he developed his *hermeneutic* approach to understanding psychological experiences in his essay entitled "The Understanding of Other Persons and Their Expressions of Life", written in about 1910 (see Dilthey, 1977).

These outer expressions of inner life can consist in concepts and judgements, in actions or in artistic products. They all need to be *interpreted* in the *context* of historical life, and "in light of the reciprocal whole-to-part and part-to-whole relations of the hermeneutic circle" (Makkreel, 1977: 15). *Interpretation*, or the systematic application of understanding to an action or text, reconstructs the whole in which the text or action was produced or took place (the biography, the historical circumstances) and places the text or action in that whole. The knowledge gained by the hermeneutic method should, according to Dilthey, be objective, but not as reductionist and ahistorical as knowledge achieved by the methods used in the natural sciences.

This method differs markedly from the one adopted by the natural sciences. Here the aim is to establish "hypotheses and laws of ever-widening scope whereby more and more phenomena can be surveyed and explained", whereas in the hermeneutic method advocated by Dilthey and his followers we are "concerned to understand historical reality in increasingly greater depth" (Makkreel, 1977: 15). Historians do not want to make probabilistic generalisations but understand particular historical actions, events, or products, something which the new psychology just does not want to do. Ebbinghaus and others want to find the general laws that govern psychic life, not understand specific products emanating from it. The modern equivalent to this dispute about methods is encapsulated in the dichotomies of nomothetic versus idiographic, and by extensive versus intensive research methods.

Now, it is astonishing to find that, when studying hermeneutically the outer expressions of inner life, Dilthey forgot to study one of the most important tools and forms of expression: *language*. The linguistic dimension of a theory of understanding was developed by two quite different but in many respects compatible followers of Dilthey: Bühler in Germany and Mead in the United States (see Nerlich & Clarke, 1998). This gap in Dilthey's theory was not spotted by Ebbinghaus, who had other points of criticism to voice. We shall come back to Mead's theory of language after a look at Ebbinghaus's critique of a descriptive psychology.

As already mentioned, Ebbinghaus received Dilthey's *Ideas* as a pre-publication copy. But instead of sending Dilthey his comments in private, he vented them publicly in his journal. In a letter to Dilthey, he explained why:

> I really was not prepared for so much injustice towards contemporary psychology and for so little clarity concerning the fact that what you are recommending to people is just what people have been doing for a long time. I was equally appalled by the insufficient acknowledgement of our experimental efforts, which shines through a thin layer of forced generosity.
>
> (Rodi & Lessing, 1984: 11)

Ebbinghaus's critique centred around two points. First of all Ebbinghaus rejected the claim that the structural system of mental life can be directly experienced, and he argued that Dilthey therefore had to proceed in the same hypothetico-deductive way as the proponents of his "new" psychology.

> Introspection does indeed reveal units of various kinds in consciousness, but it does not reveal the deep-seated unity of the whole. Dilthey's account of that unity is a hypothetical construction, put together out of fragmentary data.
>
> (Hodges, 1952: 212)

Dilthey's psychology therefore has to face up to the same problems as Ebbinghaus's. Second, Ebbinghaus pointed out that Dilthey's attack on his and others' new psychology was directed at a much older version of it, namely at Herbart's mechanical psychology of representations. Dilthey was in fact attacking an old psychological ghost which had been put to rest years ago by a systematic critique elaborated by Wundt and by Ebbinghaus himself.

Bühler (1927) points out how people like Ebbinghaus had buried Herbart's psychology in the 1890s, and how they had elaborated a new methodology for psychology. Unlike Dilthey, Bühler therefore did not dismiss Ebbinghaus's achievements, but built on them. But unlike Ebbinghaus, Bühler also took note of what Dilthey had to say about the shortcomings of the new psychology, especially since he and his colleagues at Würzburg studied higher mental processes, such as thinking in the context of what they called *Denkpsychologie*.

4. Psychology between language and society: the dialectical Aufhebung of Dilthey's thoughts

Bühler went beyond Ebbinghaus *and* Dilthey in so far as he paid explicit attention to two phenomena which are vital if we want to understand more complex psychological phenomena: the *society* we live in and the *meaning* we rely on in our linguistic interactions. It was left to people like Bühler, Vygotsky,

Voloshinov[3]/Bakhtin, and Mead to introduce into psychology what Dilthey and Ebbinghaus had left out of their two opposing versions of psychology, namely language, meaning, and society.

As a young American philosopher and psychologist Mead came to Leipzig (see Vonk, 1992: 86 and Farr, 1996), where he studied under Wundt in the winter semester of 1888/1889. On the advice of G. Stanley Hall, Mead then went to Berlin where he studied between 23 April 1889 and 24 October 1891. He went to lectures given by Ebbinghaus (in the summer semester of 1889 on experimental psychology, and in the winter semester of 1889/1890 on experimental and physiological psychology), and specialised in the study of physiological psychology and experimental psychology. He also went to lectures given by Dilthey (in the summer semester of 1890 on ethics, and in the summer semester of 1891 on the history of philosophy), and Dilthey became his supervisor. Mead's "thesis, which he failed to complete before returning to the United States, was on the perception of space and concerned the relationship between vision and touch" (Farr, 1996: 59). Mead therefore had first-hand experience of the conflict between the two positions represented by Ebbinghaus as an advocate of psychology as a natural science and Dilthey as an advocate of psychology as a human "science", which soon afterwards led to such an open controversy between Dilthey and Ebbinghaus. However, Mead did not take sides in this conflict. He can, in fact, be regarded as one of the first social psychologists to combine qualitative and quantitative methods successfully.

Mead took from Wundt the notion of the *vocal gesture* and made it a cornerstone in his social interactionist research programme in which he studied language, the mind and the self from the point of view of social interaction and mutual symbolic understanding. From Ebbinghaus he took an early fascination with physiological psychology (see Farr, 1996: 65). From Dilthey, Mead took the notion of *understanding*, but, unlike Dilthey, Mead did not regard the *I*, or the psychic nexus of inner experience, as self-evident and given, but as a product of social interaction or co-operative social, and above all, linguistic acts. For Mead:

> The conduct of the individual [can only be explained] in terms of the organised conduct of the social group, rather than [. . .] the organised conduct of the social group in terms of the conduct of the separate individuals belonging to it.
>
> (Mead, 1934: 7)

Mead founded a truly *social* psychology in which society shapes the individual and not the other way round. Here the influence of Dilthey's holistic approach to psychological phenomena is transposed from the individual psyche to society as a whole: "the whole (society) is prior to the part (the individual), or the part to the whole; and the part is explained in terms of the whole, not the whole in terms of the part or parts" (ibid.).

As for mind, meaning and mutual understanding, they too are taken away from the monological individual of the German philosophers and transposed into the dialogical setting of social interaction. Mind, meaning and under-standing are established in social interaction and are therefore social by nature. Meaning is meaning only when it emerges from and is shared by those engaged in social interaction, of which conversation or discourse is the most important type (see Tarde, 1973; Schmitz, 1987).

The "discursive turn", which has recently been observed in social psy-chology (see Harré & Gillett, 1994), and from which two of the most important qualitative methods (conversation analysis and discourse analysis) have emerged, can therefore already be located in the symbolic interactionism advocated by Mead (see Vonk, 1996: 186). However, this discursive turn was forgotten when psychology, coming under the spell of behaviourism, turned itself into a fully experimental and quantitative science in the 1940s and 1950s (a decidedly American achievement, see Farr, 1996), and when "meaning" was ousted by "measurement". Meaning has only recently been rediscovered in the context of a general re-evaluation of psychology's methodological foundations. As Harré & Gillett have pointed out:

> [The discursive turn] seems to make the mind of an individual person into a mere nexus or meeting point of social relations. In this reading, it seems as if the mind lacks any independent reality as a self-existent cluster of processes and states.
>
> (Harré & Gillett, 1994: 22)

Again one can observe an almost dialectical use of Dilthey's *Ideas*. Dilthey had claimed that psychology should not study hypothetical connections between psychical elements but should start from the already given psychic nexus of inner individual psychological experience. Mead transposed these *intra*psychical and individual phenomena onto the level of *inter*psychical and collective relations and claimed, like Vygotsky, that psychology should start from there. A similar "social" turn was brought about in sociology where Weber "sought to use tools of hermeneutics to understand actors, interaction, and indeed all of human history" (Ritzer, 1996: 223).

Mead taught courses in social psychology in the philosophy department at Chicago. These courses were also taken by many graduate students in soci-ology who then combined Mead's ideas with those they were getting in the sociology department from people like Robert Park (Ritzer, 1996: 51 and the footnotes 2, 11, 12). This contributed to establishing a new school of psycho-logical and sociological research in which social phenomena,[4] such as lan-guage and mind were studied from a perspective that was altogether different from Wundt's study of these phenomena in his "individualistic" social psychology (*Völkerpsychologie*) and from Emile Durkheim's study of these phenomena in his realist sociology of collective representations – although Mead borrowed insights from both.

In the 1930s and 1940s a new influx of German thought gave the Chicago School of Sociology yet another layer of insights.[5] This time they came mainly from Georg Simmel and Max Weber, who were themselves steeped in the tradition of Dilthey and his followers. For Simmel society *was* the same as human interaction, and Weber defined *social* action as an action, which in its subjective meaning takes account of the behaviour of others and is thereby oriented in its course. And so the task of sociological analysis involved "the interpretation of action in terms of its subjective meaning" (Weber, 1921/1968: 4). Actions cannot be explained by statistics alone. To understand actions we need to do concrete historical and empirical fieldwork.

It was in this cultural climate, filled with ideas emanating from Dilthey and Weber, that Florian Znaniecki published his work *Social Actions* in 1936 and became one of the champions of qualitative methods in early American sociology. Znaniecki and others envisaged "the study of action and social action as requiring a distinctive methodological access, which has been termed *Verstehen* in German traditions" (see Hinkle, 1994: 297). They all allude to the necessity of the inquirer "putting himself in the place of the other", what Dilthey had called *Hineinversetzen*,[6] and Charles Horton Cooley "sympathetic understanding". This is then the basis for the *interpretation* of social actions in the context of social and historical life.

In Germany Dilthey's plea for an interpretative psychology inspired a rich crop of papers arguing for and against the integration or separation of quantitative and qualitative methods in psychology (see for example Jaspers, 1913; Schweizer, 1924; Gruhle, 1948 and many more). These books and papers are largely forgotten nowadays, and did not have the impact that the American followers of Dilthey had on the shaping of social psychology and the social sciences in general. Dilthey also inspired, to some extent, the phenomenological psychology developed by Husserl, which, via Alfred Schütz, contributed to the development of qualitative methods in the social sciences.

But while sociology went qualitative in the 1930s and 1940s, psychology, including social psychology went quantitative in America and elsewhere, and that for a long time. The qualitative tradition is only now being rediscovered after a new crisis in psychology which started in the 1960s.

5. Conclusion

In 1894 Dilthey wrote:

> [. . .] the dominance of explanatory or constructive psychology, which operates with hypotheses on the analogy of the natural sciences, has extraordinarily prejudicial consequences for the development of the human studies. Researchers who devote themselves to positive investigations in the human studies seem to find themselves today under the obligation to forgo giving these investigations any psychological base whatever, or of accepting all the disadvantages of explanatory

psychology. Thus present-day science is caught in the following dilemma, which has contributed enormously to the development of skepticism and a superficial and sterile empiricism, and thus to the increasing separation of life from knowledge. Either the human studies make use of the foundations which psychology offers (and thereby they receive an hypothetical character) or they strive to fulfill their task without the support of any scientifically ordered view of mental affairs, by depending only on a subjective and equivocal psychology of life.

(Dilthey, 1977: 29)

Although he never really developed a *method* that would provide us with the tools whereby we could escape both "superficial and sterile empiricism" on the one hand and the dependence on a "subjective and equivocal psychology of life" on the other, he pointed out the shortcomings of both. In using Dilthey's insights and supplementing them by adding a linguistic and social dimension, his followers started to lay the foundations for new methods in social psychology which, after being sidelined for a quarter of a century, have gradually come to be known as qualitative methods. However, their use in psychology at large is still as controversial today as it was at their inception in the late 1890s.

In this chapter I have tried to apply the hermeneutic method to the issue of the quantity–quality debate itself. By putting it back into the whole of its historical and biographical context, I hope to have shed some light on one part of the modern debate surrounding psychology's goals and methods.

Notes

1   When tracing the roots of "grounded theory", Nick Pidgeon has pointed out that Dilthey's concept of *Verstehen* "became significant in interpretative psychology [. . .], which orients psychological inquiry towards everyday understandings and human subjectivity, as well as in the idiographic school of 1950s and 1960s psychology" (Pidgeon, 1996: 77).

2   Mead had direct experience of the quantitative/qualitative discussion in Germany, having studied under Wilhelm Wundt, Hermann Ebbinghaus and Dilthey (see end of this chapter). Under the influence of German neo-Kantian philosophy (Dilthey, Windelbandt, Rickert), Charles Horton Cooley, who inspired some of Mead's work, also discussed the concept of *Verstehen* in sociological methods. Cooley advocated the method of *sympathetic* introspection, in order to analyse consciousness. He claimed that by "analyzing what they as actors might do in various circumstances, sociologists could understand the meanings and motives that are at the base of social behavior" (Ritzer, 1996: 51). Under the influence of Dilthey (see Platt, 1985: 457), Cooley and Mead, sociologists associated with the Chicago School of Sociology, such as Florian Znaniecki (1936) and George Lundberg (1933) discussed the pros and cons of qualitative and quantitative methods in the 1920s and 1930s, the first advocating case studies, the second statistical methods (see Bulmer, 1984; Hammersley, 1992: 41). Only after the 1930s (see Platt, 1985) the influence of works by Weber and Georg Simmel (whose lecture the influential member of the Chicago sociology department, Robert

Parks, had heard in Berlin, see Ritzer, 1996: 49) made itself felt, the former reinforcing the concept of *Verstehen* used in Chicago circles, the latter reinforcing ideas concerning microsociology. However, by "the 1940s and 50s in sociology, psychology and some other fields, quantitative methods (in the form of survey and experimental research) had become the dominant approach. But since the 1960s there has been a revival in the fortunes of qualitative types of research" (Hammersley, 1992: 40).

3   In chapter three "Objective Psychology" of his book *Marxism and the Philosophy of Language*, Voloshinov deals extensively and quite positively with Dilthey's critique of 'objective psychology', but he also points out that "Dilthey and his followers *make no provision for the social character of meaning*" (Voloshinov, 1986: 27).

4   "However, Mead's work had relatively little impact on Chicago sociology in his lifetime but became important through Blumer, who wrote his PhD on *Method in Social Psychology* in 1928 and was on the staff of the Department of Sociology from 1925 until 1952. It seems to have been Blumer who coined the term *symbolic interactionism* for the kind of sociology that was directly inspired by Mead and which had a major impact after World War II through its influence on people like Shibutani and Strauss" (Murphy et al., 1998: http://www.soton.ac.uk/~hta/htapubs.htm).

5   On the history of qualitative methods, especially in sociology, read Murphy et al. (1998), especially section 2.4.3. "Qualitative research in America 1920–1960" (see also Platt, 1996). They point out that "Qualitative research was not uniquely associated with the University of Chicago" and stress the influence of Robert Park on the debate about methods. He first worked as an investigative journalist, then heard lectures by Simmel in Berlin, and finally worked at the Sociology Department in Chicago from 1914 until 1933. He was instrumental in bringing Continental thinkers to the attention of Chicago sociologists. Park tried to find "a more systematic framework for understanding societies" and the "central role in this was played by direct experience and observation".

6   There are important affinities between the notion of *Verstehen* and Adam Smith's position in *Theory of Moral Sentiments*, though it is not known whether either Dilthey or Mead read Smith's seminal work (Murphy et al., 1998). It is clear however, that economists, such as Schmoller and Menger read Adam Smith and it is also known that other social scientists, such as the early social psychologist Gustav Adolph Lindner quote him frequently (Lindner, 1871).

References

Blumer, H. (1928). *Method in social psychology*, Unpublished PhD dissertation, University of Chicago.

Bryman, A. (1988). *Quantity and quality in social research*. London: Unwin Hyman.

Bühler, K. (1927). *Die Krise der Psychologie*. Jena: Barth. (Original work published in *Kant-Studien 31*, 1926, 455–526).

Bulmer, M. (1984). *The Chicago School of Sociology: Institutionalization, diversity, and the rise of sociological research*. Chicago: University of Chicago Press.

Carroy, J., & Plas, R. (1996). The origins of French experimental psychology: Experiment and experimentalism. *History of the Human Sciences*, 9(1), 73–84.

Cloeren, H. J. (1988). *Language and thought: German approaches to analytic philosophy in the 18th and 19th centuries*. Berlin/New York: Walter de Gruyter.

Dilthey, W. (1894). Ideen über eine beschreibende und zergliedernde Psychologie.

Sitzungsberichte der Akademie der Wissenschaften zu Berlin, 2, 1309–1407. Reprinted in W. Dilthey, *Gesammelte Schriften* (Vol. 5, pp. 139–240). Stuttgart: Teubner (1957).

Dilthey, W. (1977). *Descriptive psychology and historical understanding* (R. M. Zaner, & K. L. Heiges, Trans.). The Hague: Martinus Nijhoff. (Original work published 1894)

Ebbinghaus, H. (1896). Über erklärende und beschreibende Psychologie. *Zeitschrift für Psychologie und Physiologie der Sinnesorgane, 9,* 161–205. (Reprinted in Rodi, & Lessing (1984), pp. 45–87).

Ebbinghaus, H. (1913). *Memory: A contribution to experimental psychology* (H. A. Ruger & C. E. Bussenius, Trans.). New York: Teachers College, Columbia University. (Original work published 1885)

Ebbinghaus, H. (1964). *Memory: A contribution to experimental psychology.* (Henry A. Ruger & Clara Bussenius, Trans. Introduction by E. R. Hilgard). New York: Dover. (Reproduction of 1913 translation of 1885 German *Über das Gedächtnis*)

Farr, R. M. (1996). *The roots of modern social psychology.* Oxford: Blackwell.

Formigari, L. (1994). *La sémiotique empiriste face au kantisme.* Paris: Mardaga.

Gabriel, C. (1980). Different approaches to the study of psychology. In J. Radford (Ed.), *A textbook of psychology* (pp. 33–53). London: Routledge (2nd ed. 1991).

Garfinkel, H. (1967). *Studies in ethnomethodology.* Toronto: Prentice Hall, Inc.

Gordon, S. (1991). *The history and philosophy of social science.* London & New York: Routledge.

Gruhle, H. W. (1948). *Verstehende Psychologie (Erlebnislehre). Ein Lehrbuch.* Stuttgart: G. Thieme.

Hammersley, M. (1992). Deconstructing the qualitative–quantitative divide. In Julia Brannen (Ed.), *Mixing methods: Qualitative and quantitative research* (pp. 39–55). Aldershot: Avebury.

Harré, R., & Gillett, G. (1994). *The discursive mind.* Thousand Oaks, CA: Sage Publications.

Hinkle, R. C. (1994). *Developments in American sociological theory, 1915–1950.* Albany: State University of New York Press.

Hodges, H. A. (1952). *The philosophy of Wilhelm Dilthey.* London: Routledge & Kegan Paul.

Husserl, E. (1977). *Phenomenological psychology.* Lectures, Summer Semester, 1925, (J. Scanlon, Trans.). The Hague: Martinus Nijhoff. (Original work published 1925)

James, W. (1892). A plea for psychology as a "natural science". *Philosophical Review, 1,* 146–153. (Reprinted in *Essays in psychology.* Cambridge, MA: Harvard University Press, 1983).

Jaspers, K. (1913). Kausale und verständliche Zusammenhänge zwischen Schicksal und Psychose bei Dementia praecox (Schizophrenie). *Zeitschrift für die gesamte, Neurologie und Psychiatrie, 14*(2), 158ff.

Kant, I. (1974). *Anthropology from a pragmatic point of view.* (Translated, with an Introduction and Notes, by Mary J. Gregor). The Hague: Nijhoff. (Original published in 1798)

Leary, D. E. (1982). Immanuel Kant and the development of modern psychology. In W. R. Woodward, & M. G. Ash (Eds.), *The problematic science: Psychology in nineteenth-century thought* (pp. 17–42). New York: Praeger.

Lindner, G. A. (1871). *Ideen zur Psychologie der Gesellschaft als Grundlage der Social-wissenschaft*. Wien: Carl Gerold's Sohn.

Lundberg, G. (1933). Is sociology too scientific? *Sociologus*, *9*, 298–322.

Makkreel, R. A. (1977). *Dilthey. Philosopher of the human studies*. Princeton, NJ: Princeton University Press.

Malinowski, B. (1918). Letter to Alan Henderson Gardiner, from the Trobriand Islands, 29 April 1918. Ashmolean Museum, Griffith Institute, Oxford: Gardiner MSS, AHG 42.201.1

Manicas, P. T. (1987). *A history and philosophy of the social sciences*. Oxford: Basil Blackwell.

Mead, G. H. (1934). *Mind, self, and society: From the standpoint of a social behaviorist* (Edited and with an Introduction by C. W. Morris). Chicago & London: University of Chicago Press.

Murphy, E., Dingwall, R., Greatbatch, D., Parker, S., & Watson, P. (1998). Qualitative research methods in health technology assessment: A review of the literature. *Health Technology Assessment*, *2*(16), iii–ix. http://www.soton.ac.uk/~hta/htapubs.htm.

Nerlich, B., & Clarke, D. D. (1996). *Language, action, and context. The early history of pragmatics in Europe and America 1780–1930*. Amsterdam/Philadelphia: John Benjamins.

Nerlich, B., & Clarke, D. D. (1998). The linguistic repudiation of Wundt. *History of Psychology*, *1*(3), 179–204.

Nicolas, S. (1994). Hermann Ebbinghaus (1850–1909): La vie et l'oeuvre d'un grand psychologue expérimentaliste. *Schweizerische Zeitschrift für Psychologie – Revue Suisse de Psychologie*, *53*(1), 5–12.

Parker, I. (1989). *The crisis in modern social psychology, and how to end it*. London: Routledge.

Pidgeon, N. (1996). Grounded theory: Theoretical background. In J. T. E. Richardson (Ed.), *Handbook of qualitative methods for psychology and the social sciences* (pp. 75–85). Leicester: BPS Books.

Platt, J. (1985). Weber's *Verstehen* and the history of qualitative research: The missing link. *British Journal of Sociology*, *36*(3), 448–466.

Platt, J. (1996). *A history of sociological research methods in America 1920–1960*. Cambridge: Cambridge University Press.

Politzer, G. (1994). *Critique of the foundations of psychology: The psychology of psycho-anlysis* (M. Apprey, Trans., foreword by A. Giorgi). Pittsburgh, PA: Duquesne University Press. (Original work published 1928)

Richardson, J. T. E. (Ed.) (1996). *Handbook of qualitative methods for psychology and the social sciences*. Leicester: BPS books.

Ritzer, G. (1996). *Classical sociological theory*. New York, etc.: The McGraw-Hill companies, Inc.

Rodi, F., & Lessing, H.-U. (Eds.) (1984). *Materialien zur Philosophie Wilhelm Diltheys*. Frankfurt/M.: Suhrkamp.

Schmitz, H. W. (1987). Der Begriff der "Conversation" bei Gabriel Tarde. *Kodikas/Code*, *10*(3/4), 287–299.

Schweizer, W. (1924). *Erklären und Verstehen in der Psychologie*. Inaugural diss., Bern: P. Haupt.

Tarde, G. (1973). *Ecrits de psychologie sociale*; choisis et présentés par A. M. Rocheblave-Spenlé et J. Milet ("Radamanthe"). Toulouse: Edouard Privat.

Toren, C. (1996). Ethnography: theoretical background. In J. T. E Richardson

(Ed.), *Handbook of qualitative methods for psychology and the social sciences* (pp. 102–112). Leicester: BPS Books.

Turner, R. S. (1982). Helmholtz, sensory physiology, and the disciplinary development of German psychology. In W. R. Woodward, & M. G. Ash (Eds.), *The problematic science: Psychology in nineteenth-century thought* (pp. 147–166). New York: Praeger.

Veer, R. van der, & Valsiner, J. (1991). *Understanding Vygotsky: A quest for synthesis*. Oxford: Blackwell.

Viddich, A. J., & Lyman, S. M. (1994). Qualitative methods: Their history in sociology and anthropology. In N. K. Denzin, & Y. S. Lincoln (Eds.), *Handbook of qualitative research* (pp. 23–59). Thousand Oaks, CA: Sage Publications.

Voloshinov, V. N. (1986). *Marxism and the philosophy of language* (L. Matejka and I. R. Titunik, Trans.). London, England; Cambridge, MA: Harvard University Press.

Vonk, F. (1992). *Gestaltprinzip und abstraktive Relevanz. Eine wissenschafthistorische Untersuchung zur Sprachaxiomatik Karl Bühlers*. Münster: Nodus.

Vonk, F. (1996). Linguistik und Psychologie. Sprachursprung und Sprachfunktionen. In K. D. Dutz, & H.-J. Niederehe (Eds.), *Theorie und Rekonstruktion* (pp. 181–205). Münster: Nodus Publikationen.

Weber, M. (1968). *Economy and society* (3 Vols). Totowa, NJ: Bedminster Press. (Original work published 1921)

Woodward, W. R., & Ash, M. G. (Eds.) (1982). *The problematic science: psychology in nineteenth-century thought*. New York: Praeger.

Wundt, W. (1874). *Grundzüge der physiologischen Psychologie*. Leipzig: Engelmann.

Wundt, W. (1922). *Völkerpsychologie; Eine Untersuchung der Entwicklungsgesetze von Sprache, Mythus und Sitte*. Vol. 1, first part and Vol. 2, second part: *Die Sprache*. 4th unchanged ed. Leipzig: Kröner. (Original work published 1900)

Znaniecki, F. (1934). *The method of sociology*. New York: Farrar and Rinehart.

Znaniecki, F. (1936). *Social action*. New York: Farrar and Rinehart.

3 Reinventing validity

Reflections on principles and practices from beyond the quality–quantity divide

Karen Henwood

a method by itself is neither valid nor invalid; methods can produce valid data or accounts in some circumstances and invalid ones in others. Validity is not an inherent property of a particular method, but pertains to the data, accounts or conclusions reached by using that method in a particular context for a particular purpose.

(Maxwell, 1992, p. 284)

Validity is not a commodity that can be purchased with techniques . . . Rather validity is like integrity, character and quality, to be assessed relative to purposes and circumstances.

(Brinberg and McGrath, 1985, p. 13)

The background to this discussion of validity within psychology rests in the legacy of "modernism" or "the Enlightenment" on what is often taken for granted as appropriate intellectual standards and practices. The idea that rational "man" lays the foundation for objective, scientific practice which has the potential to harness and control natural processes, leading inexorably to social progress and to an increase in human welfare, has been integral to much twentieth-century thought, including the development of the discipline of psychology. Such modernist commitments are unlikely to disappear as justification for much psychological endeavour well into the new millennium. At the same time, postmodern developments are likely to continue and strengthen. These work against modernist influences by highlighting its limitations (Gergen, 1982, 1992; Kvale, 1992). This situation raises some obvious and pressing questions about discussions of validity: can and should they be modern or postmodern, or can they be both at the same time?

This chapter suggests that, although there is no absolute requirement to turn away from modernist, and towards postmodernist psychology, we do need to appreciate and utilise the benefits of destabilising and disrupting unhelpful or worn out categories and dichotomies. The term often used by discussants of postmodernism to label this endeavour is "deconstruction" (Burman, 1994; Parker & Shotter, 1990; Richer, 1992), and this is useful in its analogy to taking down a previously built edifice so that another can be put in its place. Unfortunately the term has also become loaded with unlimited destructive intent. So it is important to note that the aim here is not to critique or undermine the supposedly essential foundations of modern psychology in some totalising or universalising way. In particular, there is no wish to undervalue psychology's historical concern to include discussions of how research is done – issues of process, procedure, and method – as integral to ways of demonstrating research quality.

However, we do need to avoid the methodogmatic (see e.g. Reinharz, 1988, 1994) view that validity is something inherent in a clearly delimited set of procedures. Quality checklists or lists of procedures have begun to proliferate in recent years (Blaxter, 1996; Elliot, Fischer, & Rennie, 1999; Stiles, 1993; Turpin et al., 1997; and see Spencer, Richie, Lewis, & Dillon, 2003, for a recent overview). These are useful not as procedures for guaranteeing truth (Murphy, Dingwall, Greatbatch, Parker, & Watson, 1998), but as resources to be used flexibly (Yardley, 2000) to promote awareness of alternative and extended ways of conceptualising validity and appropriately enhancing the validity of diverse kinds of qualitative studies (Taylor, 2001). In a manner resembling arguments in favour of "methodological feminocentrism" (Warren, 1988, cited in Wolf, 1996), this chapter articulates the case for reinventing issues of validity, legitimacy or "goodness" (Marshall, 1985) out of contemporary discussions of more contextual and practical ways of doing "inquiry guided" research (Mishler, 1990).

The insights about validity discussed in this chapter derive from a number of interrelated domains: feminist research, qualitative methodology and social science (Henwood & Pidgeon, 1995; Maynard & Purvis, 1994); the quality–quantity debate (Guba and Lincoln, 1994; Lincoln and Guba, 1985) – including arguments for mixing methods which are an outgrowth of these (Todd, 1998; Todd, Nerlich, & McKeown, this volume); and dialogue between critical and interpretive psychology and ethnography (Denzin, 1997; Lather, 1986, 1993, 1995). Engagements and disengagements between various positions expressed in these domains destabilise and question taken for granted assumptions that close off necessary avenues for discussion in respect of validity. Arguments in favour of mixing methods can serve to disrupt unhelpful aspects of the quality–quantity divide, as long as this position is formulated so as not to collapse issues of difference into a pre-existing hegemony.

Some of the immediate issues and intractable barriers confronted by psychologists when they first come across different approaches to research within an expanded methodological terrain are addressed in the first part of the chapter. The second considers efforts that have been made to work out how issues of validity apply in research that does not seek to rely on the rhetoric or norm of objectivity for its justification. Both parts concern some of the major benefits and challenges of harnessing the conversations that are taking place about validity from beyond the quality–quantity divide.

1. Emic construction of qualitative inquiry and what makes good and bad research

Discussions of culture-sensitive approaches to the institutions and practices of science have long encompassed arguments for embracing qualitative methods, and associated understandings of scientific inquiry, based on the proposition that knowledge is specific to purpose and context (Chalmers, 1982; Latour, 1987; Ravetz, 1971; Woolgar, 1988). This defining idea provided the rationale for a small scale piece of funded research that I conducted in 1996–7, and reported upon shortly afterwards (Henwood, 1998). The project aimed to evaluate a single innovation – my own teaching on qualitative methods on a clinical psychology training course. It asked: How well would my teaching, which initially had been developed for a broader psychological and social science audience, transfer across into this particular domain? How did it compare with other in vivo or externally taught developments on other UK courses? Had the changes that I had made to take account of the new teaching context provided a better focus, and had they been sufficient?

The answers to these specific questions are not relevant here, but the focus on a range of largely participant-generated (emic) constructions of qualitative research and qualitative methods generated in the course of the study is of interest, along with the assumptions about good and bad research and threats to reputable, creditable, or valid psychological science contained within those constructions. The initial analysis reported to the project funders differentiated between perspectives on the uptake of qualitative research into clinical psychology, and encoded the range of positions that it was possible to take up within the discourses of disciplinary legitimation. It used data in the form of participants' accounts gathered by telephone interviews[1] with course team leaders and methods specialists on clinical psychology training courses, and made use of a convenience classification of four (far from homogeneous or mutually exclusive) response types: "active facilitative", "passive/anxious facilitative", "reactive" and "nothing new/no change" (Henwood, 1998). Analysis of these response types pointed to the need for contextual sensitivity of efforts to introduce qualitative methods teaching within clinical psychology training. This chapter addresses connections between issues of validity and quantitative and qualitative inquiry as indicated by participants' accounts, read by the researcher, and framed by a research narrative aimed at going beyond the familiar polarities often found in discussions of qualitative vis-à-vis quantitative methods. The two maximally contrasting categories considered here are: "reactive" and "active facilitative".

1.1 *"Reactive" responses*

Within the "reactive" category, responses took up a number of specific constructions or positions, all of which posed barriers to adopting a non-dualistic approach to psychological methods. The tropes, ideas, images and arguments that recurred constructed qualitative research as lacking, bringing difficulties, and measuring up less well against assumed research standards. Instead of presenting a relational view of the ways in which qualitative and quantitative methods can serve equally and mutually informing functions within the total research process, these comments presumed a *hierarchical view of difference*. Hence the potentials of qualitative inquiry remain silent or hidden within this type of discourse, other than to reader-hearers already actively attuned, and able to access, non-hierarchical positionings.

Dubious researchers: a restatement of a dichotomy between methods

> In the past (we) have not been strong in qualitative methods. We have been more quantitative. [. . .] I am not averse to qualitative but do have reservations. While qualitative research itself may not be dubious, dubious researchers can be drawn to it for it is easier to do dubious qualitative research. It is harder work with richer data.
>
> (Precis 1, interviewee 17)

In this precis, although qualitative research methods are not seen as inherently flawed in and of themselves, they are seen as providing a haven for "dubious" researchers who find them easier to abuse (see quotation/precis 1[2]). So, within this construction, complex issues of validity are apparently reduced to the single issue of a dualism between methods. Later in the quotation, though, it is implied that, with hard work, qualitative analyses of rich data are both desirable and achievable. Two further points of critical, contextual analysis also point to further reasons for believing that claiming semi-inherent virtues for quantitative research throws more heat than light on the subject of threats to validity. First, locating perceived problems with qualitative methods within the dispositions of individual researchers resorts to an ad hominum argument that tells us little about people's preferences and behaviours when compared to more complex accounts of the meanings of psycho-social events viewed in relation to culture and to history. Second, it neglects to consider that quantitative research has been a vehicle for the expression of bias and intolerance too, especially on certain well known and widely discussed topics and issues.[3]

Hermetically sealed paradigms/world views

> we are worried about being unable to give detailed advice to trainees and training co-ordinators and an inability to evaluate and give feedback to trainees. Individual courses define what they do, their world view, what it is. It seems that trainees (doing qualitative research) need to have a high tolerance for ambiguity, and we as supervisors need to be able to limit that ambiguity. We are worried about existing guidelines, assessment

criteria, wordlimits. The place for qualitative research must fit within the philosophy of clinical psychology. For this course what is desirable must fit within the scientist practitioner model. [Researcher: Can qualitative research have a use?] Qualitative is secondary it informs and illuminates other views, at least that is one perspective from some clinicians.

(Precis 2, interviewee 21)

This second quotation takes a paradigmatic or world view approach to methodological issues (individual courses and clinical psychology have a "world view" that is different to qualitative inquiry). It questions the general acceptability of qualitative methods, and limits their uptake to occasions where they can be fitted into already established practices and disciplinary regimes.

The fact that the paradigmatic/world view approach can take on this particular role in undercutting the perceived acceptability of qualitative methods is worthy of special mention here, as it is more typically viewed as a way of establishing an autonomous place for qualitative vis-à-vis quantitative methods – for example in the arguments made in the 1960s in sociology (Glaser & Strauss, 1967; see also Bryman, 1988); in the 1970s for ethogenic psychology (Harré & Secord, 1972); and in the 1980s for naturalistic inquiry (Lincoln & Guba, 1985). Accordingly, there is some irony in the identification of qualitative and quantitative research as representing different world views serving to reposition qualitative research back in a subservient or dependent role.

The quotation/precis relates clinical psychologists' concerns about giving feedback and assessing qualitative research conducted by trainees, and proceeds to construct qualitative research in two stages. In the first, the difference between qualitative and quantitative research is described as having an apparently disabling influence on an otherwise experienced teacher and course team, who now find it difficult to give guidance to trainees based on approved standards for research and dissertations. In the second, difficulties expressed in the first are apparently resolved by drawing upon the regulatory function of the course's preferred scientific practitioner model. As a result, qualitative research is constructed as playing only a subordinate, supporting or "secondary" role.

It is possible that this quotation/precis retrenches an established disciplinary position, as a way of dealing with anxieties about change. Developing this point, Boyle (1998) suggests that some of the hidden values of numbers (e.g. in delivering status and prestige, and feelings of control over subject matter) can result in emotional resistancies to qualitative inquiry. By limiting discussion of validity to established guidelines, and to a concern for stipulating the minutiae of how to do and write up quantitative studies, it is as if a hermetic seal is formed around clinical psychology, and against those different concerns and potentials that qualitative principles and practices bring to inquiry guided research. The possibility of diverse relationships existing between researchers and regulatory/disciplining regimes also goes unrecognised. Three further issues, can be identified, however, that run

counter to the effect of such paradigmatic arguments in the elision of difference: researcher openness, observational multiplicity, and democratisation of
the research process. These issues are integral to the later section on discussions about extending and reinventing validity. "researcher openness",
"observational multiplicity" and "democratisation of the research process".

RESEARCHER OPENNESS

Although it may well be necessary to place limitations on the ambiguity and
uncertainty that are part of the research and teaching process, qualitative
research points to the necessity of attending, in equal measure, to both sides
of the dialectical inquiry process. The need for "researcher openness"[4] is one
of the major justifications for undertaking a qualitative study and, moreover,
attending to this principle is a way of increasing validity in qualitative
inquiry. This principle of openness offers guidance on the need to reduce the
risk of unreflexively constructing objects of inquiry by the theories and
methods used to study it. The same principle of openness can also be applied
more widely to members of the research community, by alerting them, for
example, to the risks attached to research that proceeds exclusively by
abstract theory testing (viz. of never looking beyond what one already knows;
Flick, 1998).

OBSERVATIONAL MULTIPLICITY

Some qualitative research principles and techniques are not easily displaced
by arguments that construct qualitative research as of only marginal importance, accept the scientist practitioner model as the norm, or in other ways
support the hegemony of quantitive methods. Central among them, and
labelled here "observational multiplicity", is the use of multiple methods,
perspectives, research sites and data sources to create more multi-faceted
accounts of a phenomenon or topic of interest (Miles & Huberman, 1994),
or to break down uniform, unified and seamless representational forms
(Henwood & Pidgeon, 1995).

Observational multiplicity often underpins a mixed methods approach to
inquiry, although without undermining arguments in favour of conducting
single method, one-shot studies should an attempt at theory verification/
falsification be appropriate. Rather, the aim is to create an equally valued role
for the principled comparing of methods, perspectives and sites/cases as an
approach to designing and analysing studies, and as a means of staking
claims to validity.

The principle of observational multiplicity is sometimes described as a
process of establishing validity through a process of "triangulation" (Marris &
Simmons, 1995). With its traditional routes in navigation practice, triangulation refers to taking measurements from different positions to increase the
accuracy of recording the single location of a known entity (a technique for

establishing reliability of measurement). However, there has been some discussion of how to merge together internal/construct/concurrent validity and reliability.[5] Moreover, revisions have been made to the navigational view of triangulation to address the critiques of naive realism underpinning the view of using different methods to identify a single spatial location. As commented upon by Flick, in the "triangulation as validity" view "the focus . . . has shifted . . . towards further enriching and completing knowledge and towards transgressing the (always limited) epistemological potentials of the individual method" (Flick, 1998, p. 230).

DEMOCRATISATION OF THE RESEARCH PROCESS

Another issue identifiable through active, critical and contextual reading of the quotation/precis 2, is its reliance upon appeals to institutional standing and to the status quo to express its methodological position. Prior to the caveat at the end of the remark ("at least that is the perspective of some clinicians"), it presumes an all powerful and all knowing position: qualitative research is simply pronounced as lacking consistency with "the philosophy of clinical psychology". The absence of any attempt to justify this claim, or to be reflexive about the assumptions that might make it possible, makes this argument interpretable as an overtly disciplining or regulatory one. Certainly, it makes no attempt to address or question its own "will to power". For this reason it provides no general solution to issues that are now pressing for clinical (and other) psychologists, who are having to find ways of delivering increased democratisation of their research.

Increasingly, within the NHS, the doors of research are being opened to include the views of service users. This movement parallels the long-standing qualitative research position that more informed and useful knowledge will often be produced by social inquiry if it takes people's personal and cultural understandings and stocks of knowledge fully into account. Clinical psychologists, themselves, are increasingly endorsing this as a commitment to qualitative inquiry, and for its possible role increasing democratisation of the research process (see e.g. Clegg & King, 1998; Patel, 1998; Phillips, 1998). Alongside long-standing assumptions about validity concerns being at the heart of the research process, therefore, stand efforts to promote the greater flexibility and practical choice offered to clinical psychology researchers by qualitative approaches and methods of inquiry. No longer is it possible to neglect key issues highlighted by qualitative researchers merely on the grounds that they are different to the scientist-practitioner norm.

1.2 *"Active facilitative" responses*

the majority still do quantitative work, but the people involved in teaching here take a practical approach – the best method for the questions, with the exception of (X) who is pro-discourse analysis (DA). Other staff do not like the epistemological assumptions of the approach, but accept that students can work with it. Different criteria are used to assess pieces of work that buy into different epistemological assumptions. We will not ask for reliability tests with DA, although students are expected to do work that matches with the epistemological positions they take.

(Interviewee 12, precis 3).

the taught research methods module combines qualitative and quantitative methods . . . We take a balanced view of both approaches, while having a leaning ourselves towards qualitative.

(Interviewee 2, precis 4)

trainees are expected to be competent in a variety of methods, including both qualitative and quantitative, so the training is pluralistic. It is guided by a philosophy of science framework to give familiarity with an epistemic framework for establishing validity from both qualitative and quantitative standpoints, and which involves deconstructing claims in favour of quantitative.

(Interviewee 1, precis 5)

Explicit alternatives to the constructions of qualitative research offered within the "reactive" category are conveyed by those classified in the original study as "active facilitative" responses. Rather than seeking to specify the contrasting properties of qualitative and quantitative inquiry, or viewing them as clearly definable entities, these responses articulated a defensible and deserving place for qualitative research and adopted a stance of methodological pluralism. Sometimes, this stance was also proposed as a possible way of redressing efforts at disciplinary legitimation and regulation.

The role and benefits of qualitative methods were discussed in terms of providing a grounding in philosophy of science and the deconstruction of quantitative research (quotation/precis 5); the need to take a practical approach linking together questions and methods (quotation/precis 3); and how to advance a more balanced approach to quantity–quality issues (referred to in quotation/precis 4). Minimal and stronger commitments to methodological pluralism were expressed. A commitment to institutional tolerance by colleagues towards others who took a different view was associated with a belief in distributed expertise between individuals. Where particular individuals had responsibility for research methods teaching in toto, they described their role as foregrounding possibilities for combining methods and presenting methodological preferences among staff. Stronger statements took pluralism out of the domain of institutional and departmental politics of methodological inclusion, and into a full discussion of ways of accommodating a recognition of epistemic difference. How to accommodate claims about epistemic difference within discussions of method and epistemology, though, is no straightforward matter. In particular it is necessary to find a way to accommodate claims to difference, while avoiding polarising arguments that position qualitative and quantitative methods as competing or incommensurable paradigms (Bryman, 1988; Henwood & Pidgeon, 1994). Such polarisation supports a tendency towards hypercriticality, instils restricted vision, and blocks new ways of embracing, extending, revisioning or reinventing existing form of understanding (Atkinson, Delamont, & Hammersley, 1988). This is particularly important within extended discussions of what it means to evaluate and legitimate research using qualitative methods, either singly or within a mixed methods design.

Some have argued that latterday discussions that seek to extend, revise, or reinvent validity issues are merely an exercise in "criteriology": the reintroduction of some of modernism's least helpful preoccupations and preconceptions in an effort to keep a tight rein on the "conceptual practices of power" (Schwandt, 1996). Yet, it is probably not helpful to become solely entrenched in arguments for or against criteria.[6] Rather, what is needed is the development of appropriate frames of reference to help qualitative and quantitative researchers appraise the relevance of an extended range of ways of evaluating psychological studies that will in some respects be similar and in others different in kind.

2. Discussions of validity beyond the hierarchical view of quality–quantity issues

How are questions about the soundness, believability, legitimacy or validity of findings from empirical, qualitative studies addressed by researchers who take on an equal rather than hierarchical difference view of quality–quantity issues? Are frameworks available, or being developed, that are able to facilitate the use of criteria for evaluating quantitative studies in thoughtful, rather than methodogmatic, ways? To what extent do such frameworks take on board the dilemmas of qualitative inquiry, or do they merely sideline them as matters to be (conveniently) associated with quantitative studies? These are the kinds of question to be addressed if discussions of validity are to be extended beyond the dualistic division between qualitative and quantitative methods. While these questions cannot be exhaustively addressed within the remaining space for this chapter, some attempt can be made to move in fruitful directions.

It is not always easy to locate or describe ways of assuring research quality within the traditions that form the backbone of qualitative inquiry (such as ethnography and phenomenology). Partly, this is because the topic of research quality/validity has tended to be "owned" (Altheide & Johnson, 1994) by scientists who define empirical inquiry positivistically (viz. by using precise, numerical measures to establish empirical facts and using these to directly test theory). Yet, there is considerable evidence within qualitative research communities of investigators orienting towards the evaluation of their studies in similar ways. In ethnographic work, for example, considerable importance is placed on the researcher's commitment to prolonged engagement in the field, to taking a principled stance on the balance between "insider" and "outsider" perspectives in fieldwork relations, and on the "thickness" of descriptions written up in fieldnotes and later in the ethno-graphic monograph itself (Burgess, 1984). In phenomenologically oriented studies, the starting point for developing good and useful knowledge is a detailed appreciation of members' unreflective, first hand, taken-for-granted stocks of knowledge, attempts to make such tacit knowledge explicit, and efforts to establish second and third order perspectives and understandings (Schütz, 1953). It would seem, then, that evaluative principles and practices do lie at the heart of qualitative inquiry traditions, but that they are not reflected upon in the same way as in quantitative research, as specific tokens of research quality.

Where efforts have been made to reflect theoretically and methodologically upon both the principles and the practices of qualitative inquiry (Hammersley & Atkinson, 1983), the result is a more accessible knowledge base that can be mined about pointers to validity. Where efforts have been made to develop difference-sensitive ways of evaluating qualitative studies, they tend to be informed by the realisation that ensuring and demonstrating validity need not remain restricted to strategies for truthfully reflecting a single, static state or entity since this view is limited to perspectives that assume a simple realist ontology and epistemology. The first of three lines of argument that follow rests on the view that researchers must provide a thorough and careful account of linkages (including any broken ones) between the various elements of the entire knowledge process: hence the first sub-heading "validating the knowledge process". The second sub-section considers the issue of transgressing the rigour/ethics divide, and the third questions ways of asserting authority in discussions of writing, representation and validity.

2.1 Validating the knowledge process

A first example is Flick's (1998) thesis that, because all qualitative research works with texts as its empirical material, a commitment to validity amounts to analysing processes of mimesis, or symbolic world making in the text. That is to say, it involves analysing the processes by which texts are transformed by, refer to, and link with, reality and with one another. Three core principles are identified as part of such analyses: demonstrate the merits of the ways in which one has reconstructed each case to be analysed (viz. though the thoroughness and appropriateness of one's fieldnotes, transcripts, etc.); demonstrate that one has adopted the requisite amount of researcher openness throughout the research process (from case reconstruction, to coding/categorising, to interpretation, analysis and explanation); show that one has instituted controls to check on such openness.

Analytic integrity and continuity, and its demonstrability, is the major theme running throughout Mason's (1996; reprinted, second edition 2002) discussion of the ways in which qualitative researchers can approach the familiar issues of reliability, validity and generalisability. For her, qualitative and quantitative researchers differ profoundly in the specific ways in which they produce sound and well founded analyses, and demonstrate that they have proceeded in a rigorous fashion – making reasonable assumptions in the process. But they differ not at all in their desire to "produce analyses and explanations that are convincing" (p. 136). Hence, the qualitative researcher's task becomes one of replacing conventional or standardised ways of forming research questions and generating explanations of findings, with the more "continuous and arduous" (p. 150) one of posing the most difficult questions it is possible to ask about the course of individual research projects.

Researchers are recommended to ask themselves whether they have ensured, and demonstrated to others, that the methods they have used to generate and analyse data are appropriate to the questions addressed, and that the various methodological operations involved in the project have been executed honestly, carefully and accurately (as opposed to truthfully or correctly, which is too narrow a formulation, since it assumes that it is possible for one uniform, seamless reality to be observed). Then questions need to be asked about "methodological" and "interpretive" validity, based on the requirement for further clarity about the ontological status of concepts and constructs that are being used, and about the epistemological framework for studying them. The following kinds of question could be asked to establish methodological validity: Is the logic of the methodology matched to the kinds of question asked and explanations sought? Were the particular methods used consistent with this broader strategy? Did the interviews or observations (for example), conducted on each specific occasion, produce relevant data for addressing these questions, and for developing these explanations? For interpretive validity: Is the quality and rigour of the means by which particular interpretations and analyses of data have been arrived at sufficient, and has its sufficiency been demonstrated? Do the interpretations offered address the issues that have been specified (both in the research project's intellectual puzzles and research questions) in conceptually coherent and appropriate ways? Have the interpretations been derived in analytically supportable ways, given the pathways through the data gathering, coding and analysis parts of the research? The adoption of two more specific kinds of questioning strategies is also said to be useful here. Is it clear that the researcher has understood and engaged with his/her own assumptions, standpoints and conceptual lenses (thereby endowing the analysis with the requisite quality of researcher reflexivity)? Has the audience been shown why any one chosen interpretation should be preferred over other possible ones (suggesting that the researcher has shown sufficient awareness of the relevance of multiple perspectives to the task of justifying interpretation)?

Mason's approach is also concerned with establishing the wider resonance of the study beyond its particular context (viz. generalisability) and, on this point, she combines her questioning stance with the requirement that researchers should identify the particular basis (out of four possibilities) upon which they are staking a claim to theoretical (as opposed to statistical) generalisability: (i) Either their claim relies upon having established that there is no reason to suspect sample atypicality; or (ii) they are arguing from a holistic analysis of one specific setting, to draw out lessons for other settings (also called the notion of transferability); or (iii) they are establishing claims about wider sets of processes from an analysis of carefully chosen pivotal or extreme cases; or finally (iv), their claims for wider resonance are based on the rigour of an analysis conducted by using sampling and analytic strategies that underpin the qualitative approaches of grounded theory (Glaser & Strauss, 1967) and analytic induction (Bulmer, 1979). The latter type of approach probably represents the most ambitious one for establishing claims to interpretive validity. By making strategic comparisons between specially chosen cases or theoretically derived sampling units explanatory theories can be developed. By seeking out negative instances, that suggest alternative explanations, emerging ideas and theories can be put to the test.

Whereas Flick's framework concerns processes of mimesis and Mason's asks difficult questions, Yardley's approach (1997) reviews various approaches to validity, but similarly establishes the need for non-realist formulations. In particular, she argues against a hypocritical approach which, having critiqued the norm of objectivity, claims objectivity for its own materials and findings. But in talking of a rift between qualitative and quantitative researchers, her case is that this has been exaggerated and that both need to express more tentative, thoughtful, and limited forms of validation that are apprised of the dilemmas of research since "these tentative and thoughtful forms of validation have the immense value of stimulating awareness of methodological issues other than sample size and statistical significance, [and also] continually expose the intellectual and ethical dilemmas inherent in research" (Yardley, 1997, p. 40).

Yardley's consideration of a range of dilemmatic ways of establishing validity adds depth and complexity of appreciation of validity issues. Theoretical sampling is said to depend mainly on variability, but also on typicality concerns. Coding schemes have different uses extending across realist and non-realist goals. Striving for rigour and coherence can function as a non-objectivist alternative, or as a form of objectivist rhetoric. Reflexivity is useful in disclosing how conclusions are reached, and can thus defend against accusations of subjective bias/covert prejudice, but it can also degenerate into futile narcissism; moreover, if presented as an objectivist account of motives, it is an impossible aim. Triangulation can easily be misunderstood as a procedure for checking that measures converge upon a unitary conclusion, but it can have the advantage of opening up avenues for multiple interrogation and observation (see also earlier comments on p. 42–3). Respondent validation or member checking is a useful procedure when the research aim is to describe participants' views, but one would not expect analytic outcomes to be easily recognisable by participants (if at all) from studies with other kinds of goals (such as to deconstruct accounts, or to seek out the rhetorical strategies in use).

While validity is presented as an impossible goal, in Yardley's treatment this view is yet subject to compromise. There may be no gold standards, but more limited authority can be claimed. For example, interpretations may be presented as "comprehensive and coherent, consistent with the data and theoretically sophisticated, and meaningful to both participants and peers" (Yardley, 1997, p. 40). Or they can be seen to rely "on a combination of thorough and conscientious exploration and reporting, intellectual excellence, consensus of opinion, and productive utility" (Yardley quoting Guba & Lincoln, 1994, p. 40). None of these attributes, either in combination or singly, are expressions of absolute guarantees of validity, even in relation to the specific circumstances of the study to which they have applied. However, they are a way of strengthening confidence that any particular study has been conducted with serious research intent, and in accordance with an appropriate understanding of the kinds of activities that research should involve.

2.2 Transgressing the rigour/ethics divide

Another way of aiding the project of reinventing validity is by being explicit about the diversity of goals and values that are relevant to the task of producing knowledge. Having recognised that there can be no assumptionless science, researchers' next task is to reflect upon the kinds of assumptions, goals and values that one's approach to inquiry entails and how, in turn, these have consequences for the process of validation. Two extreme possibilities would seem to have little to recommend them. One is seeking to to reassert the supremacy of the values and practices of logical-empiricist inquiry, such as those of disengagement and control, by proclaiming abstract, intellectual goals as justifiably dominant personal, disciplinary or societal values. But neither is it satisfactory to assert competitor goals, such as liberation/ emancipation, artistic creation, and action for change if, in so doing, the intrinsic value of the pursuit of knowledge is completely effaced. A preferable, middle way, is to jointly promote standards of ethics and standards of inquiry so that each is able to transgress the other's ways of evaluating inquiry when taken alone. By considering them it is possible to break out of the assumption that one is limited to thinking about validity in terms of a "rigour/ethics divide" (Lincoln, 1995).

Attempts have begun to be made to provide not fixed and regulatory criteria but emergent, relational ones that have relevance for a community of interpreting scientists and scholars who are committed to a research ethic of conducting their inquiries in the manner of dialectical, mutually respectful, critical inquiry (Lincoln, 1995). The criteria that have emerged are developments from the earlier criteria for establishing trustworthiness in naturalistic inquiry, and from specialist ways of evaluating case study reports (Lincoln & Guba, 1990), but they have also taken into account some principles and practices whose genealogy lies more closely at the interface between critical and postmodernist inquiry (Lather, 1986, 1995). By exposing the potential non-contradictoriness of different, value-sensitive ways of appraising inquiry, or by discussing the reasons for contradictions when they occur, they can effectively "collapse the distinction between quality(rigour) and research ethics" (Lincoln, 1995, p. 275). For example, being committed to displaying the partiality and social situatedness of one's own positioning or standpoint as researcher guards against silencing the claims of other voices, as well as being an appellation of quality and rigour. The formulation of such non-dichotomising or relational kinds of criteria for assessing empirical/fieldwork investigations is also broached within frameworks that discuss the issues of writing and representation.

2.3 Writing and representation

A third area of contemporary analyses that is now also generating insights about validity is concerned with the interrelated issues of writing and representation, especially when conducted in dialogue with reflections upon the processes of fieldwork and other forms of qualitative inquiry (Clifford & Marcus, 1986; van Maanan, 1988; Wolcott, 1990). The connection between validity issues and these concerns follows inevitably once the metaphor of directness and immediacy has been displaced by a concern for intervening processes of mediation, interpretation and transformation in conceptualisations of the principles and practices of science. The seeds of the view that empirical and interpretive work can be integrated within one and the same epistemic domain were sown much earlier this century by phenomenological and hermeneutic research traditions, but now these have been consolidated by critical, postcolonial and postmodernist perspectives on knowing that have specifically focused upon the concepts of writing and representation (Denzin, 1997). By extending the metaphor of "world as text" to "science as text", the ways in which events and persons (including self and other) are portrayed – or represented – in scientific texts and other writing genres have become both a fashion and a serious concern within a wide range of social science disciplines, including psychology in recent years (see e.g. Fine & Wiess, 1996; Henwood, Griffin, & Phoenix, 1998).

As a result of these kinds of deliberation a framework has been proposed for comparing craftskill, communicative and pragmatic concepts of validity (Kvale, 1995). Another development is the examination and use of new writing forms as a vehicle through which critical and interpretive researchers can effect various "transgressions of validity" (Lather, 1993, 1995). One of the important points conveyed is that it is far more complex than once thought to move beyond traditional authoritarian ways of knowing, in which assumptions about epistemic privilege are used to retain a power-appropriating grip on the claim to expertise. Where attempts have been made to democratise the research process, these have often involved the introduction of multiple perspectives, interests and voices into the inquiry process, and into the constructions of reality it produces. So doing can create a more diffuse set of power relations, and take into account a far more diverse range of the values, goals and purposes that play an important role in guiding inquiry. From a phenomenological point of view, a main concern has been to make it more difficult for the author of research texts to over-write internally structured subjectivities with a single layer of externally structured meanings. The promise of democratisation from an interpretive-textual point of view is to replace the researcher's single authorial voice with a polysemic account, containing a greater diversity and texture of perspectives and viewpoints, so that the latter also become positions that it is possible to read from within the text.

However, while all of these aims do, indeed, counter the dangers of an unreflexive, authoritarian appropriation of expertise, it is probably too idealistic to expect to exchange an authoritarian position for a purely democratic one. Once the multiplicity of interests and viewpoints, the relevance of power dynamics, and the impossibility of ever finally fixing meanings have been brought into the research equation, this suggests taking up a less easily categorised stance on one's own perspective on knowing and on the practices of knowing. No matter how well intentioned one's goals at the start of inquiry, there can be no guarantee that the outcome will be less problematic modes of representation. Researchers retain the role of organising and ordering the way research is done and the way reports are written, and will always be writing for audiences who demand that they make authoritative (if not necessarily precise) knowledge claims. Perhaps all that can be hoped for is that, by being more aware of the power-appropriating stance research can take, and by being more reflexive in one's mode of reporting, one can become accountable to a greater diversity of audiences or, at least, place the issue of to whom we are accountable more firmly on the research agenda.

It is possible that the foregoing remarks might be interpreted as making a simple case in favour of postmodernist recommendations on the issues of writing and representation. This would include the claim that a more evocative and hence less representational mode of writing is a way of avoiding the abuses and misrepresentations that are inherent in the practice of authorship. Such a claim is not the one being made here, although some movement towards recognising the non-literalness of standard scientific reporting does seem appropriate. Evocative, multi-voiced texts are still themselves framed by genres or metanarratives that tell their own story – even if it is one about the importance of seeing beyond representation. For this reason, it is understandable that postmodernist texts should come under fire for elitism and for an apparent lack of concern for the writing and representational concerns of non-elites, in a way that parallels criticism of traditional authoritarian/ authorial styles of writing for obscuring their own power-knowledge interests.

If researchers are, indeed, to be more accountable to diverse audiences, and less liable to create colonising representations of their participants, a further issue is to counter the implicit message conveyed by some postmodernist writers that accounts of research merely amount to efforts at storytelling. As long as researchers claim to locate their claims and interpretations in investigations of the world of any kind, then accounts of the process must be written that are more than just stories. In consequence, our work necessarily involves trying to communicate as responsibly and honestly as we can how it was that we came to the knowledge that we generated, and what the bases are for the claims that we make to interpretive validity (Altheide & Johnson, 1994).

Concluding remarks

The concern of this chapter has been with enhancing understandings and ways of delivering validity, as discussed by qualitative researchers within a methodologically pluralist, mixed methods or difference-sensitive frame. Other chapters in this volume will have identifed and illustrated the value of mixed methods inquiry in many dimensions and for many kinds of reasons. It can, for example, bring multiple perspectives to bear on the knowledge process; critique a singular method, embed or question institutional norms; and be a useful response to the concerns of funders (see also Marris & Simmons, 1995). The special contribution of this chapter has been to add a sustained consideration of validity to the broader discussions about what is involved when researchers seek to mix or combine qualitative and quantitative methods, or when they transgress boundaries between methodologies and epistemologies often or typically construed as different.

The first half of the chapter identified how barriers continue to exist amongst (a not atypical group of) psychologists against taking qualitative methods seriously, despite the fact that these methods now occupy an obvious and necessary place within psychology when it is constructed as a methodologically pluralist discipline. Analyses of these psychologists' remarks prompted the insight that it is not straightforward to accommodate issues of epistemic difference, or to avoid exacerbating presumptions of difference, despite the widespread adoption of a pluralist frame. Arguments about the value of differentiated, specialised criteria for evaluating qualitative studies were also put on the agenda. The second part of the chapter then proceeded to identify a host of productive ways of reinventing validity in domains that have rejected, and managed to supersede, the hierarchical view of epistemic difference.

Each of three sub-sections on reinventing validity added to the chapter's general arguments for avoiding an unhelpful dualism between qualitative and quantitative methods by providing more specific reasons for extending approaches to and practices for validating inquiry.

- Asking questions about the intellectual coherence and practical linkages between various elements in the knowledge process provides a less parochial view of how validity can be established than applying a priori strictures and standards that are appropriate only with a simple realist ontological and epistemological frame.

- Establishing the validity of different kinds of projects may require reflexively incorporating the (potentially much more diverse) goals, purposes and values of the conducted inquiry, and being aware that emerging relational criteria are now available that provide a means of transgressing the ethics/rigour divide.
- Discussions of the issues of writing and representation provide a framework for dealing with criticism of authoritarian styles of researching and reporting, but without assuming that qualitative methodologies are necessarily free of the dilemmas associated with the will to power, authority and expertise.

A wide range of perspectives on science, method and psychology inform the claims and arguments that have been put forward in this chapter. They have been selected for their preparedness to put difficult quandaries and challenging dilemmas onto the psychological agenda, rather than claiming to provide false hopes of solutions and guarantees. Valid inquiry is likely to be inquiry that turns reflexively in on itself and outwards to its position in society, so that it can interrogate and not just sustain its own values, purposes and goals. It may be more comfortable to remain cocooned within a singular and insular package of past practices. But this is less likely to equip researchers with the powers of reflection and practical ways of working they need to evaluate their own work and that of others outside a narrow disciplinary frame.

Acknowledgements

A small grant from the Welsh Office for Research in Health and Social Care (SG96/005) supported work informing part of this paper. My thanks to all those who agreed to be interviewed for this part of the research, and who prompted me to consider a wide range of positions in relation to quality–quantity issues.

Notes

1   The interviews were loosely structured and addressed course directors' and/or research coordinators' views about their course team's provision of methods training, and their views of qualitative methods within clinical psychology more widely. The research proceeded by the researcher taking down full notes at the time of the interview, filling in missing details immediately after the interview had ended, and recording verbatim quotations whenever possible.
2   The extended inserts are precis of participants' comments that keep as close to the actual words used as possible given limitations on note taking (see note 1). Place, person names and any other identifying information have been deleted in an effort to preserve respondent anonymity.
3   The history of psychology's relationship with issues of cultural difference, and especially with ethnicity and "race" is one such topic (Henwood & Phoenix, 1996; Richards, 1997).

4   The term researcher openness describes a motivation to do justice to one's object of inquiry, by suspending overly rigid commitments that might construct it only in a priori ways (Flick, 1998).
5   According to Kidder (1985), to be able to repeatedly measure a construct with the same (and not just related) instruments which have an acceptable degree of accuracy is to find support for its "real existence".
6   A point made at the Day Conference "Qualitative Research: Criteria for Evaluations" (1986). Notes of the discussions can be obtained either from Ian Parker (Manchester Metropolitan University) or from the author.

References

Altheide, D. L., & Johnson, J. M. (1994). Criteria for assessing interpretive validity in qualitative research. In N. K. Denzin, & Y. S. Lincoln (Eds.), *Handbook of qualitative research*. London: Sage (pp. 485–499).

Atkinson, P., Delamont, S., & Hammersley, M. (1988). Qualitative research traditions: A British response to Jacob. *Review of Educational Research, 58*(2), 231–250.

Blaxter, M. (1996). Criteria for the evaluation of qualitative research papers; criteria adopted by the Medical Sociology Group of the British Sociological Association. (Reprinted in Clive Seale (Ed.) (1999), *The quality of qualiative research*. London: Sage).

Boyle, M. (1998). Endnote: Reflections on promoting the interchange. *Clinical Psychology Forum, 114*, 34–35.

Brinberg, D., & McGrath, J. E. (1985). *Validity and the research process*. Newbury Park, CA: Sage.

Bryman, A. (1988). *Quality and quantity in social research*. London: Unwin Hyman.

Bulmer, M. (1979). Concepts in the analysis of qualitative data. In M. Bulmer (Ed.), *Sociological research methods*. London: Macmillan (pp. 241–262).

Burgess, R. G. (1984). *In the field: An introduction to field research*. London: Allen and Unwin.

Burman, E. (1994). *Deconstructing developmental psychology*. London: Routledge.

Chalmers, A. F. (1982). *What is this thing called science?* (2nd ed.). Milton Keynes: Open University Press.

Clegg, J., & King, S. (1998). Three outcomes of qualitative research in learning disabilities: Reconceptualising models, enhancing clinical practice and developing services. *Clinical Psychology Forum, 114*, 7–35.

Clifford, J., & Marcus, G. E. (1986). *Writing culture: The poetics and politics of ethnography*. Berkely, CA: University of California Press.

Denzin, N. (1997). *Interpretive ethnography: Ethnographic practices for the 21st century*. Thousand Oaks, CA: Sage.

Elliot, R., Fischer, C., & Rennie, D. (1999). Evolving guidelines for publication of qualitative research studies in psychology and related fields. *British Journal of Clinical Psychology, 38*, 215–229.

Fine, M., & Wiess, L. (1996). Writing the wrongs of fieldwork: Confronting our own research/writing dilemmas in urban ethnographies. *Qualitative Inquiry, 2*(3), 251–274.

Flick, U. (1998). *An introduction to qualitative research*. London: Sage.

Gergen, K. (1982). *Toward transformation in social knowledge*. New York: Springer.

Gergen, K. (1992). Toward a postmodern psychology. In S. Kvale (Ed.), *Psychology and postmodernism*. London: Sage (pp. 17–30).

Glaser, B. G., & Strauss, A. (1967). *The discovery of grounded theory*. Chicago, IL: Aldine.

Guba, E., & Lincoln, Y. (1994). Competing paradigms in qualitative research. In N. K., Denzin, & Y. Lincoln (Eds.), *Handbook of qualitative research*. London and New York: Sage (pp. 105–117).

Hammersley, M., & Atkinson. P. (1983). *Ethnography: Principles in practice*. London: Routledge.

Harré, R., & Secord, P. (1972). *The explanation of social behaviour*. Oxford: Blackwell.

Henwood, K. L. (1998). Qualitative research and clinical psychology: A Combined report on the outcomes of two small grants (SG96/005 and SG97/050), Welsh Office for Research and Development in Health and Social Care, April 1998.

Henwood, K. L., Griffin, C., & Phoenix, A. (1998). Introduction. In K. L Henwood, C. Griffin, & A. Phoenix (Eds.), *Standpoints and differences: Essays in the practice of feminist psychology*. London: Sage (pp. 1–17).

Henwood, K. L., & Phoenix, A. (1996). "Race" in psychology: Teaching the subject. *Ethnic and Racial Studies*, *19*(4), 841–863.

Henwood, K. L., & Pidgeon, N. F. (1994). Remaking the link: Qualitative research and feminist standpoint theory. *Feminism and Psychology*, *5*(1), 7–30.

Henwood, K., & Pidgeon, N. (1995). Beyond the qualitative paradigm: A framework for introducing diversity in to qualitative psychology. *Journal of Community and Applied Social Psychology*, *4*(4), 225–238.

Kidder. L. (1985). Qualitative research and quasi-experimental framworks. In M. B. Brewer, & B. E. Collins, *Scientific inquiry and the social sciences*. London: Jossey-Bass (pp. 226–256).

Kvale, S. (Ed.) (1992). *Psychology and postmodernism*. London: Sage.

Kvale, S. (1995). The social construction of validity. *Qualitative Inquiry*, *1*(1), 19–40.

Lather, P. (1986). Issues of validity in openly ideological research: Between a rock and a soft place. *Interchange*, *17*(4), 63–84.

Lather, P. (1993). Fertile obsession: Validity after poststructuralism. *The Sociological Quarterly*, *34*(4), 673–693.

Lather, P. (1995). The validity of angels: Interpretive and textual strategies in researching the lives of women with HIV/AIDS. *Qualitative Inquiry*, *1*(1), 41–68.

Latour, B. (1987). *Science in action*. Milton Keynes: Open University Press.

Lincoln, Y. S. (1995). Emerging criteria for quality in qualitative and interpretive research. *Qualitative Inquiry*, *1*(3), 275–289.

Lincoln, Y. S., & Guba, E. G. (1985). *Naturalistic inquiry*. Beverly Hills: Sage.

Lincoln, Y., & Guba, E. G. (1990). Judging the quality of case study reports. *Qualitative Studies in Education*, *3*(1), 53–59.

Marris, C., & Simmons, P. (1995). Current methodological issues in the study of risk perceptions. Unpublished Manuscript, School of Environmental Sciences, University of East Anglia.

Marshall, C. (1985). Appropriate criteria of trustworthiness and goodness for qualitative research on education organisations. *Quality and Quantity*, *19*, 353–373.

Mason, J. (1996). *Qualitative researching*. London: Sage (reprinted 2002, 2nd ed.).

Maxwell, J. A. (1992). Understanding validity in qualitative research. *Harvard Educational Review*, *62*(3), 279–300.

Maynard, M., & Purvis, J. (1994). *Researching women's lives from a feminist perspective*. London: Taylor and Francis.

Miles, M. B., & Huberman, A. M. (1994). *Qualitative data analysis: A new sourcebook* (2nd ed.). London: Sage.

Mishler, E. (1990). Validation in inquiry guided research: The role of exemplars in narrative studies. *Harvard Educational Review*, *60*, 415–442.

Murphy, E., Dingwall, R., Greatbatch, D., Parker, S., & Watson, P. (1998). Assessing the validity of qualitatative research. In *Qualitative research in health technology assessment: A review of the literature. Health Technology Assessment*, *2*(16), 178–199.

Parker, I., & Shotter, J. (Eds.) (1990). *Deconstructing social psychology*. London: Routledge.

Patel, M. (1998). Black therapists and cross cultural therapy: Issues of power dynamic and identity. *Clinical Psychology Forum*, *114*, 13–15.

Phillips, L. (1998). Community psychology: Theory, practice and the link with qualitative research. *Clinical Psychology Forum*, *114*, 16–18.

Ravetz, J. R. (1971). *Scientific knowledge and its social problems*. Oxford: Oxford University Press.

Reinharz, S. (1988). Feminist distrust: Problems of context and content in sociological work. In D. N. Berg, & K. K. Smith (Eds.), *The self in social inquiry: Researching methods*. London: Sage (pp. 153–172).

Reinharz, S. (1994). *Feminist methods in social research*. Oxford: Oxford University Press.

Richards, G. (1997). *"Race", racism and psychology: Towards a reflexive history*. London: Routledge.

Richer, P. (1992). An introduction to deconstructionist psychology. In S. Kvale (Ed.), *Psychology and postmodernism*. London: Sage (pp. 110–118).

Schütz, A. (1953). Common sense and scientific interpretation of human action. *Philosophy and Phenomenological Research*, *XIV*(1), 1–38.

Schwandt, T. A. (1996). Farewell to criteriology. *Qualitative Inquiry*, *2*(1), 58–72.

Spencer, L., Richie, J., Lewis, J., & Dillon, L. (2003). *Assessing quality in qualitative evaluations*. Nat Cen, 35 Northampton Square, London.

Stiles, W. (1993). Quality control in qualitative research. *Clinical Psychology Review*, *13*, 593–618.

Taylor, S. (2001). Evaluating and applying discourse analytic research. In M. Wetherell, S. Taylor, & S. Yates (Eds.), *Discourse as data*. London: Sage (pp. 311–330).

Todd, Z. (1998). Mixing methods. *Clinical Psychology Forum*, *114*, 32–33.

Turpin, G., Barley, V., Beail, N., Scaife, J., Slade, P., Smith, J. A., & Walsh, S. (1997). Standards for research projects and theses involving qualitative methods: Suggested guidelines for trainees and courses. *Clinical Psychology Forum*, *108*, 3–7.

van Maanan, J. (1988). *Tales of the field*. Chicago: University of Chicago Press.

Warren, C. A. B. (1988). *Gender issues in field research*. Qualitative Research Methods Series. London: Sage.

Woolgar, S. (1988). *Science: The very idea*. London: Tavistock.

Wolcott, H. F. (1990). On seeking – and rejecting – validity in qualitative research. In W. Eisner, & A. Peshkin (Eds.), *Qualitative inquiry in education: The continuing debate*. New York: Teachers College Press (pp. 121–152).

Wolf, D. L. (1996). Situating feminist dilemmas in field work. In D. L. Wolf, *Feminist dilemmas in fieldwork*. Boulder, CO: Westview Press (pp. 1–55).

Yardley, L. (1997). Introducing discursive methods. In L. Yardley (Ed.), *Material discourses of health and illness*. London: Routledge (pp. 25–49).

Yardley, L. (2000). Dilemmas of qualitative research. *Psychology and Health*, *15*, 215–228.

Part II
Mixing it up

4 Discursive analysis and the interpretation of statistics

Rom Harré and David Crystal

Introduction

Current complaints about methodology

In recent years there has been growing uneasiness with the use of statistical methods in psychological research when applied to groups of subjects in a search for causal relations between initial conditions and the subsequent outcomes of subjecting people to those conditions. This has come about for various reasons. First of all there has been the growing awareness of the prevalence of elementary statistical fallacies in the interpretation of results. For instance it is quite common to find a conclusion about individual propensities drawn from a statistical distribution of attributes over a population to which those individuals belong. Then there has been the turn from looking for group averages towards the search for individual cognitive procedures, whether in the form of abstract AI models or of more concrete cases of symbol using. Complaints about the loss of idiographic data have been voiced for at least the last twenty years. Finally there has been the changing character of psychological "experiments". The trend has been more and more to the use of questionnaires and commentaries on vignettes as ways of exploring many aspects of psychological functioning. The traditional practice of interpreting correlations revealed by factor analysis of the answers to questionnaires as indicative of causes has been strongly criticised. However, we believe that a judicious combination of statistical analyses using data expressed in numerical form, and semantic and narratological interpretations can be a very powerful method of revealing the sources of regularities in psychological phenomena, combining the virtues of numerical analysis while avoiding the errors of a blanket and unexamined assumption of a causal metaphysics.

Two distinctions of importance

Since the 1970s there have been a variety of methodological debates, emphasising two main polar contrasts. On one axis lies the distinction between causal and discursive explanations for observed regularities. On the other lies the distinction between intensive and extensive designs. For many critics the main stumbling block to creating a scientifically respectable discipline has been the use of numerical "measures" and statistical analysis, as if there were a third axis of opposition between quantitative and qualitative procedures. In this chapter we step away from the third opposition to illustrate how the Cartesian product of the other two oppositions can help us establish a fruitful way of mixing methods. The main casualty of our analysis will be the causal metaphysics of much current psychological explanation. We hope to show how the extensive design can be salvaged when it is combined with a discursive analysis of the results of employing it. We also hope to show that the criticisms of statistical methods, however valid they may be for attempts to use them to back up causal explanations, are not germane to their use in the search for semantic rules and narrative conventions.

Stepping aside from the quantitative/qualitative polarity gives us four possibilities. There is extensive-causal; extensive-semantic; intensive-causal; and intensive-semantic. We shall rule out two of the four from our discussion in this chapter, in particular the two that involve causal explanations. It may be the case that successful causal explanations can be constructed within one or both of the "inductive" designs, but for the purposes of the discussions in this chapter we are agnostic.

Meanings and causes

It is important to be clear about the difference between a discursive and a causal explanation of some psychological regularity. Suppose it had been shown that there was a strong correlation between the frequency with which someone claimed to have met another person, and that person being a friend. A causal interpretation (for example Zajoncs, 1968) would be that frequency of meeting was the independent variable and liking, as a component of friendship, was the dependent variable; therefore "frequency of meeting causes liking, e.g. friendship". This explanation presupposes that there is some causal mechanism which is set running by the asking of the question, or whatever "treatment" is imposed on the participants. What could such a causal mechanism possibly be? From the discursive point of view the question to be considered is all about the semantics of the *words* "friend" and "likes". An examination of the fine details of the huge majority of "experiments", studies, in contemporary psychology make use of verbal *reports*. These are statements made on the occasion of the "experiment". And since the vast majority of experiments are either commenting on a vignette (Egerton, 1995) or answering a questionnaire, the conditions and the outcome are both linguistic. According to the discursive interpretation the explanation of the correlations revealed by the "experiment" is to be found in the meanings of the words used: "the word 'friend' is used, inter alia, for people we often see". Instead of "Similarity of opinions causes people to feel (be) friendly (be attractive) to one another" we have the semantic convention, that we use the word "friend" for someone with whom we have common opinions.

Types: concrete and abstract realisations

Most intellectual enterprises aspire to some degree of generality. Chemists aspire to an account of the reactions of chlorine that will be useful in many different times and places. Literary theorists offer accounts not just of *Bleak House* and *Genji* but of a wide variety of novels. The trick is to find the *type*. We are not interested in this or that sample of chlorine, but in the chlorine-type, and eventually perhaps in the halogen-type. To declare "The novel is dead!" is not to announce the demise of a particular work, but to assert that a certain type of literary production will find no more instantiations. One can arrive at a knowledge of the types in a domain in two different ways. In an intensive design one picks a concrete instance as typical, and investigates it in detail. The class or group of which it is a representation of the type is all the instances sufficiently similar to it. This is the method used for the most part in the natural sciences. Very few instances of a chemical reaction are required before the reaction is found a place in chemistry. One does not average the characteristics of numerous oak trees before giving a description of the species *Quercus quercus*. In an extensive design a large number of instances are studied and a statistical procedure is used to abstract a type. For example a physical anthropologist might make measurements of a great many members of a population and arrive at a type-description from them. Of course these measurements would also permit a profile of the population to be created but that is a quite different enterprise. It is a law of logic that intension varies inversely as extension. Thus the use of the extensive design will always yield a less detailed type-description than will the use of the intensive design. It is perhaps mostly for that reason that the extensive design is rare in the natural sciences.

"Factors" and narrative conventions

When the replies to a questionnaire cluster into groups, the traditional causal interpretation requires the postulation of a "factor" to account for the group-ing. The aim is to introduce as few factors as possible to account for as much of the variance as possible. Logically a "factor" is a stand-in for some causal mechanism, at present unknown. Psychologists have fun finding names for "factors". Ontologically "factors" must be, somehow, aspects of a general abstract cognitive engine, or something of the sort. Of course there are no such engines. According to the discursive interpretation the clustering is due, not to some mythical mechanism, but to one of three possibilities: there is a meaning relation between the *words*; or there is a narrative convention that requires that in answering this class of *question* a certain class of *answers* are appropriate; or the person answering has seen these features correlated often in his/her experience, reading, cultural tales and so on. Neither the extensive nor the intensive design can sort out the three main cases. For this purpose an investigator must make use of some means for distinguishing to which of the three possibilities a cluster belongs.

Introjecting the discursive analysis into the "mix of methods"

Repertory grids are built up by people displaying the characteristics of their friends by the use of technique that analyses *what they say about them*. The usual "experimental" methods, getting people to answer a questionnaire, say by checking a five point Likert scale, are also collecting up what people say about some topic, for example *about other human beings*. When this is done in accordance with the extensive design the original discursive phase of question and answer, or vignette and commentary, is followed up by a statistical analysis revealing how types of answers cluster. These types are generally not syntactic but semantic, that is they are arrived at by first "coding" the answer; again that is providing them with interpretations from a generic repertoire. Old paradigm or mainstream psychological method then provides a ready made interpretation of these clusters with "factors", allegedly the underlying *causal* sources of the correlations. But one can reinterpret results within a different metaphysical framework, looking for the semantic rules and narrative conventions that explain the correlations in what people say about their friends and other people. That this is the more natural interpretation is obvious once one steps back from the methodology and asks oneself what one has been doing – asking people questions and recording their answers!

How is this done? Smedslund's method is aimed at bringing out the "psychologic" or *system* of semantic rules that are current in a community like those we have used for our studies. A set of about 30 sentences are constructed, using the words that appear in the construct correlations that we think might be semantic in origin. The questions are like this: For example "Is 'friends have similar beliefs' always true, sometimes true, never true?" The participants are asked to select those they think belong to each category. The second category can be rejected without further ado, as not semantic in character. The remainder, both positive and negative, can be worked up, in so far as that is possible into a system of logically related linguistic commonplaces, a "psychologic". The remainder will be assigned, *pro tempore*, to the category of strong empirical generalisations. With a semantic hypothesis in hand the investigator can now return to the material to test the proposed semantic rules on the materials obtained in this and other discursive interactions, such as accounts. By building a hypothetical semantic hierarchy out of the relevant pairs one tests the plausibility of assigning regularities between question-types and answer-types to the semantic category, rather than narratological or the empirical.

The idea is to illustrate these proposals for mixing methods by permuting statistical and semantic methods in the following pattern:

1   Repertory grid analysis as a representative of the intensive design.
2   Statistical distributions interpreted as odds on a type of event occurring as a representative of the extensive design.
3   The distinction between semantic and empirical concept patterns used to develop a discourse analysis of the results of studies of types 1 and 2.
4   Finally to use the techniques of Smedslund's "psycho-logic" to test the semantic rules that we tentatively drawn from the discursive "take" on studies of types 1 and 2 for linguistic plausibility.

Repertory grids and statistical analyses lead to correlations between outcomes, say "friendship", and conditions, say "likeness of opinions". But these and other correlations can have two quite different kinds of explanations:

A. Mainstream: there is a causal relation between the correlates, e.g. "similarity of beliefs causes X to feel friendly to Y". Or Zajoncs "Frequency of meeting causes X to feel friendly to Y".
B. Discursive: "having similar beliefs is part of what 'friendship' means". "We call people 'friends' if we see them often".

The Smedslund procedure enables us to distinguish between these rival explanations for particular cases of correlations.

Study One: An intensive design. The use of repertory grids to reveal the semantic rules behind culturally diverse conceptions of friendship[1]

Repertory grids are one convenient way of following the real time uses by individual people of their personal cognitive resources in carrying out some cognitive task. In the example to be discussed participants are asked to describe six of their friends. The descriptors were elicited by the usual Fransella–Bannister (1977) method, namely by asking participants in what way two of their friends were alike and different from a third. Permuting the possible combinations of six friends gave a semantic repertoire for each participant who was then asked to use these paired words to rate all six friends. We worked with twenty students from the Universidad de Santiago de Compostella, and with twenty students from Chung-ang University in Seoul.[2]

The statistical analysis of the answers to the task of describing one's friends in a repertory grid format allows us to identify how each person thinks about their friends. The correlations among both elements and constructs allow us to see which among their friends they considered very similar, according to whatever characteristics were salient for *that person*. It also allowed us to identify which characteristics were used by that person in similar ways. The results are twenty cognitive-semantic structures, one for each participant.

According to the intensive design, we select one person to be the exemplar of the type, for example we select a Spaniard man, let us call him

"José-Carlos", as the concrete bearer of the type and a Spanish woman, let us call her "Marie-Carmen" as another exemplar of a type. There are two obvious logical points to be emphasised about the intensive design. On the plus side, so to speak, since the exemplars are real people and not mathematical abstractions we could return to them to find out more about their cognitive resources and how they put them to use. On the minus side the logical principle that extension varies inversely as intention kicks in. The more detail we assign to the exemplar the narrower the range of similar persons is likely to be.

For the illustrative purposes of this discussion we took the next step, the construction of a Smedslund psychologic by concentrating on the construct patterns only. If one finds that two or more characteristics are used by a person in very similar ways there are two possible strong hypotheses:

H1: They are related semantically, and the relevant relation is probably a semantic rule of the discursive practices or narratological conventions of the culture. For instance if the words "greedy" and "fat" are used similarly this may be because there is a subtle semantic relation, such that bulk in a greedy person is construed as fat.

H2: They are related as the result of the experience that a person has had of their appearing together. Thus if the words "gordo [fat]" and "holgazano [lazy]" are used together it may be because in the experience of the person constructing a repertory grid which displays this correlation, in the thinking of the participant their fat friends are lazy. However experiential correlations fall into two further subclasses: those that reflect psychological generalisations in the culture, "fat people are cheerful", and those that pick up only local and personal experience of the idiographic characteristics of one's friends.

There may be intermediate cases. For example a person may have experienced the copresence of a pair of attributes so often that they begin to treat the relation as semantic rather than causal. From the point of view of the cognitive psychologist the two hypotheses are very different. If the relation is semantic it is immune to experience as if learned in the course of learning the language. If it is causal then it has developed from experience and as such can be refuted, exceptions might be tolerated and so on. Whereas a semantic rule or narratological convention does not require a *ceteris paribus* clause, causal relations must be so accompanied.

Finally a word of caution about language: in each case we are using translations of local vocabularies in this report. It hardly needs pointing out that the semantic field of an expression like "diligent" may not be exactly coincident with the semantic fields of Spanish and Korean words of which it is the best translation. This report is being written in British English, and one of the authors not being an American, there are nuances of American usage of the vocabulary that are lost on him.[3] These difficulties have been discussed a great deal. The consensus seems to be that greater and greater attention to detail does lead to step by step refinements, without the possibility of ambiguities and misunderstandings being finally eliminated.

What are the other nineteen participants of each national group doing in our study, if our purpose is to find a concrete exemplar? The intensive design requires that we build an extension for the class of which the characteristics of the exemplar represent the intension. Is our chosen exemplar some *rara avis*, or are there others that are similar? Notice here we build out towards an extension. In the extensive design we will be "building in" from a given extension to an intension.

In practical and applied psychology, for example in the work of clinical psychologists or parole boards and juries or Congressional committees, the very same research technique, the single case study, serves the purposes of the third design possibility – the idiographic design. In deciding whether to parole a prisoner or impeach a President, whether this film actor killed his ex-wife, and so on, the question of whether this murderer or this President or this actor is an exemplar of some class or group is irrelevant.

The Spanish material: "José-Carlos" and "Marie-Carmen" as exemplars[4]

Here are the results of the statistical analysis of the friendship-discourses provided by our chosen exemplars.[5]

Exemplar SA: "José-Carlos", a 24 year old Spanish man

He describes his six friends in a fairly restricted vocabulary, three of them being seen as very much alike. His vocabulary is used with strong contrasts between the polar terms of his constructs. He finds one of his friends very "seguro" and another very "inseguro". Looking at the inter-relations between constructs we find a pair of constructs "FUERTE [strong] (seguro) [secure] – DEBIL [weak] (inseguro) [insecure]"[6] used in a very similar pattern. Our intuition is that this pair might reflect a semantic relation, to be tested by the Smedslund procedure. Another fairly similarly used pair "CONSTANTE (alegre) [happy] – INCONSTANTE (triste) [sad]" seems to be more likely to express an empirical generalisation. By including these words in the Smedslund procedure we hope to be able to take these intuitions one step further.

Exemplar SB: "Marie-Carmen", a 23 year old Spanish woman

"Marie-Carmen's" friends are described in remarkably similar ways. Her vocabulary, like that of "José-Carlos", is used in a strongly differentiated way, the poles of her construct pairs being treated as very distinct. There are no very closely similar uses of a pair of constructs. The pair that is used the most alike is "COMPREHENSIVA [understandable] (no atractiva) – INCOMPREHENSIVA [non-understandable] (atractiva)". This pair strikes us as unlikely to express either a semantic rule or a cultural generalisation. The Smedslund procedure should enable us to determine more securely whether this pair is an idiosyncratic feature of "Marie-Carmen's" circle of acquaintances. Both constructs in this pair are used similarly to the construct the poles of which are "burlona – respetuosa". While it seems likely that the pair "NO ATRACTIVO (burlona) [mocking] – ATRACTIVA (respetuosa) [respectful]" could be semantically linked, in that one of the criteria for some-one being attractive is that they are not always mocking one, the other pair "COMPREHENSIVA (burlona) – INCOMPREHENSIVA (respetuosa)" strikes us as likely to be shown to be highly contingent when tested in a psychologic analysis.

We could now make comparisons between the conceptual resources of our chosen exemplars and other young Spaniards. This is best facilitated by pre-senting the material in a Cartesian space from which visual comparisons of degrees of clustering on constructs and similarities and differences can be recovered (cf. Smith, 1990).

But our interest in this chapter is in mixing methods, not in the details of the use of the intensive designs. We turn now to applying a semantic analysis to the words which appeared in the construct patterns of all of those who took part in our study. By extracting correlated constructs from all twenty of the participants' grids, we can begin to address the question of whether their uses of words are characteristic of the Spanish language and culture – that is representative of the semantics of a dialect – or are they *sui generis*, display-ing the semantic structure of an idiolect? To pursue this question further we return to Spain, so to speak, with our Smedslund technique, armed with a list of candidate semantic rules. For the purpose of constructing a Smedslund psychologic it is not necessary that the people who answer the Smedslund set of questions are just the very same people that created the grids. But it would be wise to recruit some young people from Santiago de Compostella, in particular since the mother tongue of most is probably Gallego and Castillaño their second language.

Here are some candidate cases for semantic rules and narrative conven-tions, drawn from the entire Spanish construct corpus.

Semantic rules and empirical generalisations: Santiago de Compostella

"NO ESTUDIO – ESTUDIO", that is [not studious – studious], is matched to "estupido – inteligente" as "NO ESTUDIO (stupido) – ESTUDIO (inteli-gente)".[7] Interpreted as a semantic rule it expressed the thought that what it is, among others things, to be stupid is to be casual in your studies. Interpreted as an empirical generalisation it expressed the thought that on the whole those who are not studious are also, by some other criterion, found to be stupid. The Smedslund technique allows us to resolve the issue: is the above paired construct relation semantic or empirical? Another candidate case for a semantic rule is "DIVERTIDO (forte) – ABURRIDO [boring] – (debil) [feeble]", that is what it is, among other things, to be interesting is to be strong and to be boring is to be feeble.

Candidate cases for an empirical generalisations included the following: "RAPIDO (bajo) [short] – LENTO [slow] (alto) [tall]", expressing the thought that as a matter of fact short people are generally quicker than tall people. Another might be "IDEALISTICO (activo) – NO IDEALISTICO (no activo)", that is as a matter of fact it turns out that idealistic people are generally more active than non-idealistic.

There are many more cases of groupings that seem to be good candidates for semantic rules, for instance (omitting the negative pole) "COMPREHEN-SIVE (atractiva)" that is [Understandable/attractive]; "TRABAJERA (responsible)" [Hard working/responsible]. And there are others that seem likely to turn out to be the result of an empirical generalisation from experience, for instance "VALEROSA (escrupulosa)" [Brave – scrupulous], and so on, while there were others that seemed not only to be empirical but to reveal locally valid criteria, matters of fashion, for instance "ATRACTIVA (alta)", [Attractive – tall {for women}], for which one expects to find lots of exceptions.

As a general principle we would say that there cannot be exceptions to semantic rules, while there is always the possibility of an exception to turn up to an empirical generalisation. This contrast is not quite as rigid as it might seem, since it presupposes a strictness and determinateness to the meaning rules that define a culture which is rarely fully exemplified strictly. Most words that are used for describing and evaluating people have subtly varying fields of application, ordered not by semantic essences, but by what Wittgenstein called "family resemblances", networks of similarities and differences in the ways that they are applied. Nevertheless it is generally true that the negation of a semantic rule seems to have no application, rather than being simply false, that is it could not be applied to anything.

The next step is to create a set of statements using the elicited vocabulary of which our participants are asked to say whether any one is always true, never true or sometimes true and sometimes false.

The psychologic stage

A set of thirty statements was devised (see Appendix 1), including, for example "Los hombres quienes son juergistos son amargandos" ["Men who are party people are embittered"]; "Las mujeres debiles son vagas" ["Weak women are lax"]; "Una mujer hipocrita es antipática" ["A hypocritical woman is unlikeable"]; and submitted to a group of young Spaniards from Santiago de Compostella.

The semantic probe yielded four candidates for verbal patterns reflecting semantic rules. These were positive: "idealistic and active", "hard-working and responsible", "hypocritical and unlikeable" and negative: "incomprehensible and respected". It seems to us that it is part of what one means by "responsible" to be hard-working, and similarly that being hypocritical is a species of unlikeability. These two then seem to us to be semantic. However, we can easily conceive of a person who is both idealistic and lazy, and comprehensible and held in contempt, indeed we both know such people. The numerically strong showing of the first of these patterns in the results of the semantic probe must be put down, we think, to a narrative convention, current in Spain, where idealistic young people are expected to be active. Finally the fourth seems to be neither semantic nor narratological, but rather to be a rule of self-presentation. Of course these preliminary analyses are not definitive and suggest all sorts of further follow-up studies.

Nor do we have sufficient material to carry out a full scale psychological construction linking up the various semantic rules we have come across into a systematic and ordered structure.

The Korean material: "Mi Hyun" and "Mang Ho" as exemplars[8]

To remind the reader of the general principle underlying the interpretation of material of the sort we are studying here, there are two main reasons why a person would use words in such a way that they form clusters. One way is because the words are related by their meanings, for example "wife" and "woman". Another way is because the words are related by having been called for by experience, for example "April" and "rain" might be associated in Western European discourse. When Chaucer uses these words together we do not explain it by a meaning relation.

Here are the findings of a repertory grid analysis of the results of asking two young Koreans, a man and a woman, chosen from twenty single cases, to describe their friends.

Exemplar KA, "Mi Hyun": A twenty six year old Korean woman

Her grid data show that she makes fairly strong assessments of her friends, using the extremes of the rating scales she has created during the elicitation process. However the grid analysis shows that she describes two of her friends in very similar terms, and while three of her friends are described by her as very similar, three are alike, but very different from the first trio, though their characters and so on are the polar opposite of the first group. Thus though the two groups of people are very diverse, semantically the grid is very "tight". Among her constructs, that is polarised concept pairs, two, "diligent–lazy" and "strong–weak" are used in exactly similar ways, that is written in our convention the semantic structure is "DILIGENT (strong) – LAZY (weak)". Three of her other constructs, "keen–dull [as character traits]", "fun–not fun" and "clever–stupid" are also used in very similar ways to the first two. Her last pair, "pretty–not pretty" correlates hardly at all with the others. Graphically her cognitive profile for talking about friends looks like this:

CONSTRUCTS

Diligent/lazy

Keen/dull

Strong/weak

Fun/not fun

Competent/incompetent

Pretty/not pretty

Distance from the ordinal axis represents descending degree of correlation.

Exemplar KB "Mang Ho", A 21 year old Korean man

The analysis shows that this man uses his six constructs in rather divergent ways if compared with the semantic system employed by KA. But his conceptual repertoire is still only moderately "loose". The best candidate for a semantic cluster among his constructs is "SERIOUS (frank) – FRIVOLOUS (bashful)". Having a similar pattern of use is the pair "STRONG (opinionated) – WEAK (easy going)". While the former strikes us, at first glance, as empirical, the second seems to reflect meanings. A person might be called "strong" if he is opinionated, so that the attribute "strength" and the correlated attribute "opinionated" are internally related. It is also noteworthy that "Mang Ho" talks of all his friends in very similar terms, that is he describes them as very much alike. Like "Mi Hyun" he also tends to use the strongest contrasting senses of the poles of construct pairs in describing his friends. Graphically "Mang Ho's" semantic repertoire for talking about his friends looks like this:

CONSTRUCTS

serious/frivolous

frank/bashful

writes well/does not write well

messy/neat

weak/strong

easy-going/opinionated

Semantic rules and empirical generalisations: Seoul

To reiterate the analytical principles involved: a regularity in the results of study of how people use words could be due to one of several influences. Taken generally people might favour a certain semantic pattern either because it realises a semantic rule of the language, or because it realises a narrative convention for telling stories about the topic in question, or because it expresses an empirical generalisation, what people notice about other people. In any study of this sort there will be very great variation in the results for individuals. These are unlikely to be semantic or narratological, since all are native speakers of the language used. We would expect there to be some idiosyncratic answers because of the unique characteristics of the people that any one participant comes across in daily life.

Here are some candidate cases of regularities in patterns of word use drawn from the whole Korean corpus. For example a semantic rule might be the following: "KEEN (fun) – DULL (not fun)". "Fashionable (tall) – unfashionable (short)". Another candidate might be "ALTRUISTIC (open minded) – SELFISH (closed minded)". Remember that we are not claiming to be able to make the distinction between the two kinds of conceptual relations by some power of intuition. At this point we are picking out candidates which would serve as the material for the carrying through of a Smedslund analysis.

As possible cases of empirical generalisations widely manifested by Korean participants we suggest the following: SMART (strong) – DUMB (weak) and GREGARIOUS (kind) – LONESOME (mean). And our material contains many more possibilities.

Finally there seem to be some clear candidates for ranking simply as expressions of the idiosyncratic experience of the participant who used these constructs in pairs: for example "HONEST (conceited) – CHEAT (modest)", and "MANAGES ALCOHOL BADLY (tall) – MANAGES IT WELL (short)".

Here then we have some construct groupings that arise because that is the way that linguistic convention prescribes the use of words, groupings which express generalisations about psychological types learned by experience, and groupings which reflect the idiosyncratic characteristics of particular persons. To distinguish these possibilities we must turn to the techniques of psychologic, explicit explorations of putative semantic hypotheses.

The next step would have been to devise thirty statements using the words that figured in the candidate grammatical rules and to have some Koreans of the same age, class and educational standard rank them as "always true", "never true" and "sometimes true and sometimes false". One could then set about trying to construct a psychologic using the "filtered" vocabulary.

Since our study here is exemplary only we have only carried out the Smedslund psychologic stage for the Spanish material.

What has the Spanish and Korean material revealed?

It would be quite improper to construe any of the above results in causal terms. We have not revealed causal laws by which "friends" as stimulus objects cause the "subjects" to describe them thus and so. We are analysing the way some people[9] talk about people. What we have been able to abstract from the material is at least some of the semantic rules that are obeyed in talking about people, and some of the generalisations about people that are held among some members of this category of persons in Spain and Korea. Since assessments of people and judgements about them are made by the use of the available linguistic resources, the semantics of the "talking about people" vocabulary will constrain the possibilities of such assessments and judgements. And at the same time, the available vocabulary necessarily constrains how people can think about themselves.

Study Two: A traditional statistical analysis used on discursive data can be interpreted as disclosing semantic rules and narrative conventions

The second study with which to illustrate the value of mixing statistical and analytical methods (Crystal, Weinfurt, Watanabe, & Wu, 1998) was based on the answers to a questionnaire given to children in the United States, Japan and China. For our illustrative purposes we have abstracted results only for the American part of the study. It has been necessary to retrace the steps taken by the authors of the original study, in order to recover the words used by the participants, prior to reinterpretations and selections made in the course of "streamlining" the data to fit it for statistical analysis. "The coding scheme developed for categories of human differences [the authors mean not 'differences' but 'human attributes'] was first based on an analysis of the answers from subsamples of 40 respondents in each culture. It was then modified through lengthy discussion among [the authors] ... to accommodate new responses that did not fit the original coding categories" (ibid., 1998). In this chapter we are not concerned to discuss the methodological legitimacy of such interpretative procedures. We simply take into account that they have been performed on the original answers, which, to legitimate the "in depth" study sketched here, must be recovered. In the original publication of this material only the reinterpreted replies were used. This contrasts sharply with other studies in which such concrete descriptions as "He is a loud mouth" and "When there's a quarrel he can't resist having the last word", are employed. Our metastudy, then, begins with a description of the statistical results obtained on the interpreted data, from which, by back-tracking to the original words used, we arrive at a version of the result that is relatively free of the effects of "streamlining". This seems to us legitimate in this chapter, since we are using only the American data to construct the semantic probe for developing a Smedslund "Psychologic".

The Crystal et al. (1998) study is not concerned with friendship *per se* but with ways of talking about other people. At least some of the ways of talking about those people who are singled out as friends, must be drawn from the general semantic repertoire of ways of talking about people, be they semantic, narratological or empirically based. The statistical analysis amounted to a study of the distribution of already categorised answers over various populations, such as "U.S. children" or "Chinese 5th Graders". Comparisons of rates of use of certain kinds of descriptive predicates were made between comparable populations, such as "Chinese 5th Graders", "Japanese 5th Graders" and so on. The comparative rates were reinterpreted as "odds that a certain 'response' category would be used by a member of the relevant population". One final ambiguity in the presentation of the results of the original study needs to be noted. The notion of "odds" is multivocal. It may mean the distribution of a certain outcome in a population of outcomes, so that odds of .9 means that 90% of a population deterministically display a certain attribute. It may mean that every member of the population has a strong propensity to display the attribute. We shall interpret the notion of odds in the original study in the former sense.

Starting with the interpreted categories we have the following statistical results: The chances of someone from the American sample choosing to describe other people in words concerning their attractiveness is 4.44 times greater than the chances of someone from China using comparable expressions; with words concerning their demographic status the ratio is 9.62 times as likely; with words concerning their material possessions and life style it is 8.24; while words for personality traits and physical attributes are 2.79 and 2.06 times as likely respectively, at whatever the base rate of likelihood in the comparison group might be.

The first job for the analyst would be to recover the base rates so that we can decide whether a usage is common or rare. If among Chinese the probability of using a certain expression is only .005 and the use of that expression is 9 times more likely in the United States, it has a probability of only .45 of being used by an American young person. No estimate of the depth by which a certain concept is embedded in the cultural resources of a culture can be made with comparative, only with absolute rates of usage. For our illustrative purposes we simply took a representative sample of words to create our semantic probe for young American, native speakers of English.

As a preliminary to developing a semantic probe to access the semantic rules for the use of the concept of "person" it seems that only demographic and material attributes are candidates. If there are many people whose descriptions do not use words for personal attractiveness, personality and physical characteristics, other than those relevant to demography, then those words cannot be linked to "person" by semantic rules. The vocabulary that we need to recover from the interpretive phase of the original study will be those words for which Crystal et al. (1998) used their common-sense intuition to classify in the semantic categories such as "attractiveness", and so on.

By recovering the original vocabulary we have constructed a semantic probe (See Appendix 2). The results of using a semantic probe with a group of young Americans, comparable in age, class and educational level to those who took part in the original study are described below.

In commenting on the results in the original study the authors make use of the idea of a discursive convention without identifying it as such. For instance they comment on ". . . the greater tendency of Chinese respondents, relative to that of their Japanese peers, to report somatic complaints and to somatise psychological disorders, such as depression" (Crystal et al., 1998, p. 721). We note the use of the Western category "depression" in the metadiscourse of their paper, reproducing a Western story-line in the analysis. This suggests a further refinement in the reworking of the data of the original study. The Smedslund technique reveals semantic rules in contrast to empirical generalisations as explanations of patterns of verbal responses. But one might also devise another type of probe that would be designed to distinguish patterns that exemplified the conventions of local story-lines. But to pursue this further analytical step would take us too far from the focus of this chapter which is intended to be focused sharply on the distinction between causal and semantic explanations of the discursive patterns revealed by statistical analyses of answers to questionnaires.

Thus, given the discursive approach to these results which rules out any causal interpretation, we have two main explanatory formats. High odds on the use of a word in a certain context means only that it is often used, that is many people using it and using it often, may be because the context and the word are semantically related. Thus in contexts defined by the concept of "friends" the preponderance of the word "trusts", say, is to be explained by the semantic fact that the word "friend" is used of those one trusts. However in a particular study the other format may be necessary in case we find someone using "fat" in all "friend" contexts, expressing an empirical regularity among his or her friends.

Having extracted likely candidates for semantic explanations and also some which would be very unlikely to have semantic explanations we can now construct a semantic probe, as in Appendix 2. The results of the probe were very clear. The word "friend" was tightly associated with "kind" and "nice", and fairly tightly associated with "funny" and "clean". That is the statements "My friends are kind" and "My friends are nice" were picked out as always true by nearly everyone, while "My friends are funny" and "My friends are clean" by a substantial majority. (Note that we have no recourse to numerical measures at this stage of the research, since we are dealing with a non-quantitative phenomenon, namely maintenance of semantic conventions or narrative story-lines.) We also found a very tight disassociation between "friend" gender, in that almost no one declared that "My friends are of the same sex as myself" is always true. And again we found fairly strong associations of "friend" with "ugly", "stupid" and "slow".

At this preliminary stage in the investigation we are inclined to see the meaning of the word "friend" as incorporating the concepts "nice" and "kind". It would not be false but semantically odd to declare that friends (including mine) were all horrid and cruel. Despite the universal rejection of the idea that friends are always of one's own sex we are less inclined to see this relation as semantic, indeed it seems to us a prime candidate for a story-line or narrative convention, a "sign of the times", so to speak. In the youth of one of us the semantic tie of "friend" to own gender was so strong that close female acquaintances were not the unmarked "friends" but the marked "girl-friend" and "boy-friend" for girls. The semantics of these expressions was sharply different from "friend", "mate", "pal", "chum" and so on. Again we are inclined at this stage of the research to classify the "friend" to "ugly", "stupid" and "slow" as internal relations but expressing a narrative convention.

As with the Spanish and Korean material we remind the reader that the purpose of this chapter is the demonstration of the value of mixing methods, rather than that of making a contribution to the cross-cultural study of friendship. The results we have obtained point towards further studies in depth of the way these concepts are used among young Americans.

Summary

We have shown, we hope, not only the possibility of mixing statistical and analytic (semantic) methods but that adopting mixed methods leads to a powerful tool for gaining access to the fine structure of working cognitive systems. The mix we have adopted has the further advantage that it remains very close to the phenomena, eschewing, as much as possible, the kind of reworking and reinterpreting of concrete linguistic data that can only be a reflection of the informal intuitions of psychologists as to the grammars of the languages, dialects and idiolects of the people they are studying. Each of our studies could be further developed. In the present study they serve merely as illustrations of the power of mixing methods that have been thought, by many, to be radically antithetical. In most cases where there are significant correlations between discursive elements, for instance words, there are three possible explanations:

1   The correlation is a reflection of a semantic rule, for example one of the words could be an element in the definition of the other. And there are other semantic relations, such as those we find in type-hierarchies.
2   The correlation is a reflection of a narrative convention, particularly in the examples we have used in this chapter, that of how to tell stories about people in the three cultures the language usages of which we have sampled.
3   The correlation is empirical, expressing a pattern of concomitances that the speaker or speakers have noticed in the group of people they have been asked to describe.

Choice between these possibilities calls for the use of semantic probes, such as those which can be developed within the framework of Smedslund's Psychologic. Much more extensive use of semantic probes of this and other types, such as story writing, would be needed before we could venture on the construction of a full scale semantic analysis of fields of family resemblances and the dynamic type-hierarchies which express the "grammatical" structure of friendship, as a lived and as a spoken reality. Finally we should emphasise that there can be no sampling problems at the stage of the use of a semantic probe. There are probably 500,000,000 native speakers of English, so no sample has any traditional formal validity. But, of course, any linguistic study whatever must be based on the intensive design, that is that one chooses an exemplar, and indeed just one native speaker would do in principle. There are idiolects, so that logical point must be qualified to allow at least some sampling and spread of cases. But mathematical concepts of sampling have no application to intensive designs.

Notes

1 The material used in this study is taken from a cross cultural study of "friendship" currently in process.
2 We have also collected data from Japan and the United States, which could be used in a more extensive study on the substantive question of how "friendship" is understood. We remind the reader that our purpose here is to illustrate method.
3 The well known quip that Americans and British are divided by a common language does have a smidgen of truth.
4 We are grateful for the invaluable assistance of Professor José-Luis Falguera of the Universidad Santiago de Compostella in obtaining this material, and for administering the follow-up semantic probe (Appendix 1) to a group of his students.
5 For the technically minded the "GRAN" programme written by Christopher Leach was used, which is based on the Pearson correlation formula.
6 We adopt the convention for pairing construct-pairs by interposing a bracketed lower case pair into an unbracketed capitalised pair.
7 We remind readers not well acquainted with romance languages that when an adjective ends in "-o" it is being used of a man, and when it ends in "-a" it is being used of a woman. It is an interesting question, not to be pursued here, whether the inflexion changes the semantic rules for the use of the adjective.
8 We are grateful to Professor Uichol Kim of Chung-ang University, Seoul, for his invaluable assistance in collecting our Korean material, and to Julie Kim of Georgetown University for translations.
9 It should be pointed out that the participants in each country were drawn from comparable social classes, that is upper middle class university students in their early twenties. Part of the point of the study is to see whether these criteria also pick out trans-national groups which have similar discursive conventions for talking about those they take to be their friends. At the same time the study could be regarded as an exploration of the concept of "friendship" in each of the cultures. That implies that at a higher order of abstraction the concept of "friendship" makes sense in much the same way in each culture. A much larger scale study would be needed to investigate that assumption, but without it the work reported here would make no sense at all.
10 Translations have been inserted in square brackets where it seemed advisable.

References

Crystal, D. S., Weinfurt, K., Watanabe, H., & Wu, C. (1998). Concepts of human differences: A comparison of American, Japanese and Chinese children and adolescents. *Developmental Psychology*, *34*(4), 714–722.

Egerton, M. (1995). Emotions and discursive norms. In R. Harré and P. Stearns, *Discursive psychology in practice* (pp. 183–193). London and Los Angeles: Sage.

Fransella, F., & Bannister, D. (1977). *A manual for repertory grid technique*. London: Academic Press.

Harré, R. (2004). Concepts of friendship: Young people in Spain and in Korea. *Asian Journal of Social Psychology*. Forthcoming.

Smedslund, J. (1988). *Psychologic*. Heidelberg and New York: Springer-Verlag.

Smith, J. A. (1990). Transforming identities: A repertory grid case-study of the transition to motherhood. *British Journal of Medical Psychology*, *63*, 239–253.

Zajoncs, R. B. (1968). Attitudinal effects of mere exposure. *Journal of Personality and Social Psychology*, *9*, 2–27.

Appendix 1

The Spanish 30 question semantic probe[10]

Considera cada una de estas frases. ¿Es verdadera siempre (S), jámas (J) o algunas veces si y algunas veces no(V)? Escoge y marca, per favor, una de las tres posibilidades, S, J, V.

1 Un hombre quien es fuerte es seguro [reliable]. S, J, V?
2 Una mujer quien es inconstante [fickle] es triste [sad]. S, J, V?
3 Una mujer quien es burlona [jokey] no es atractiva. S, J, V?
4 Un hombre incomprehensivo es respetuosa [respected]. S, J, V?
5 Una mujer stupida no es estudia. S, J, V?
6 Los hombres divertados [amusing] son fortes. S, J, V?
7 Las mujeres idealisticas son activas. S, J, V?
8 Un hombre feble [feeble] es aburrido [boring]. S. J. V?
9 Un mujer quien es trabajera [hard-working] es responsible. S, J, V?
10 Una mujer valerosa [brave] es escrupulosa. S, J, V?
11 Los hombres juerguistos ["party people"] son amargandos [embittered]. S, J, V?
12 Un hombre quien es responsible es alto [tall]. S. J. V?
13 Los hombres activos son obstinados. S, J, V?
14 Un hombre deportisto [sporting] tiene un caracter bueno. S, J, V?
15 Una mujer quien es débil es estupido. S, J, V?
16 Los hombres críticos son rapidos [quick]. S, J, V?
17 Un hombre quien es fuerte [strong] es listo [clever]. S, J, V?
18 Las mujeres estupidas son holgazanas [lazy]. S, J, V?
19 Los hombres lentos [slow] son altos [tall]. S, J, V?
20 Un hombre quien es alegré [cheerful] es practico. S, J, V?
21 Una mujer insegura no es practica. S, J, V?
22 Un hombre alto es fuerte. S, J, V?
23 Las mujeres debiles son vagas [vague]. S, J, V?
24 Los hombres holgazanos son torpes [clumsy]. S, J, V?
25 Una mujer quien es pacifica es altruistica. S, J, V?
26 Las mujeres guapas [pretty] son simpáticas. S, J, V?
27 Una mujer agobiada [depressed] es cariñosa [affectionate]. S, J, V?
28 Los hombres débiles son lentos. S, J, V?
29 Una mujer hipocritica es antipática. S, J, V?
30 Las mujeres inteligentes son cariñosas. S, J, V?

¡Muchas gracias!

Appendix 2

The American 30 question semantic probe

Your task is simply to read each sentence and then to indicate whether you think it is always true, never true or sometimes true.

 1   My friends are smart. A: N: S
 2   My friends are stupid. A: N: S
 3   My friends have attitude. A: N: S
 4   My friends are tall. A: N: S
 5   My friends are nice. A: N: S
 6   My friends are kind. A: N: S
 7   My friends are selfish. A: N: S
 8   My friends are generous. A: N: S
 9   My friends are fat. A: N; S
10   My friends are strong. A: N: S
11   My friends are popular. A: N: S
12   My friends are ugly. A: N: S
13   My friends wear glasses. A: N: S
14   My friends have lots of money. A: N: S
15   My friends are easy-going. A: N: S
16   My friends are all the same colour. A: N: S
17   My friends are funny. A: N: S
18   My friends are mean. A: N: S
19   My friends are weird. A: N: S
20   My friends are cool. A: N: S
21   My friends have great clothes. A: N: S
22   My friends are clean. A: N: S
23a (For men respondents): My friends are all men A: N: S
23b (For women respondents): My friends are all women. A: N: S
24   My friends are slow. A: N: S
25   My friends are considerate. A: N: S
26   My friends are blue-eyed. A: N: S
27   My friends are shy. A: N: S
28   My friends are bossy. A: N: S
29   My friends are sport-mad. A: N: S
30   My friends are party people. A: N: S

Thanks for taking the trouble to help us.

5 "Structured judgement methods" – the best of both worlds?

David D. Clarke

Counting, describing and understanding

> In truth, a good case could be made that if your knowledge is meagre and unsatisfactory, the last thing in the world you should do is make measurements. The chance is negligible that you will measure the right things accidentally.
>
> (George Miller, 1962: 79)

Until now, psychology has had its greatest successes with problems that lend themselves to experimentation, quantitative surveys, or computational modelling, where there are numerous equivalent cases, with precise and complete data, and ample time for analysis. But there are other kinds of problems which are common and very important, yet notoriously intractable by these means, problems in the real world, where orderly situations unravel over time and have to be repaired. These situations are too intricately structured for standard experiments; too poorly understood for survey methods; too rich for the stochastic mathematics of sequences; and so on. They are "chain reactions", with no standard initial conditions, or clearly separable causes and effects.

Such problems call for a radically new approach, which starts with the kind of information that is available in practice (often incomplete, idiosyncratic, fragmented, partly qualitative, and rapidly changing) and works out increasingly effective ways of dealing with it, on its own terms. The methods may sometimes have to work with single cases and in real time. Better tools are essential to extract the relevant patterns from data, to extrapolate them into the future, and to steer them away from bad outcomes. This has been the aim of developing the "SERIAL" (**SE**quential **R**eal-time **In**-depth case **AnaL**ysis) approach to research. If we could understand how the present generates the future, we should have the key to conflicts, accidents, the breakdown of relationships, and crises of various kinds.

Sometimes the information we need to consider is qualitative, sometimes quantitative, most often a mixture – hence the importance of being able to "mix methods", but the qualitative/quantitative distinction is not really fundamental. One can describe things qualitatively or quantitatively, and often the two blend into each other. There is no hard and fast boundary between quality and quantity. Similarly one can carry out qualitative experiments or quantitative experiments. The two are not all that different. The distinction between descriptive and experimental research is much more fundamental, in terms of the logic involved, and the purposes they serve. Experimental methods are the only ones which allow causes to be matched unequivocally with their effects, but the price that has to be paid for doing this, in terms of artificiality and inappropriate explanatory frameworks, can sometimes be very high indeed (e.g. Harré, 1993; Harré, Clarke, & de Carlo, 1985).

The process of research can be thought of in many ways: answering questions, solving puzzles, finding the truth, discovering causes. One of the best metaphors, and the closest to the way research is done, is Campbell's (1974) notion of "evolutionary epistemology", in which the evolution of ideas is likened to the evolution of organisms. Just as in biological evolution, there has to be a process of diversification, without which evolution stagnates; and a process of restriction or selection, without which it goes wild and produces arbitrary and unstable results. The crucial thing is the balance between the two. Theoretical creativity without enough critical assessment produces bizarre intellectual ramblings. There are certain disciplines where this appears to go on. But excessive critical assessment coupled with insufficient theoretical creativity is no good either. This is a recipe for "dustbowl empiricism". The situation is rather like a factory where all the designers and inventors have been co-opted into quality control. Very little is produced that is worth having, but the mundane products are quality tested to the very highest degree. It is an error into which (social) psychology is always tending to slide.

In principle, "qualitative methods" should include any methods which are qualitative. It seems obvious, but in practice it is not the case. The field of qualitative methodology, which has been rapidly gaining in popularity over the last ten years or so, has centred very largely on methods for the analysis of language, and more specifically conversations, as in Conversation Analysis following the tradition of Harvey Sacks and his colleagues (Sacks, Schegloff, & Jefferson, 1974; Schegloff & Sacks, 1973) and interviews, as in Discourse Analysis (Potter and Wetherell, 1987). It is good that language has come back into view in this way, having been neglected by social psychology for so long, but it is regrettable that it has now come to eclipse the study of most other kinds of activity that are not conducted in language, and research materials other than linguistic texts, such as films, videos, photographs, maps, and so forth. The "turn to language" is in danger of becoming a retreat into language, while social psychology constructs a new mythical world to explore. Gone is the realm that experimental social psychology used to inhabit, where people looked, smiled and gestured but never spoke. Now we have entered Talkworld where people converse, argue, negotiate, and the rest, but never fight, eat, shop, drive or make love.

This strange turn-about seems to have been prompted by three things. One is the fashion for giving a post-modernist spin to everything in psychology which aspires to be social (and therefore politically correct). The social world we now try to understand is a text, or like text, or constructed through inter-textual devices, or "understood" by playing certain kinds of language games with it. Everything is language, so when language has been captured everything has been captured. This allows or encourages a flight from realism and into relativism. Gone too are truth and falsity, for some researchers, together with accuracy, validity and reliability. Instead we have alternative readings of the text, each as good as another.

A second impetus for the retreat into language seems to be the rise of computer technology, and with it the Internet and the Web. These new media provide a greatly expanded arena for interaction. The global conversation has begun. But it is *only* a conversation. Those of us who inhabit the net no longer touch or hear or smell each other. We may occasionally see each other. Everything is text. We type at each other for hours on end. And the way to understand all this is (arguably) through the analysis of language.

Third, the general loss of faith in laboratory experiments as the primary paradigm for social psychology, has shifted the focus of the subject from observation, recording and measurement to accounts of action, and texts as action.

I want to take a different line, however. I want a psychology and a methodology that deals with everything people do, in language and otherwise. One which strives for accurate descriptions and valid explanations. This would be a kind of qualitative neo-positivism (which is not a contradiction in terms, however undesirable it may seem to some people) or a hybrid neo-positivism where qualitative and quantitative methods are mixed and used together.

Values

Such a combination of quantitative and qualitative approaches may also help us to reunify scientific and everyday psychological ideas, using methods which are more accessible to the lay people to produce findings which are more understandable, more credible, and easier to use in the context of everyday beliefs and practices. I call this activity "Natural Psychology" (Clarke, 1988). In some respects it parallels Lave's (1988) work on the relation between abstract and everyday knowledge, except that Natural Psychology aims to reintegrate our *own* abstract and everyday knowledge as researchers, *about* the people we study, rather than reconciling the different forms of knowledge that occur *in* the people we study.

The usual way of doing and teaching psychology is to start with our view of what science is like, and then to apply it to "human nature". But we also need the opposite approach, which starts from our existing conception of human nature, and then works to make it more systematic and scientific. This is a complementary, but quite different enterprise from the usual approach, and is urgently needed in some parts of psychology (although, admittedly, quite inappropriate for others). After all, if we cannot find room for lay people's psychology in what we do, there is not much chance of them finding room for our psychology in what they do.

The aim of a psychological education should be to refine and supplement the interpersonal insightfulness of the student, not to replace it with something which is entirely explicit and objective (and therefore bound to be crude and incomplete for a long while yet). If I lived on a hill and wanted to see further, I would build a tower on the hill. It would be foolish to reject the hill as a mere peculiarity of nature, and to build a tower in the valley, hoping that one day I could make it tall enough to give a better view.

One obligation of psychology, as a publicly funded enterprise, is to find out what is of general benefit or general interest, not just to pursue more and more arcane minutiae of the subject in the hope of greater scientific credibility and respectability. The two objectives are not necessarily in conflict, but when they do clash we are much too willing to sacrifice utility for scientistic mystique and impressive complexity.

There is so much of great importance that psychology as a practical discipline could do, but much of it is ruled out by our present conception of what is scientifically proper and appropriate. Instead, psychology has worked very effectively to move its components into the clusters of natural, physical and engineering sciences that provide the most institutional prosperity and political influence. But this has been at the expense of the social and personal insights we could have been developing, and of the preferences of generation after generation of students, who have to be socialised into the discipline by persuading them to like the subject they have ended up with, instead of getting the one they wanted. This misdirection of the field has been further exacerbated (in Britain at least) by the current fashion for using certain kinds of "performance indicators" to determine the distribution of research funds for universities. The indicators in question are narrow and conservative, so individuals and institutions are forced to concentrate on orthodox, and often quite sterile, lines of research in order to survive and prosper. If we continue to penalise innovation and reward conformity in this way, the long-term health of the discipline must surely suffer.

We need to be more pragmatic, and perhaps more daring. Rigour is not everything. Saying only what you can say with (a high degree of) certainty is often less important and less useful than doing the best you can with the information available, and in the time available. Good sound evidence is the (expensive) "fuel" on which science travels forward. What we need in these hard times is a way of going as far as we can on as little fuel as possible.

Orthodox research methods are slow and painstaking. They work at a fixed pace, cautiously, and in great detail. In practical matters though, especially where real-time problems (and possibly forecasts) are concerned, the need is not to work at a fixed level of detail and precision, no matter how long it may take; but to work in as much detail and precision as time allows. Methods are needed which can systematically trade-off detail against speed, as required.

In traditional psychological research, rigour counts above everything. Novelty, utility, originality, and cost-effectiveness are appreciated as well, but the basic purpose of standard research methods is the avoidance of "false positives" or "type I errors". Nothing must be claimed as "true", "found" or "discovered", unless there is sufficiently watertight evidence that it really is the case. However, no method is infinitely powerful. In a messy and complex world we shall never achieve a perfect partition, where every true proposition is shown to be true, and every false one is shown to be false. We know from signal detection theory that imperfect discriminability means a reduction in false positives will lead to more "false negatives" or "type II errors" (all other things being equal). The more cautious you are, the more you miss. Surely, it would be more reasonable to strike a considered balance between false positives and false negatives, in an appropriate way for each field of enquiry and each issue we deal with. In the first instance this may be just a matter of journal editors and referees recognising that relatively speculative papers are fruitful in some areas (and of course downright dangerous in others).

Our present philosophy of science, with its emphasis on minimising false positive errors, regardless of the price in false negatives, is creating a further paradox in our relations with the wider public. People expect psychologists to be insightful, to notice and understand what they would miss. The reality is often quite the reverse. We acknowledge *less* of human nature than the person in the street, because our "threshold of belief" has been set inappropriately high. Somewhat to our cost, we would rather miss much of what is true in the world, than believe a little of what is false. (I am not dealing here with type I and type II errors in just their narrow statistical sense, as they occur in the design of particular experiments. There, of course, we have detailed techniques for considering and balancing the two. I am using the terms in a broader, rather metaphorical sense, to refer to more general issues, like our prevailing preference for experimental over all other methods, because they deliver more certain conclusions, even though they restrict the scope of the subject quite severely.)

Understanding complex episodes of human behaviour requires synthesis just as much as analysis. We should always be trying to piece things together to see what they are part of, as well as taking them to bits to see what they are made of.

To a considerable extent, the studies that make up psychology at any stage in its development will not be the ones that are needed, or that any one of us would choose as an ideal selection. The invisible hand is at work. Some lines of research exist rather than others for the same reason that some animal species exist rather than others – because they are better at keeping themselves in existence. Science is a cultural replicator. Operationalised procedures that are easy to disseminate make good replicators. Methods which require insight and creativity to produce novel results do not. Research that makes good sense will always be under threat from research that makes a good bandwagon.

Our methods remove us from our subject matter, they do not bring us closer to it. We have created a body of technique, an abstract machine, for generating information about human nature. Meanwhile, our understanding, our expertise, is focused more and more on that machine. Psychologists (or at least academic psychologists) are not individuals who understand people. They are individuals who understand the business and the technicalities of doing psychology. There is a major difference. Suppose you wanted to play the violin. There are various approaches you could take. You could study and practise in the usual way, training your ears and your fingers to appreciate and respond to the nuances of the instrument and the music. Alternatively, you could study robotics, calculating exactly the number and arrangement of actuators required to build a robotic violinist's arm. Even if the music sounded the same at the end of the day (which it might well do), I would say the person who played directly was the one who had mastered the violin, while the other person had achieved the (equally difficult and worthwhile) task of mastering advanced robotics. So which is the role we want for ourselves as psychologists – to be understanders of people, or the creators of a people-probing technology? And which are we turning out to be?

It is time to make a strategic choice. Shall we ask ourselves what is worth knowing about human conduct and experience, and try to discover it? Or shall we carry on doing what we do at present, simply because that is what we do – its momentum is hard to resist – reproducing what is easiest to replicate because the invisible hand guides us that way? There is nothing in an evolutionary process to steer it in "sensible" or "desirable" directions. Good replicators just replicate. That is all there is. In the same way, some research paradigms are easier to reproduce in a thousand minor variations than others, so more student projects can be based on them quickly and easily, leading to more PhDs and academic careers. People in these fields write more than the average number of journal articles for their students to cite, and to base their own work on. Maybe the students carry on themselves into the same lines of research, and so it goes on. But what is the point of all that? Were there not real problems to be solved, and needs to be met? We must break out of the loop of runaway positive feedback that drives the discipline, and decide on a worthwhile direction to go in, and an effective way to get there.

Structured judgement methods

As far as methodology is concerned, the essence of the problem is this. The things we observe in the world, which we want to understand and explain, are the visible products of unseen processes. The job our methods have to do, is to get us from descriptions of individual instances of the product (be they individual cases, problems, people, events, or whatever) to a generalised account of the underlying processes. There are two steps involved, from the particular to the general, and from description to explanation. In most research they are taken in that order. First the data are aggregated. Then, in the aggregate, explanations are sought or checked (pathway **a** in Figure 5.1). But the data-coding and aggregation stage tends to obscure the structure of

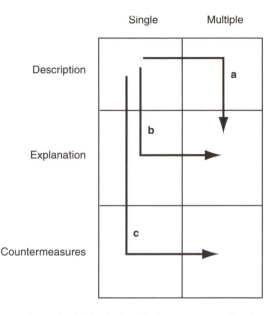

Figure 5.1 Pathways from individual description to generalised explanations and countermeasures. From Clarke (1992). Reproduced with the permission of The Institution of Electrical Engineers.

each case, making it harder for the researcher to use real-world knowledge and domain expertise. Very often the comprehensibility of the research material which is apparent at the outset is lost early on, and then laboriously recovered or replaced by the use of large data sets and elaborate statistics.

Sometimes though, especially in multiple case studies, it can be productive to do things the other way round. This means analysing each case in turn, moving first from description to explanation, and only later aggregating over the explanations or conclusions (pathway **b**). That too can be problematic, though. It is often said that one limitation of case study methods is that as each case is more and more richly understood, it becomes harder and harder to compare and combine it with others. If the research is "applied", and has the objective of producing practical remedies or countermeasures for a problem, the answer can be to defer the aggregation stage still longer, and to move from description to explanation and on to the identification of countermeasures in each case in turn, and then to aggregate over the countermeasures (pathway **c**).

In road accident research, for instance, it can be relatively hard to aggregate the results of a detailed accident-causation study over the cases involved. The explanation for each case is elaborate, time-based, and highly structured. Conceptually it seems more like a molecule than a list of features (and it would be nonsensical to invent a generic molecule to capture the properties of several rather different compounds). However, the countermeasures appropriate to each case are easier to describe as a list, and to summarise quantitatively. It is even possible to redescribe the cases according to the patterns and combinations of countermeasures which fit them, and to map them and cluster them in 'countermeasure-space" (Clarke, Ward, & Jones, 1998, 1999).

However, the "explanation-before-aggregation" strategy means that causes have to be detected in individual cases. Conventional wisdom holds (sometimes correctly) that this cannot be done. Sometimes, the causal mechanisms are not apparent, and the influence of one event over another can only be revealed by looking for concomitant variation in many cases. But in other situations, involving everyday behaviour, interaction and language, it is quite straightforward to interpret individual events, using the same sense-making capabilities we use as lay people rather than researchers.

This use of the researcher's (or other experts') judgement to ascribe causes to events has other advantages as well, besides the chance to analyse cases individually. Other kinds of knowledge and experience of the topic can be brought into play, which often cannot be incorporated in the more mechanical kinds of analysis. Furthermore, once the judgemental skills of the researcher have been exercised and evaluated in this way, they can be refined as the research proceeds, whereas conventional research methods would leave them unused, and hence untested and undeveloped. "Structured judgement methodology" sets out, not only to use judgemental skills where appropriate, but also to refine them at the same time.

Judgement is flexible in various ways. For one thing, it meets the requirement for flexibility, proceeding slowly, carefully and in detail, or faster and more crudely, as the needs of the situation dictate. It can also take account of context more easily than rigid algorithmic and quantitative methods. Events may change their significance in the presence of other events. The human interpreter is aware of this (so much so in fact, that allowance is often made automatically, and without awareness). Non-judgemental methods tend to code events at face value, and then remove them from their context, so if different instances have different significance, it can no longer be recognised.

We have just seen that the stage of aggregating over cases is sometimes best left until late on in the research process. The same can be true of reliability and validity checking. The usual procedure is to remove "threats to validity" before analysing a batch of data – checking the reliability and accuracy of each measure, for instance, before proceeding. But this can be very wasteful and inefficient. There is an alternative strategy, which works better in some cases, when relatively few striking findings likely to be extracted from a large mass of data, for example. This is to do the analysis first, and then to consider just those threats to validity which are relevant to the (apparent) findings. This produces two savings. First, there may be relatively few cross checks to carry out if there are relatively few results. This is easier than screening and cleaning the whole data set to begin with. Second, the nature of the findings can sometimes indicate which threats need to be considered and which do not. For instance, if a particular group of informants turn out to be much more self-critical than expected, this cannot be the result of self-serving biases. However, to remove all possible problems from the data before analysis, one would have to consider and deal with the potential for self-serving biases, before realising that it was unnecessary.

So much for the benefits of putting (qualitative) judgement at the heart of the investigative process. There are drawbacks too. Judgement can bring distortion and inconsistency as well as insight and flexibility. That is why a systematic (quantitative) framework is needed to discipline and standardise the judgements, and so to give "the best of both worlds". The business of reading case reports or other qualitative research materials, and arriving at explanations and interpretations in consultation with colleagues, is likely to need structuring in at least the following ways if it is to provide a repeatable, teachable, and valid method of investigation.

- There should be an explicit written step-by-step protocol, documenting the procedures to be applied in each case, or listing the issues and questions to be addressed.
- There should be explicit (and preferably quantitative) assessments of the reproducibility of interpretations, by different researchers and on different occasions.
- There should be explicit attempts to identify details which need corroboration, and to use whatever methods of triangulation or "converging operations" are appropriate, to ensure the validity of factual information.
- The nature of the initial information and the final conclusions should be described in an accessible form which is commensurable with other studies, so that complementary or conflicting findings are recognisable, and so that variations in the accuracy of interpretation between researchers, procedures or occasions are brought to light.

At its simplest, the essence of structured judgement methodology, or any systematic, "scientific" method, is that researchers may draw whatever conclusions they like (whichever ones seem most interesting, novel and useful to them), *provided adequate precautions have been taken against false positive error and false negative error*. In practice this tends to mean scrutinising the research materials and procedures first for the possibility of false negative errors, looking for omissions and oversights in the types of cases sampled, the issues raised, and the explanations considered. Later comes the task of screening out false positives: patterns in small groups of cases that do not generalise to others; key facts that cannot be corroborated; causal ascriptions whose implications are not borne out; and so on.

The reduction of false positives is a matter of testing ideas to destruction, or the "falsification" of potential conclusions wherever possible (Popper, 1963, 1972), rather trying to prove or verify selectively those ideas that are true. (This principle of falsificationism, which can be seen as a particular approach to the task of reducing false positives, should not be confused with the reduction of false negatives, which is a separate matter, the importance of which has already been discussed.)

Structured judgement methodology is not a single research technique, rather it is a style of research, with its own guidelines and rationale, which embraces many specific techniques, some of which are new, others of which already have an established history. Grounded Theory (Glaser & Strauss, 1967) is one of the best known examples of this kind of idea. It is a technique which is widely known and used in the social sciences, where the interpretations of the researcher are central, and the process by which they are created, revised, used, and recorded is carried out in a highly structured way through the medium of "theoretical memo writing". There are some differences of emphasis though between that form of structured judgement methodology and the general principles discussed here (the structuring is not quantitative, and there is no explicit focus on the benefits of late aggregation). Nevertheless, Grounded Theory is clearly one of the first and best of the established research methods to which the label of "structured judgement" could be applied.

Let me close this chapter with a specific example of one form of structured judgement methodology, called "Matrix Forecasting". This technique mixes qualitative and quantitative elements. It fits the general framework of "structured judgement methodology" principles described above. And it can be used with a variety of research materials, whether language-based like interviews, conversations and speeches; non-language-based like films, videos and direct observation; or a mixture, like case reports containing pictures, maps, test results, and so forth, in addition to statements, interviews, and so on. As such it is intended to provide a useful counterpoise to the majority of qualitative methods that have come forward in recent years, which are exclusively aimed at the analysis of verbal activities and materials.

Matrix forecasting

Behavioural forecasting should be a general aim and an interest of psychologists and social scientists, for several reasons. First as a practical matter, various kinds of prognosis, advice or decision depend on judging what is likely to happen in the near future, and how the course of events might be affected by the actions we take ourselves. Well-developed methods already exist for predicting highly aggregated behaviour, in sales forecasts for example, but there is no real equivalent for the prediction of single actions by individual people, even though for some purposes these can be just as important.

Second, the most rigorous way of testing ideas about the psychological processes underlying any sequence of actions, is to look at the accuracy of the predictions they make. This is usually taken to mean that controlled (laboratory) experiments are required, where a price may have to be paid in terms of simplification and artificiality. Theory-based predictions of free-ranging behaviour, on the other hand, have many of the advantages of experimental methods, but without the same disadvantages.

Lastly, forecasting studies provide a way of achieving the aims of "Natural Psychology", making psychological findings more widely accessible and useful by keeping research procedures as close as possible to the concepts and methods of everyday life. This is a matter of building on and refining everyday and scientific knowledge *taken together*, to produce findings which are easier to incorporate into the beliefs and practices of everyday life. One way of doing this concretely is to formulate process hypotheses in real-time, as some naturally occurring course of events unfolds, and to retain the ideas whose implications for later events are borne out, while discarding the rest. This is essentially how much of our everyday epistemology works. Cyclical, iterative forecasting procedures allow all manner of scientific and everyday predictive beliefs and intuitions to be tested side-by-side, and assimilated into composite models in a straightforward, flexible and effective way, which is not possible with most other research techniques.

However, the forecasting methods that are available at present divide between quantitative techniques which are easily (in most cases *better*) implemented computationally, and qualitative methods which rely on human judgement. Since neither sort of technique can do the job of the other, and most problem domains have both quantitative and qualitative aspects, it is difficult to create a comprehensive and coherent approach to behavioural prediction. Matrix forecasting allows predictive judgements about actions and events over time to be systematically collected, evaluated and refined, in a way which iterates towards increasingly accurate predictions, produces an increasingly sophisticated list of predictive heuristics as the method progresses, and is skill enhancing for the participants.

Over about the past twenty years, the various subjects involved in forecasting, from meteorology to economics, have created a general forecasting discipline, sharing and developing their common methods through agencies such as the International Institute of Forecasters. They have developed objective methods (which are quantitative, and rely on mathematical modelling or time series analysis and extrapolation), and judgemental methods (which may also be quantitative, or may be qualitative).

A lot of work has gone into the development of better trend extrapolation techniques for cyclical, and other complex data, and the methods have been extensively evaluated and compared, most notably through the "M Competition" computer tournaments, in which different prediction algorithms were played off against each other on a range of economic data sets. The great problem though is with "structural change", meaning that a model which has been carefully fitted to past data often makes poor predictions, because the phenomenon being predicted has changed its underlying rules meanwhile. As a result, the correlation between how well a model fits the past and how well it predicts the future is only 0.3 for predictions one time-unit ahead, and it falls to zero for predictions four time-units ahead! (see Makridakis, 1988).

In quantitative judgemental forecasting research, the emphasis has been on identifying and reducing cognitive errors and biases (e.g. Hogarth, 1987), and on improving the ways in which the judgements of individuals in a group can best be combined to form a single decision. Sniezek (1989) found, for example, that different heuristics for combining the opinions of group members can affect forecast accuracy, with initial results favouring the "dictator method", in which group members all state a forecast, and then make a consensus choice as to whose opinion should stand for the group as a whole.

The "poor relation" of the field remains the methodology of qualitative judgemental forecasting, where the techniques have been less developed and are harder to evaluate. This is the area which mainly concerns us here. Certain approaches stand out, such as scenario-writing, cross-impact matrix analysis, and morphological analysis, but the field is wide open for new developments.

An idea of some of the key findings of forecasting research comes from Armstrong's (1988) overview of work since 1960, which includes the following:

- Role-playing is especially valuable when conflict outcomes are to be predicted, increasing accuracy from about 20 per cent to about 70 per cent.
- Structured methods improve judgemental forecast accuracy significantly.
- Domain expertise is associated with accuracy of short range predictions, but not long range ones.
- Highly complex quantitative methods have not so far proved to be more accurate than some of the simpler ones.

A second precedent for Matrix forecasting comes from the field of machine learning, or more specifically of "genetic algorithms" (Forsyth, 1989). These are rule-inducing programs that search a problem space very efficiently by borrowing the mechanism of Darwinian evolution. Random predictive or classificatory rules are created and evaluated, and then the worst performers are abandoned, and the best ones retained, "bred", mutated, and re-evaluated. The process iterates towards an optimal solution. In forecasting too, it is possible to incorporate evolutionary, self-adapting strategies. Predictive beliefs, heuristics and procedures are systematically used, evaluated and modified, in such a way that the overall forecasting activity does not just deliver the best possible predictions at any one time, but more importantly, improves its own procedures and performance as it goes along.

Psychological research has contributed to forecasting in a number of ways, including the study of errors and biases, and of group judgemental processes, but there is also potential for suitable forecasting methods to add a great deal to the methodological range of psychology itself. A rolling forecast of a series of events (whether in real time or *ex post facto*) provides a good compromise between the rigorous experimental way of testing hypotheses according to their predictive accuracy, and the need to study free ranging uncontrolled phenomena. Furthermore, as we have seen, it provides a concrete way of implementing the aims of "Natural Psychology".

This approach can be used with all kinds of materials and problems, but the simplest to imagine, and in some ways the most straightforward to do, is the forecasting of everyday conversation (or arguments, debates, meetings, etc), where each event is a single conversational "turn". Here too the central idea of "natural psychology" can be seen in action, namely that the researcher's personal beliefs about the domain in question, gained through everyday experience, should be used and tested together with knowledge from reading and scholarship. According to natural psychology, the two kinds of information should be deliberately made to engage each other, and to compete, displace or complement each other piece-by-piece, according to their contribution to the (forecasting) task in hand.

The basis of the Matrix Forecasting family of methods is a technique called "Seven Column Forecasting" (Clarke, 1992). It is designed for use with a group of experts, who may bring formal professional expertise to the task, or may be family members or acquaintances of an individual being studied, say. They consider a structured series of events as they occur. Alternatively, for research purposes, they may work step-by-step through a record of events from the beginning, while artificially maintaining their ignorance of later events at each stage. This is called "rolling horizon" forecasting. There is one iteration of the procedure for each event in the sequence, during which the expert panel records the seven kinds of information shown below.

1) **An *ad hoc* prediction** of the next event
2) **A rationale** for the prediction
3) A summary of **the *real* next event** as it becomes known
4) A quantitative estimate of the extent of **the match** or mismatch between 1) and 3)
5) A summary of the *nature* of **the discrepancy** between 1) and 3)
6) **The changes** in predictive strategy which might prevent such errors arising in future
7) A cumulative list of **predictive guide-lines and system principles**, incorporating all the revisions from 6).

A record of the group's decisions is displayed in front of them on a board or display screen, as a summary table with seven columns for the different kinds of information (hence the name of the method), and one row for each event. The layout is shown in Figure 5.2.

This creates a multi-loop feedback process where item 1) influences 2), 4) and 5); 2) influences 7); 3) influences 1), 4) and 5); 4) influences 7); 5) influences 6); 6) influences 7); and 7) influences 1) as shown in Figure 5.3.

	1 Forecast	2 Rationale	3 Real	4 Accuracy	5 Discrepancy	6 Correction	7 Heuristics
Event 1							
Event 2							
Event 3							

Figure 5.2 Layout of "Seven Column Forecasting" Matrix. From Clarke (1992). Reproduced with the permission of The Institution of Electrical Engineers.

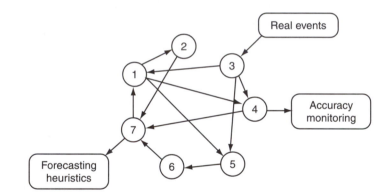

Figure 5.3 Feedback loops in "Seven Column Forecasting". From Clarke (1992). Reproduced with the permission of The Institution of Electrical Engineers.

The method is self-adapting and skill-enhancing. As it proceeds, causal hypotheses are created, tested, and selected according to their predictive accuracy, so that a list of provisional findings is produced at each stage, and continually updated and refined as the method iterates, together with accuracy measures and successful predictive heuristics.

This is a procedure which should be experienced at first hand, rather than just read about. It is a common reaction of group members, when encountering the method for the first time, to be unimpressed by the briefing on what is to be done, but then intrigued by the feel of the session itself, and the sense that their own understanding of the area is being tapped, challenged and modified in quite unexpected ways.

However, the full procedure tends to be somewhat cumbersome, as it has no way of focusing attention on key events, and reducing unnecessary detail. A variant called the "Three Cycle Procedure" works better for some purposes, especially when the application is time-critical. Here the expert group performs three cycles of judgements, the first applying to all events at a low level; the second involving rarer and more abstract judgements; and the third being the rarest and most abstract of all.

In cycle one, the task is merely to monitor the stream of events and to decide when a worthwhile prediction is possible, or when a previous prediction can be evaluated. When either condition is satisfied, control passes to cycle two for a prediction to be made or evaluated, and for the possibility to be considered of adding a new predictive heuristic to the stack, or of evaluating an existing one. If either of these steps is appropriate, the procedure passes to cycle three to modify the current heuristic stack. Once this method is established, it represents a real saving in time, but the very scarcity of cycle-three operations which gives it its economy, means that it has to run for some time before any heuristic-level products emerge at all. This method also tends to mix together substantive hypotheses about the process being predicted, and procedural guide-lines about the best ways to structure the available information and the task. For some purposes, these considerations need to be kept apart, especially if the technique is being used primarily to investigate the underlying process, and not to make predictions *per se*.

This brings us to the question of just what the various different kinds of forecasting technique might be trying to achieve. What exactly do we expect a good forecasting method to do, or to produce? There are at least five possible answers to this, which may require rather different approaches to be taken.

- Most obviously, forecasting methods should produce (accurate) forecasts. However that is not a sufficient, or even for some purposes a necessary end-product of forecasting research.
- We may want a given method or project to produce (complete, explicit and optimal) techniques for making forecasts at a later date, rather than immediate predictions about the research data or domain. This is especially important when the events are very fast moving, so the researchers' most useful role is to develop methods for others to use "in the field", rather than involving themselves in the flux of events as they occur.
- The aim may be to discover the processes that underlie the events being predicted.
- Meta-forecasts may be needed, that is to say ways of distinguishing between the situations which are predictable and those which are not. This is one of the ways in which meteorology has been able to deal with the problems posed by Chaos Theory.
- In some problem areas, it may be that forecasts are already being made intuitively, and quite successfully by the participants. It may not be feasible in the short term to replace the existing methods completely, or to go

to the lengths of making them explicit in order to refine them. The real need may be to find a way of improving the quality of existing judge-mental forecasts progressively and reliably, without interrupting the process by which they are made. This is the aim of the final version of Matrix forecasting to be described below. This is called "forecast enhancement".

A forecast-enhancement procedure works best if it is not just an abstract research technique, which then has to feed its results back into practice some-how, but is rather a complete method of forecasting which can operate in either of two modes – "standard" and "evolutionary". For "everyday use" it should produce predictions straightforwardly, without evaluating or changing its own procedures. When used for research, on the other hand, it should include evolutionary components which feed lasting improvements back into the standard version. Looked at in this way, the question becomes not "How could a good forecasting procedure be produced from scratch?" but rather "How could the way people set about forecasting at present be supplemented with an optional evolutionary component?"

To answer that second question, consider how intuitive forecasting works, and how a systematic learning component might be added. The essence of qualitative prediction is mapping from a given history of events to a set of explanatory beliefs or causal attributions, by using (often tacit) knowledge of the people or activities concerned, and then inferring the future consequences of those processes continuing to operate, perhaps by drawing further on similar knowledge. What is missing from all this is the systematic use of feedback to eliminate erroneous sources of prediction. That requires the primary, or forecast-making, procedure to be embedded in a second, evolutionary, procedure. A simplified version of the original seven-column technique may be all that is needed for this. Once again there is a panel of forecasters who consider events in turn, deliberating and setting out the record of their work in tabular form. Again there is one row for each event, but only four columns are used in this case: a) a record of the events; b) the group's analysis of the underlying causal processes; c) their predictions; and d) the possible problems and improvements to the method that occur to them while making the forecasts. Three forms of cross-checking and improvement can then occur. They can be employed at each step; or else periodically, taking account of a whole block of predictions; or even as a separate "off-line" exercise, maybe carried out by other people, perhaps when the whole sequence has run its course.

First, the modifications occurring to the forecasting group while making predictions can be tried out, and retained subject to further evaluation. Second, and more importantly, past errors can be examined and diagnosed, and potential remedies devised. In principle any false positive or false negative prediction is an error which can be detected, analysed and addressed. In other words, every prediction in column c) should correspond to a later event in column a), and vice versa. Whenever that is not so, the error can be compared with the process beliefs that informed the prediction – recorded on the same row as the prediction, in column b), and with the errors and omissions in the record of events – contained in the same and earlier rows, in column a). On that basis, further modifications can be made to the primary forecasting procedure. However, even that would not be guaranteed to improve matters, unless apparent remedies were always real remedies, and improvements in one regard could never create knock-on problems elsewhere, which is not the case. The final safeguard, the third level of feedback, working in the longer term, is to collate the forecasting error types and rates which occurred over a series of past trials with the supposed enhancements and remedies which were introduced at the time. Only the changes in procedure that had produced detectable improvements in performance would then be retained in the long term. All these learning cycles can continue to iterate continuously in search of further improvements, without hampering the primary forecasting procedure which remains viable at all times, and always employs the best set of guidelines to be discovered up to that point.

The method has been tried out in exploratory studies of a number of problems, including the study of international crises, everyday discourse, autobiography, and football, with interesting results. A number of issues and possible enhancements have been identified. A more elaborate and structured way of setting out the main options of the principal actors seems to be desirable, as does a more detailed breakdown of the possible choice factors in each situation, including the main actors' aims, beliefs, resources and expectations. Typically, each prediction involves the enumeration of the main options for each actor, which is relatively easy, followed by an estimate of their choice strategy, which is a good deal harder. This may be a suitable point at which to incorporate other techniques from decision analysis, and from the study of conflict resolution (between courses of action) in Artificial Intelligence (AI).

Clearly, the "evolutionary strategy" behind these methods can only work effectively if changes in forecast performance can be measured satisfactorily, and that raises particular problems of specificity, and base-rate probability, when the forecasts are of this qualitative kind. A count of true and false predictions alone is misleading if it gives equal weight to vague and to precise predictions, or to obvious and to surprising ones. Neither problem arises in quite the same form with quantitative predictions because specificity is constant and one value is (assumed to be) as hard to predict as another. Furthermore, the magnitude of individual errors can be gauged quite straightforwardly.

One of the advantages of forecasting as a research paradigm, is that it is relatively straightforward (and of course all-important) to tell how well a given method is working. Predictions soon become true or not. (Or in the rolling horizon case, they are soon found to have been true or not.) Some preliminary evaluations can already be made of the methods presented here. First, it has become clear, working with and developing the prototype versions, that they have a real relevance and usefulness in the analysis of complex situations. They are flexible in their requirements for time, people, equipment and expertise. They are interesting, enjoyable and easy to use. And they give users a sense that their insights are being recruited and used to the full, in a new and challenging way which also exposes weaknesses and misconceptions, and so encourages adaptive change. It is still too early though to say for sure if these methods meet the stronger criteria of providing increased, and *progressively increasing* forecast accuracy.

For the specific purpose of enhancing intuitive predictions of a kind that are already being made, a very simple strategy suggests itself. The improvement of forecast accuracy is, on the face of it, the same as the reduction of common errors. That seems to require three kinds of information: the main types of error that occur; the circumstances in which each type arises; and the appropriate safeguards to apply against each type. However, it is entirely possible that the first kind of information will do the duty of all three. The nature of each error type may in itself indicate the situations that call for special caution, and the safeguards to employ, as is commonly the case with errors and biases of judgement, and statistical fallacies in general. In that case, all that will be needed for a major improvement in forecast accuracy will be for the commonest errors to be documented, a task which is already well under way in attribution theory and cognitive psychology. If the catalogue of errors is well known to forecasters at the time of making predictions, it could turn out to be self-evident how they can be avoided. Whether such a simple philosophy can produce significant improvements in accuracy will be an empirical issue, once we know enough about the nature of forecasting errors to put it to the test.

Conclusions

Qualitative and quantitative methods are not as different as we sometimes think, and not as difficult to combine, in principle at least. In many cases, the important issues are the same for qualitative, quantitative, and hybrid researchers, such as the need to establish the reliability and validity of the methods being used. There are much more fundamental differences between experimental and non-experimental methods, for instance, or between explanation by meaning and explanation by causal process. It is this latter which often underlies the apparent opposition of qualitative and quantitative methods. Highly formalised methods have many advantages including repeatability and self-evident complexity, but they sometimes rob the research process of the subtlety, flexibility and creativity that have been fundamental to the success of the advanced sciences.

Areas of psychology should be developed which are more pragmatic, more concerned with the users of psychological knowledge and what they need to know, and more willing to meet lay people halfway in the terms and concepts they use. Lay people, after all, are participants in the research, and are supposed to be the beneficiaries. We should be more concerned with finding out what they need to know for their purposes, and less concerned with extracting the information from them which we need for ours.

Structured judgement methods fit in with these values by using researchers' interpretations of individual cases as the central method of investigation, while surrounding and confining them with a framework of more conventional and quantitative techniques. This helps to assure reliability and validity, and to pick out and communicate the findings which generalise successfully over different groups and types of cases.

Examples which illustrate the properties and values of structured judgement methodology include some familiar and long-established techniques such as Grounded theory, as well as novel research methods such as Matrix Forecasting. Here, intuitions about the processes governing a series of events, and what they might lead to in the future, can be systematically stated, checked and refined, until the predictions become sufficiently accurate, and the predictive skills of the researchers suitably developed.

References

Armstrong, J. S. (1988). Research needs in forecasting. *International Journal of Forecasting, 4*, 449–465.

Campbell, D. T. (1974). Evolutionary epistemology. In P. A. Schilpp (Ed.), *The philosophy of Karl Popper*. La Salle, IL: Open Court (pp. 412–463).

Clarke, D. D. (1988). *In defence of "natural psychology"*. Paper to British Psychological Society, Social Psychology Section Annual Conference, University of Kent at Canterbury, 24th September.

Clarke, D. D. (1992). Qualitative judgemental forecasting methods for use in strategic decision making. In *Proceedings of IDASCO '92: International Conference on Information-Decision-Action Systems in Complex Organisations*. London: Institution of Electrical Engineers, Conference Publication, No. 353 (pp. 75–79).

Clarke, D. D., Ward, P. J., & Jones, J. (1998). Overtaking road-accidents: Differences in manoeuvre as a function of driver age. *Accident Analysis and Prevention, 30*(4), 455–467.

Clarke, D. D., Ward, P. J., & Jones, J. (1999) Processes and countermeasures in overtaking road-accidents. *Ergonomics, 42(6)*, 846–867.

Forsyth, R. (1989). Inductive learning for expert systems. In R. Forsyth (Ed.), *Expert systems: Principles and case studies* (2nd ed.). London: Chapman and Hall (pp. 197–220).

Glaser, B., & Strauss, A. L. (1967). *The discovery of grounded theory: Strategies for qualitative research*. Chicago: Aldine.

Lave, J. (1988). *Cognition in practice*. Cambridge: Cambridge University Press.

Harré, R. (1993). *Social being* (2nd ed.). Oxford: Blackwell.

Harré, R., Clarke, D. D., & de Carlo, N. (1985). *Motives and mechanisms*. London: Methuen.

Hogarth, R. M. (1987). *Judgement and choice: The psychology of decision* (2nd ed.). New York: Wiley.

Makridakis, S. (1988). Metaforecasting: Ways of improving forecasting accuracy and usefulness. *International Journal of Forecasting, 4*, 467–491.

Miller, G. A. (1962). *Psychology: The science of mental life.* New York: Harper and Row.

Popper, K. (1963). *Conjectures and refutations.* New York: Basic Books.

Popper, K. (1972). *The logic of scientific discovery* (3rd ed.). London: Hutchinson.

Potter, J., & Wetherell, M. (1987). *Discourse and social psychology: Beyond attitudes and behaviour.* London: Sage.

Sacks, H., Schegloff, E., & Jefferson, G. (1974). A simplest systematics for the organization of turn-taking in conversation. *Language, 50,* 696–735.

Schegloff, E. A., & Sacks, H. (1973). Opening up closings. *Semiotica, 7*(4), 289–327.

Sniezek, J. A. (1989). An examination of group processes in judgemental forecasting. *International Journal of Forecasting, 5,* 171–178.

6 Q methodology and qualiquantology

The example of discriminating between emotions

Paul Stenner and Rex Stainton Rogers

Qualiquantology: a monstrous hybrid?

As the aim of this book is to encourage the "mixing" of qualitative and quantitative methods, we propose a monstrous new word – *qualiquantology* – to express this discomforting hybridity. In our view the hybridity *ought* to be discomforting, since any genuine hybrid represents a significant reformation in the bodies that are brought together in forming it. Hybridity pierces the boundaries of identity and opens up the difference of Otherness. By contrast, merely adding a qualitative dimension to a quantitative study or vice versa does not constitute hybridity and may be far from discomforting.

The choice of discomfort when comfort is an option requires account. Is this, perhaps, some New Medievalist discourse of methodological self-flagellation? Certainly some users of Q methodology can occasionally be heard saying that they like Q methodology precisely because it is so *disliked* by qualitative and quantitative researchers alike. But the dynamic at play here is no mere endogenous masochism, trait-rebelliousness or perverse will-to-shock. Rather it is a functional critical device. As any psychoanalyst will attest, *dislike*, and *discomfort*, are interpretatively informative of subjective dynamics; and as any ethnomethodologist will affirm, the violation of rules brings those rules, most likely via a mob of angry rule-enforcers, to the surface. Discomfort and discovery, as a long line of persecuted un-coverers from Socrates through Lavoisier and Galileo to Darwin would avouch, go together like paranoia and delusions of grandeur.

[Stage direction: uncomfortably, as between either two stools, a rock and a hard-place, or the devil and the deep blue sea.]

Perturbating qualitative researchers

Q methodology, involving as it does factor analysis, is an eminently quantitative procedure. Sadly, this familial association alone is sufficient grounds for its dismissal as "another atomising numerology" in the eyes of some qualitative researchers. The charge *per se* has substance but, to us, is misplaced when applied to Q methodology which addresses emergent *Gestalten* – a form of

output most often associated with qualitative work. Indeed, Q methodologists (Brown, 1980; Stainton Rogers, 1995) side with the very critique that
it often laid upon them, namely, the fundamental ontological and epistemological constraints and prefigurations of conventional quantitative work. Q
methodologists, from its originator Stephenson (1935) onwards, are not born
but made. Like most qualitative researchers they have become so through
a fundamental dissatisfaction with the "positivism" and "empiricism" of
"conventional" psychology.

Is it then fair to say that one of the key advantages of qualitative research is
that it is *not quantitative*? This is only a rhetorically quantitative question, its
qualitative impact is what we seek in asking it, not a percentage, index or
weighting! Our aim is to highlight the well-sedimented and well-rehearsed
Protestant rhetoric that accounts for and warrants conversion. Key, within
the current line of argument, is that received training in qualitative methods
leads a person to be very good at insisting on attention to the specific context
out of which data (or more likely *creata* [Andersen, 1994]) emerge. The
averaging and regularising that go on in the ideal-typical quantitative study
(with its focus on means, normal distributions, standard deviations and so
on) immediately violate this rule of specificity. Likewise, the laboratory setting – designed to create a standard and controlled backdrop against which
different responses can be statistically compared – violates the principle of
naturalistic contextualisation. Finally, forcing participants into a simplified
response range and then re-coding their responses into operationally defined
categories violates the principle of respecting participants' own definitions of
the situation at hand.

Violations lead to perturbations. When qualitative researchers see the
quasi-normal distribution of a Q-sort made up of provided items; hear talk
of eigenvalues; and see the decontextualised output of a cluster of factors cut
out and laid before them like bloody organs severed from the organic whole
of the body within which they served their function – they get perturbated.
For us, however, this discomfort speaks more of an interminable battle
between "positivists" and "constructionists" than of an understanding of the
aims of a Q study. What we mean by this will, we hope, be clarified as we
continue our journey, turning away from the teeth of horrible Scylla and
towards the raging whirlpool of Charybdis.

Perturbating quantitative researchers

Despite being statistically identical to many other forms of psycho*metrics*,
for us, Q methodology lays no claim to be *measuring* anything, and hence
adopts a completely different relationship to questions of validity and reliability (it makes no sense to ask if you are measuring what you intend to be
measuring if measuring is not your intention). This, as a collective store of
personal experience demonstrates amply (*your* reaction to this statement
may well position you in the quanti-quali tension), *perturbates* conventional

quantitative researchers in fairly (if not justly) predictable ways. On one level this discomfort is an understandable and justifiable response to what seems a flagrant ignorance of the rules of psychometrics. How can we ensure our participants are telling the truth unswayed by "social desirability" and "self-serving biases" – never mind downright lying? How can we be sure they will respond the same way on all occasions? How can we be sure a normally distributed sort reflects the actual structure of their attitude? How have you ensured that your items tap what you intend them to? – and so on. Were Q methodology just another psychometric technique, then this discomfort and these questions would be right and proper (for they inform us about mensurative rules that indeed ought not to be violated).

On another level, however, the discomfort becomes more interesting. The fact that Q methodology yields clear results via factor analysis yet makes no claim to be measuring anything, demonstrates that the connection *psychometrics* (and not just psychometrics) makes between its factors and the supposedly measured intrapsychic phenomena is a *theoretical* or, worse, merely a *conventional* connection and not an axiomatic that can be unproblematically assumed a priori. Factor analysis was once the jewel in the crown of essentialising nomothetic psychology. Raising the horror that the jewel might be paste after all (a phantasm first raised by Stephenson amongst the likes of Spearman and Burt in London back in the 1930s) cannot but excite deep perturbation amongst those who prostrate themselves before that particular sceptre, sword and crown. Needless to say, Stephenson was effectively convicted of heresy and outcast to the USA (a context no less in the thrall of mental mensuration but easier to pass in). But times change, and even scapegoats occasionally come home to pasture – if only in the field of "alternative" methods! If there is indeed "a return of the repressed" it behoves us not to forget, as we bask in the new found popularity of Q methodology, that indicative discomfort.

So, to keep up the analysis: if Q methodology is not *measuring*, what is it doing?

Homo Exemplans, the neglected twin of *Homo Mensurans*

"Man", said the politically incorrect sage, "is the measure of all things." Did he mean that humans measure all things? Or perhaps that all things that matter do so relative to humans: that things "show up" for us according to human concerns? The former reading might give people the title *Homo Mensurans* (the *measurers*) whilst the latter might call us *Homo Exemplans* (the *pattern-makers*). The former, in pondering the night sky, would be concerned with questions such as how far away, in light years, a given star is from the earth. The latter, following the work of Greco-Roman mythographers, would find connections between points of light and identify patterns such as Orion and The Plough. Give human beings an array of points, suggested the Gestalt psychologists over 60 years ago, and they will make connections and "find" patterns. We would argue that this distinction between *Homo Mensurans* and *Homo Exemplans*, posing a mutual complementarity, expresses, better than that between quantitative and qualitative approaches, two orientations to scrutinising the human condition. In doing so, we are also positioning Q methodology as an exemplar of the pattern-making mode.

To illustrate this, we now turn to a Q methodological study investigating culturally shared representations of the four social emotions of joy, love, embarrassment and jealousy. The research will be presented as a way of demonstrating the pattern analytic powers of Q methodology. In other words, how those emotions are commonly configured or "patterned". The research strategy makes possible a sensibility over which moral judgements, self-perceptions, subjective experiences, bodily movements and evaluative attributions define or characterise which emotions. This task is approached by asking people to Q-sort (as explained below) a set of propositions encompassing a diverse range of thoughts, feelings, judgements, perceptions and so on into a distribution which they think best describes a given (set of) emotion(s). The factor structure resulting from Q pattern analysis (in this case, a by-person factor analysis, as described below) should, if our rationale holds, give an indication as to which propositions "hold together" in common-sense knowledge as descriptive of various contextualised emotional episodes (for further detail on the practicalities of conducting a Q study, consult Brown, 1980 or Stainton Rogers, 1995).

Q as a discriminatory taxonomic device?

In setting this task then we are able to directly assess the capability of Q methodology as a taxonomic technique. The research involved each participant sorting the same sample of items (see below) on four separate occasions corresponding to the four social emotions Love, Jealousy, Joy and Embarrassment. Thus four different conditions of sorting were asked of each participant, making it possible to test directly the utility of Q as a means of making adequate discriminations between these provided parameters. Given an adequate pool of items (i.e., one fairly sampling the concourse or domain of propositional expression brought to social emotions; cf. Stainton Rogers, 1995) we would expect the Q pattern analytic to be sensitive enough to detect shared knowledges or "social representations" (Moscovici, 1988) of these emotions.

This study sought to investigate, not only the shared representations of these four emotions, but also the possibility that the emotions are plurally represented. The claim that the same emotion word can be used to describe a plurality of related, but recognisably different experiences and situations is an important one in terms of arguments against the normalising and normatising practices of conventional quantitative research. For this reason participants were asked to perform each sort according to a contextualised example of each of the four emotions under study (the source of the example was left to the participants). That is, following a procedure developed by Stenner (1992), each of the fifteen participants was asked to think of, and write down a short scenario which for them epitomised the emotion in question making it clear which actor was experiencing the emotion. They were then asked to sort the 54 individual items from the Q set according to the provided quasi-normal distribution (see Figure 6.1, pp. 108–109). Once sorts based on all four emotion scenarios had been completed, the data were Q data analysed (principal components) and Varimax rotated using S.A.S. Q-sort data are analysed by-person, yielding emergent factors that can serve to identify groupings of similarly sorted Q-sorts. Each Q-sort is therefore expressed as a correlation on each factor, and Q-sorts which correlate (load) significantly with one factor alone (±0.5 or over in this study) are highlighted as *factor exemplars*. To be interpretable, a Q factor must have an eigenvalue greater than 1 and must have at least 1 factor exemplar. Here, 7 of the 9 emergent rotated factors met these criteria and were interpreted. Appendix 1 shows the Factor Pattern Matrix for all 9 factors, including factors 5 and 6, which were not interpreted since they lack factor exemplars. The factor exemplars for each factor are indicated in bold. As can be observed, most load at considerably over the ±0.5 threshold on one factor, with only negligible loadings on other factors. The letters in the left-hand margin indicate whether the sort was (**E**) embarrassment, (**L**) love, (**Jo**) joy, or (**Je**) jealousy.

The factor pattern matrix shows a large number of high loading Q-sorts on the first three factors, indicating a considerable degree of convergence upon whatever is being configured by these factors. Now comes the exciting part, namely how the emotion episode labels distribute across these factors! The Q-sorts loading on Factor 1 are either representations of "joy" or "love" episodes. All of the "joy" Q-sorts bar 1 and 9 of the 15 "love" Q-sorts are high loaders. Thus, we have identified a compound affect **joy–love** which was expressed through the episodes selected by these participants. Of the "love" sorts that did not load onto Factor 1, Q-sort 18 loaded at +0.60 onto Factor 7, and Q-sort 14 loaded at 0.62 on Factor 9. Thus the study reveals that love is not constituted as a singularity for it split into three separate factors, one of which is the joy/love of Factor 1.

An even greater clarity attached to Factor 2. All the sorts that loaded upon it were of embarrassment episodes: specifically, 10 of the sample total of 15 embarrassment sorts load at over 0.7, again indicating considerable convergence of representation. Note, however, that one of the two embarrassment sorts that did not load on Factor 2 (17) is the sole exemplar of a second embarrassment factor, Factor 8. In other words, the study showed that embarrassment can be constituted as other than that expressed through Factor 2.

The third factor was defined by the remaining social emotion: jealousy. However, like love and embarrassment, jealousy proved not to be singularly represented. While eleven of the jealousy sorts loaded onto Factor 3, three of the remainder loaded onto Factor 4.

This initial data review demonstrates that:

- there are discernible shared configurations of the four emotions under study (and that joy subsumes one meaning of love);
- embarrassment, love and jealousy are not represented as singularities, but fragment into two or more discernible representations; and
- the Q factor-analytic can successfully discriminate between shared representations of these different emotions, and between different representations of the "same" emotion.

There are two sources of information available in order to examine the fine-grain content of the above results. These conveniently, divide into a "qualitative" and a more "quantitative" format. First, there are the scenarios accompanying the highest loading Q-sorts of each factor. These will be presented for each factor along with (if relevant) a brief comment about their content; second there is the configuration of the exemplifying Q-sorts themselves.

The further analysis begins with an overtly "quantitative" step. For each interpretable factor a single "best approximation" sort was created by merging – where more than one Q-sort is involved – the highest loading Q-sorts. Thus for Factor 1 the five Q-sorts which loaded at 0.8 or over (all were "joy" sorts) were combined (cf. Brown, 1980). This material will be presented in three main ways:

- by presenting (for Factor 1 only) a reconstruction of the "best approximation" sort (this enables the reader to view at a glance the distribution of items which characterises the factor);
- by way of a concise summary of the definitive properties of the best approximation sort; and
- by comparing and contrasting the ranking of significant items *between* factors in order to explore key differences.

We will turn first to the scenarios upon which the highest loading Q-sorts from Factor 1 are based.

Factor 1: *"Joy and love"*

Exemplary scenarios

Q-sort 27 (Participant 7); loading of 0.913
"Source: The News. East Berliners [subjects] being let into West Berlin and being reunited with their family and friends."

Q-sort 31 (Participant 8); loading of 0.803
"Source: *She* magazine. A married couple fed up with the commercialism and hype of Christmas decided on impulse to go away on a camping trip. They borrowed a friend's car and drove to a forest some miles away from where they

lived. The woman describes her feelings on arriving in the forest just as Christmas day was dawning. It was bitterly cold and everything was covered in a thick white hoar frost. The sun was shining through the trees and picking out some deer grazing nearby. A pheasant scrabbled about in the undergrowth, a fox ghosted by after a night's hunting, and long eared owls hooted to each other across the clearing."

Q-sort 43 (Participant 11); loading of 0.823
"In a true life television interview, an old East German lady [central character] expresses her joy at the Berlin wall coming down."

Q-sort 51 (Participant 13); loading of 0.850
"Taken from a TV advert. A man rushes through the traffic to a hospital just in time to see his new born baby come into the world. Central character – father of baby."

Q-sort 59 (Participant 15); loading of 0.854
"A young child [the main character] loses her puppy and is very upset. Her parents offer to buy her another pet, but she insists she only wants her own little puppy. Then someone returns the pet and the girl is delighted."

Comment on scenarios

The above scenarios share a sense of structure that involves a transition followed by a state of joyful resolution. We have two Berlin Wall stories which focus on the joy of East Berliners, one of which reaches its resolution with a theme of "reuniting". Similarly Participant 15's scenario tells of a child reunited with her pet. The scenarios therefore feature personally significant melodramatic events (it is not every day that you see your baby for the first time, or that the Berlin wall is destroyed!) which are "out of the ordinary" in an extremely positive way. The scenarios deal with something more than mere personal "happiness". The situations have an interesting "trans-individuality" to them: we are confronted with the true beauty of "nature" in contrast to the "commercialism and hype" of human life; with the "miracle of childbirth"; with a child's love "of her own little puppy" transcending the mere financial; and with the spectacle of "humanity" overcoming the constraining structures of political oppression. The joy described in these scenarios, therefore, appears to represent a "higher", more "principled", more valuable emotion than simple human happiness.

We can now turn to the reconstructed best-estimate sort for Factor 1.

Factor 1 "joy / love": summary

The reconstructed best-estimate sort indicates that the subject of Factor 1 "joy/love" feels a strong sense of meaning to life and feels that they are an important, significant person. They feel giving and caring and are particularly non-aggressive. As suggested by the scenarios, they are in a situation that truly matters. They are confident, competent and yet not self-conscious.

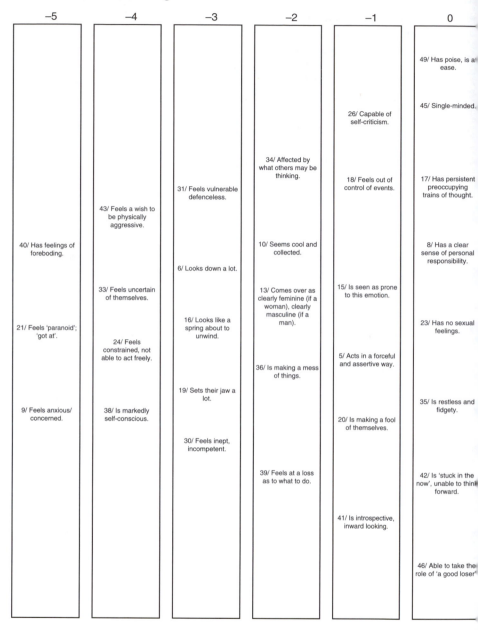

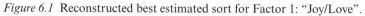

Figure 6.1 Reconstructed best estimated sort for Factor 1: "Joy/Love".

+1	+2	+3	+4	+5
25/ Thinks in inventive/innovative ways.				
	2/ Is a figure who arouses nurturant, caring feelings.			
2/ Is understanding and forgiving.		52/ Has a pounding heart.		
			14/ Seems 'in a world of their own'.	
	22/ Takes things on face; trusting.			
4/ Seems negotiable		1/ Is in a context /situation that makes it easy to describe the emotion.		7/ Feels excited/stimulated.
			32/ Feels giving and caring.	
3/ Finds any attention from others pleasant.	28/ Is more a 'hero' than a 'villain'.	29/ Seems oblivious to their image.		11/ Tends to smile.
			50/ Is 'moist eyed', even tearful.	
13/ Comes over as clearly feminine (if a woman), clearly masculine (if a man).		37/ Feels an important, significant person.		27/ Feels a strong sense of meaning to life.
	47/ Moves their eyebrows a lot.		54/ Feels in a situation that truly matters.	
48/ Feels 'In the right'.		51/ Has clear 'insight' into what they are feeling.		
	44/ Has a 'realistic' perception of things.			
53/ Feels out of control of their body. Unable to influence its reaction.				

They are not concerned with the usual mundane anxious preoccupations with self-image or personal vulnerability. Indeed they seem to be in a world of their own; sure of themselves and unaffected by the thoughts of others. They smile, their heart pounds, and they are excited and stimulated to the point of tears.

Factor 2: Embarrassment

Exemplary scenarios

Q-sort 1 (Participant 1); loading 0.807
"When I was about nine years old our teacher was very angry with the class, and one girl [central character] was too scared to ask to go to the toilet and wet herself in front of the entire class. This was immediately noticeable to everybody."

Q-sort 25 (Participant 7); loading 0.833
"I was once told a story of someone [the subject] who travelled from one side of Cardiff to the other to visit a friend and did not realise until she got there that she still had two rollers in the front of her hair."

Q-sort 29 (Participant 8); loading 0.873
"A man awaiting a grand banquet waited in nervous anticipation for his turn to deliver an after dinner speech. His turn finally arrived. As he rose to his feet, somehow he got caught up in the tablecloth, pulling it up with him so that glasses, coffee cups, etc. flew in all directions, spilling their contents over the whole linen table cloth and into the laps of the people sitting either side of him."

Q-sort 41 (Participant 11); loading 0.850
"This comes from my social observation of a fellow student [central character] tripping in a hall of residence dining hall. He smashed his food filled plate whilst everybody in the room clapped. After the incident he explained how embarrassed he felt."

Q-sort 49 (Participant 13); loading 0.821
"Taken from the film *Wilt*. Mr Wilt, who has been tied to a life sized inflatable doll and stripped naked against his will suddenly finds himself in full view of an audience of party guests. Central character – Mr Wilt."

Comment on scenarios

In each of these examples an *audience* is witness to a counter-normative and *accidental* mishap on the part of an individual. This "infraction" is embarrassing to the extent that it damages the self-esteem of the central character, thus it is significant that three of the five scenarios take place in *formal* settings (a "grand banquet", a dining hall and a class-room). The recognition of infraction by the audience seems to be of central importance to these scenarios: Mr Wilt finds himself "in full view of an audience of party guests"; the girl in participant 1's scenario wet herself and this was "immediately noticeable to everybody"; and participant 11's scenario provides a fine example of what Germans call *Schadenfreude* (pleasure in another's discomfort), "everybody in the room clapped". The reconstructed "best-estimate" sort from factor 2 provides an almost classic description of embarrassment, summarised as follows (See Stenner, 1992, chapter 4, for full data from this study).

Factor 2 "Embarrassment": summary

The subject of "Factor 2 embarrassment" is markedly self-conscious, highly concerned with what other people think of them, and ill at ease. They find the attention they receive from others highly unpleasant. They are making both a mess of things and a fool of themselves. They feel out of control of events, inept, incompetent, uncertain of themselves, and they lack a realistic perception of things. They feel vulnerable, defenceless, paranoid, and are bitter, untrusting and uncomfortable. They feel out of control of their body and are unable to prevent their heart from pounding. They are restless, fidgety and unsmiling.

Factor 3: "Jealousy"

Exemplary scenarios

Q-sort 16 (Participant 4); loading 0.801
"Othello's jealousy led him to murder the one woman he loved . . . on their wedding night! [sic] Othello by W Shakespeare."
Q-sort 28 (Participant 7); loading 0.844
"Sons and Lovers: D H Laurance [sic.]. Mrs Marel [subject] is jealous of her son Paul's relationship with his girlfreind [sic.] Miriam."
Q-sort 40 (Participant 10); loading 0.828
"There are two sisters who are at the beginning friendly with each other. A young man comes into their lives. One sister is married, the other is widowed but they both fall for the man. The married sister is so jealous that her sister is single and hence has a better chance with the man that she kills her."
Q-sort 56 (Participant 14); loading 0.863
"This example comes from Shakespeare's play, "Othello". Othello has been falsely persuaded that his wife, Desdemona, has been unfaithful. So great is Othello's jealousy that he kills his wife."

Comment on scenarios

Significantly, three of these four scenarios are taken from famous literary works and are, therefore, good examples of what Berger and Luckmann (1967) call "socially sedimented" constructions. All of the scenes involve three significant characters (although the *Othello* scenarios do not mention Iago), where the third person is an "outsider" (a "young man" for participant 10,

Miriam in *Sons and Lovers*, Iago in *Othello*). The examples are particularly extreme in their consequences. In three of the four scenarios the jealous person ends up by murdering one of the other characters.

Factor 3 "jealousy": summary

The subject of "Factor 3 jealousy" is caught in an emotional rut: they have persistent preoccupying trains of thought, are "stuck in the now" and unable to think forward, and they seem in a world of their own. They strongly feel that they are in the right and are incapable of self-criticism. They are single-minded and non-negotiable, and they act in a forceful and assertive way. However, despite their rigidity, they certainly do not have a realistic perception of things or a clear insight into what they are feeling. They do not arouse sympathy or caring feelings: they are unforgiving and non-understanding. They are "wound up" and feel a strong wish to be physically aggressive. They feel paranoid, restless and excited, and their heart pounds.

Factor 4: "Jealousy"

Exemplary scenario

Q-sort 12 (Participant 3); loading 0.737
"A friend [female, central character] had been going out with someone for a few weeks, who [male] had agreed (before they met) to go travelling with an ex-girlfriend and went because everything was already arranged."

Factor 4 "jealousy": summary

This factor describes a tearful, confused and vulnerable person who is at a loss as to what to do. They feel anxious and defensive, inept, incompetent, insignificant and uncertain of themselves. There is a lack of meaning to their life. They certainly do not feel giving and caring or understanding and forgiving. In fact, they feel that they have been wronged, and wish to be physically aggressive. Despite this they are still more "hero" than "villain" and their feelings are understandable given their circumstances. They find attention from others pleasurable.

Factor 7: "Love"

Exemplary scenario

Q-sort 18 (Participant 5); loading 0.6
"This is a kind of illness. A friend of mine had this illness. She didn't eat for a few days after meeting the boy. Love-sick it is called. Well! After the phone call from him she still couldn't eat because she is so happy."

Comment on scenario

This scenario unquestionably lacks the trans-individual, "out of the ordinary" sense of those gathered on Factor 1. Instead we are presented with an easily recognisable, "human, all too human" construction of love as "love sickness".

Factor 7 "love": summary

Factor 7 describes a person with an unbending certainty as to what they desire. They are single-minded, non-negotiable, forceful and assertive. They nevertheless feel anxious, out of control of events, and out of control of their body. They feel highly sexual and their heart pounds. They lack a clear sense of personal responsibility. They are in a world of their own. However, they are not making a mess of things: they feel giving and caring, and they arouse caring, nurturing feelings in others.

Factor 8: "Embarrassment"

Exemplary scenario

Q-sort 17 (Participant 5); loading 0.58
"This happened in the lecture room. In the peace and quiet atmosphere, suddenly someone farted loudly. It seemed like that person's bottom might be bursted. I can't imagine how that person felt."

Factor 8 "embarrassment": summary

This person is making a mess of things and a fool of themselves. Their heart is pounding, they are self-conscious and they feel inept. Despite this, however, they smile and seem oblivious to their image. Indeed, they seem to find the attention and notice from others pleasant. They are certainly not prone to this emotion.

Factor 9: "Love"

Although the one Q-sort (Q-sort 14) which loaded on to Factor 9 also had a 0.41 loading onto factor 1 (which makes it an impure loader and thus strictly not suitable as a factor exemplar), we will nevertheless describe it as it is a coherent and recognisable understanding of "love".

Exemplary scenario

Q-sort 14 (Participant 4); loading 0.62
"Edward VIII was "in love" with Wallis Simpson ... so much so that he abdicated for her." [sic]

Factor 9 "love": summary

This person feels giving, caring and also *trusting*. They are in a situation that truly matters to them, but they do not feel excited or stimulated or out of control of events in any way. Indeed they are cool and collected and have a clear sense of personal responsibility. They certainly do not feel out of control of their body or aggressive in any way. They are confident that they are doing the right thing, and they are introspective and capable of self-criticism.

Discussion of detailed results

The above results demonstrate a high degree of consensus between participants as to how to describe the four emotions under study. The discriminatory taxonomic powers of Q methodology have therefore been demonstrated.

The study also demonstrates variation in the representations of the emotions. This variation can be explored by way of a fine-grained comparative analysis of the relevant factors. Such analysis indicates that the variation found can by no means be explained away as "the same emotional experience elicited by different social stimuli". The three "love" factors, for instance, are in many ways markedly contrasted. We have the joyful, non self-conscious, deeply meaningful and trans-individual love of Factor 1 (F1); the out of control, non-negotiable, single-minded, forceful, assertive and self-conscious "love-sickness" of Factor 7 (F7); and the mature, trusting, caring, responsible, calm and self-critical love of Factor 9 (F9). Of course there are also similarities. Consider the respective rankings of the following items for example (note that the bracketed number in the left-hand side below indicates the item number, and the + or − ranking in the right-hand side indicates the ranking that item was given in each of the "best approximation" sorts under comparison, where, for instance, F1 would indicate the "best approximation" sort for Factor 1, and F7 that for Factor 7):

	F1	F7	F9
32) Feels giving and caring	+4	+5	+5
54) Feels in a situation that truly matters	+4	+2	+5

But the differences are in many ways more interesting:

22) Takes things on face; trusting	+2	−2	+5
8) Has a clear sense of personal responsibility	0	−3	+4
39) Feels at a loss as to what to do	−2	−4	−5
45) Single minded	0	+5	−1
53) Feels out of control of their body unable to influence its reactions.	+1	+4	−5
43) Feels a wish to be physically aggressive	−4	+2	−5
18) Feels out of control of events	−1	+2	−4

31) Feels vulnerable, defenceless	−3	+1	−4
7) Feels excited/stimulated	+5	+1	−3
10) Seems cool and collected	−2	−1	+2
41) Is introspective, inward looking	−1	−3	+3
11) Tends to smile	+5	0	0

The two jealousy factors emergent from this study are equally interesting (a more extensive Q methodological study of jealousy is reported in Stenner and Stainton Rogers, 1998). The results clearly show that jealousy is a highly *moralised* emotion. However, even though the characters from both jealousy factors (F3 and F4) feel "in the right", justifiably aggressive, and highly intolerant and unforgiving, they are certainly not *seen* to be morally equal:

	F3	F4
3) Is a figure who arouses nurturant, caring feelings	−5	+1
20) Is more a "hero" than a "villain"	−4	+4

To examine some further differences: Factor 4 lacks the forceful sense of purpose that is so characteristic of Factor 3:

	F3	F4
39) Feels at a loss as to what to do	−2	+5
5) Acts in a forceful and assertive way	+4	−2

Factor 3, unlike Factor 4, is characterised by delusion:

44) Has a realistic perception of things	−5	0
51) Has a clear insight into what they are feeling	−4	0

The feeling of Factor 4 is more of a sad and pitiful powerlessness than the angrily directed self-righteousness that defines Factor 3:

39) Feels at a loss as to what to do	−2	+5
50) Is moist-eyed, even tearful	+1	+5
30) Feels inept, incompetent	−1	+4
33) Feels uncertain of themselves	+1	+4

Reflections and conclusions

We began by coining the term qualiquantology and by suggesting that it has the perturbating power of the hybrid. In the process, some aspects of that discomfort to researchers of both a quantitative and a qualitative persuasion were considered. Through an actual research example we then went on to show what our favoured qualiquantology (Q methodology) can achieve when brought to bear upon a complex challenge to investigation – contextualised social emotions. The outcome, we hold, is impressive. However, we are also well aware that for all the increasing presence of Q methodological studies in scholarly life (Eccleston, Williams, & Stainton Rogers, 1997; Senn, 1996; Stainton Rogers, 1991; Stenner and Marshall, 1996) there remains what can be called an Amish-effect. The Amish (along with other tight-knit communities adhering to clear beliefs at odds with surrounding mainstream culture) enjoy a number of widely valorised "goods". These include, low rates of crime, stable families and a low drain upon social welfare. Yet, movement into these communities is a rarity. Two factors may well be at work in the Amish-effect. On the one hand, what people express as goals may not be what they pursue. On the other hand, choice may well also be influenced by perceived down-side costs. These dynamics are at least as operative in academic life as they are for life more generally and deserve consideration both by *aficionados* of Q and by those considering its use.

It is commonly held in psychology that people are "cognitive-misers" and one feature of Q methodology should be clear from our example – it is a rich and attention-demanding technique, yielding information which has depth and breadth. This down-side cost is well recognised and can show itself from the very start of reporting research. As Kitzinger (1999) remarks:

> I was not being criticised for failing to do Q methodology the way a good Q methodologist should . . . but rather criticised for using Q methodology at all – for failing to do conventional R methodological, or even conventional qualitative, research. Researchers should, of course, be able to defend the methods we choose to use: but to have continuously to explain and justify the basic premises (at the expense of any informed discussion of one's application of them, let alone any discussion of one's results) is very tiresome.

Equally, we need to be aware of the first mechanism in the Amish-effect: expressed goals may not be the goals actually pursued. Whatever may be said in statements about the wonders of science, very little research is actually concerned with overthrowing established ideas. Generally, it is a conservative and conservatising endeavour. The modal social circumstances surrounding research (from funding through to the gate-keeping of journals) require that research is warranted by established traditions, concepts, and procedures. Everything, that is, which Q methodology seems not to offer.

Alternative research, as we suggested right at the beginning, perturbates because it gainsays these warrants and their "comfort blanket" resonances. For those who have become attracted to alternative approaches precisely because of that, there is perhaps also a need to recognise the implication: If mainstream research is "in need of treatment", alternative research will find it hard to avoid certain dynamics redolent of therapy. Resistance, to borrow Kitzinger's phrase, can indeed become very "tiresome". *Caveat emptor.*

References

Andersen, M. L. (1994). The many and varied social constructions of intelligence. In T. R. Sarbin, & J. I. Kitsuse (Eds.), *Constructing the social* (pp. 119–138). London: Sage.

Berger, J., & Luckmann, T. (1967). *The social construction of reality*. Harmondsworth: Penguin.

Brown, S. R. (1980). *Political subjectivity: Applications of Q methodology in political science*. New Haven: Yale University Press.

Eccleston, C., Williams, A. C., & Stainton Rogers, W. (1997). Patients' and professionals' understandings of the causes of chronic pain: Blame, responsibility and identity protections. *Social Science and Medicine, 45*, 699–709.

Kitzinger, C. (1999). Commentary: Researching subjectivity and diversity: Q-methodology in feminist psychology. In E. B. Kimmel and M. Crawford (Eds.), *Innovations in feminist psychological research*. Cambridge: Cambridge University Press.

Moscovici, S. (1988). Notes towards a description of social representation, *European Journal of Social Psychology, 18*, 211–250.

Senn, C. Y. (1996). Q-methodology as feminist methodology: Women's views and experiences of pornography. In S. Wilkinson (Ed.), *Feminist social psychologies: International perspectives* (pp. 201–217). Buckingham: Open University Press.

Stainton Rogers, W. (1991). *Explaining health and illness: An exploration in diversity*. Hemel Hempstead: Harvester Wheatsheaf.

Stainton Rogers, R. (1995). Q methodology. In J. A. Smith, R. Harré, & L. van Langenhove (eds.), *Rethinking methods in psychology* (pp. 178–192). London: Sage.

Stenner, P. (1992). *Feeling deconstructed? With particular reference to jealousy*. PhD thesis, University of Reading.

Stenner, P., & Marshall, H. (1996). A Q methodological study of rebelliousness. *European Journal of Social Psychology, 25*, 621–636.

Stenner, P., & Stainton Rogers, R. (1998). Jealousy as a manifold of divergent understandings: A Q methodological investigation. *European Journal of Social Psychology, 28*, 71–94.

Stephenson, W. (1935). Technique of factor analysis. *Nature, 136*, 297.

Appendix 1

		Factor1	Factor2	Factor3	Factor4	Factor5	Factor6	Factor7	Factor8	Factor9
(E)	Q sort 1	-0.2872	**0.8069**	0.2818	0.0016	-0.0925	0.1593	0.1790	0.0163	0.0078
(L)	Q sort 2	0.3554	**0.5211**	0.3311	-0.0851	0.1515	0.0851	0.3538	-0.1529	-0.1449
(Jo)	Q sort 3	**0.5698**	-0.4502	-0.1033	-0.1976	0.0192	-0.3446	0.1090	-0.2625	0.0327
(Je)	Q sort 4	-0.3232	0.1769	**0.6658**	0.2265	0.0261	0.1588	0.0521	-0.0721	-0.0027
(E)	Q sort 5	-0.2051	**0.7446**	0.0283	0.0637	-0.0626	0.0553	-0.2485	0.1262	-0.0941
(L)	Q sort 6	0.4669	0.2387	0.0387	0.0351	**0.5661**	0.0298	0.1880	-0.0454	-0.1076
(Jo)	Q sort 7	**0.6402**	0.0668	-0.1275	-0.0349	0.0786	0.0698	0.0220	-0.0958	0.0578
(Je)	Q sort 8	-0.1356	0.0649	**0.7005**	0.1545	0.2851	0.0695	0.0874	-0.0547	0.0613
(E)	Q sort 9	-0.1661	**0.7344**	0.2029	0.1088	-0.0236	-0.1022	-0.0048	0.0400	-0.3054
(L)	Q sort 10	**0.5840**	-0.3901	-0.1162	-0.0871	0.3065	-0.0382	0.2036	0.2899	0.2373
(Jo)	Q sort 11	**0.7616**	-0.1327	-0.0895	-0.0139	0.0632	0.0585	0.0739	0.0624	-0.1814
(Je)	Q sort 12	-0.2178	0.3202	0.2668	**0.7372**	0.1285	-0.0157	-0.0285	-0.1432	-0.0024
(E)	Q sort 13	-0.1434	**0.7127**	0.0790	0.2463	0.2338	0.0745	0.0103	0.0092	0.0312
(L)	Q sort 14	0.4107	-0.2824	-0.3345	0.0463	-0.0631	-0.0917	-0.0562	0.0282	**0.6237**
(Jo)	Q sort 15	**0.6891**	-0.2061	-0.3029	0.0561	-0.2566	-0.0156	-0.0195	-0.2049	0.2934
(Je)	Q sort 16	-0.0741	0.1033	**0.8011**	-0.0294	-0.0240	0.0251	0.0808	-0.0686	-0.1077
(E)	Q sort 17	-0.0684	0.3022	-0.0475	-0.0541	0.0085	-0.0114	0.1261	**0.5822**	-0.0064
(L)	Q sort 18	0.2360	-0.0903	0.0534	0.0797	0.0352	0.0539	**0.6000**	0.1103	-0.0004
(Jo)	Q sort 19	0.4803	-0.2812	-0.1450	0.0436	0.1221	-0.0894	0.2536	-0.0931	-0.0207
(Je)	Q sort 20	-0.2758	0.2606	**0.5771**	0.0562	-0.3092	-0.2353	-0.0206	-0.0415	-0.0809
(E)	Q sort 21	-0.0222	**0.7112**	0.1159	0.0359	-0.0385	0.0063	-0.1560	0.4062	-0.0041
(L)	Q sort 22	0.4851	0.1005	0.2434	0.1060	0.1568	**0.5999**	0.1629	-0.0302	-0.0915
(Jo)	Q sort 23	**0.7571**	-0.1987	0.2133	0.0130	0.0682	-0.0593	0.0745	0.0023	-0.1798
(Je)	Q sort 24	-0.0982	0.3919	**0.5774**	0.4892	0.1074	0.1145	-0.0768	0.1794	-0.0762

(E)	Q sort 25	-0.0845	**0.8331**	0.1819	0.1511	-0.0397	-0.0201	-0.0657	-0.0989	0.0885
(L)	Q sort 26	-0.0059	0.2376	**0.5702**	0.3309	-0.0715	0.2352	0.2055	0.0211	0.1095
(Jo)	Q sort 27	**0.9130**	-0.1235	-0.0364	-0.0707	-0.0721	-0.0388	-0.0123	-0.1082	0.0337
(Je)	Q sort 28	-0.1076	0.1271	**0.8439**	0.0537	0.0749	-0.0010	0.0792	-0.0459	0.0374
(E)	Q sort 29	-0.0599	**0.8729**	0.0636	0.0165	-0.0319	0.0322	0.0226	0.1668	0.0701
(L)	Q sort 30	**0.7105**	-0.3623	0.0173	-0.0606	0.1075	-0.0484	0.2660	0.1459	0.1776
(Jo)	Q sort 31	**0.8027**	-0.1252	-0.2801	-0.1212	-0.0536	-0.0316	-0.0686	0.1051	0.0266
(Je)	Q sort 32	0.1051	0.1325	0.4439	**0.5780**	-0.1311	0.0835	0.1040	-0.0604	0.0443
(E)	Q sort 33	-0.1138	**0.7683**	-0.1724	-0.0509	0.2306	-0.1247	0.0573	0.0149	-0.1859
(L)	Q sort 34	**0.7378**	-0.1261	-0.2111	0.0421	0.1278	-0.2413	0.2239	-0.2435	0.3097
(Jo)	Q sort 35	**0.7653**	-0.0624	-0.1827	0.1058	0.0789	-0.0601	0.0248	-0.2224	0.1116
(Je)	Q sort 36	-0.2433	0.3796	**0.5849**	0.3596	-0.1230	-0.1713	0.1821	-0.0191	-0.0717
(E)	Q sort 37	-0.2982	**0.6922**	0.2382	0.2307	-0.1603	0.3755	-0.0185	-0.1280	-0.0941
(L)	Q sort 38	**0.7634**	-0.1053	0.0219	-0.1543	0.1214	-0.1835	0.2278	0.0574	0.0162
(Jo)	Q sort 39	**0.7836**	-0.2301	-0.2095	0.0334	0.2380	0.0686	-0.1214	-0.0627	-0.0956
(Je)	Q sort 40	-0.0819	-0.0547	**0.8283**	0.0163	-0.1375	-0.0436	-0.1127	-0.1027	-0.0605
(E)	Q sort 41	-0.1483	**0.8503**	0.2772	0.0466	-0.0264	0.1107	0.0707	-0.0384	0.0744
(L)	Q sort 42	**0.7452**	-0.1752	-0.0505	-0.1912	0.0502	0.1373	0.2057	-0.0686	0.3142
(Jo)	Q sort 43	**0.8233**	-0.0813	0.1883	0.0378	-0.0353	0.2248	0.0587	0.0601	0.0652
(Je)	Q sort 44	-0.2555	**0.5306**	0.3866	0.1672	0.2112	0.1098	0.2082	0.0875	0.0255
(E)	Q sort 45	-0.2597	**0.7240**	0.2311	0.0593	0.0019	-0.0259	-0.1356	0.1338	0.0162
(L)	Q sort 46	**0.7044**	-0.0334	-0.0909	-0.1556	0.0206	0.2338	-0.0499	0.2234	0.0919
(Jo)	Q sort 47	**0.7848**	-0.1784	-0.0531	-0.2437	-0.1547	0.0787	0.0620	-0.1052	0.0151
(Je)	Q sort 48	-0.2055	0.4520	0.2838	**0.5429**	0.0258	0.2752	0.0343	-0.0252	0.0082
(E)	Q sort 49	0.1415	**0.8211**	-0.1079	0.1376	-0.0231	-0.1839	0.0184	0.1611	-0.2034
(L)	Q sort 50	**0.7096**	-0.2092	-0.3361	-0.0734	0.0465	0.0937	0.0673	-0.1037	0.1020
(Jo)	Q sort 51	**0.8502**	-0.2591	-0.1741	-0.1167	-0.0757	0.0649	-0.0980	-0.1383	-0.0878

		Factor1	Factor2	Factor3	Factor4	Factor5	Factor6	Factor7	Factor8	Factor9
(Je)	Q sort 52	−0.1070	0.1368	**0.7245**	0.1850	−0.1049	−0.0762	−0.1004	0.2391	−0.2165
(E)	Q sort 53	−0.2364	0.4584	0.2933	0.4905	−0.0414	−0.2460	0.2182	0.2062	−0.0524
(L)	Q sort 54	**0.6198**	0.0286	0.2164	−0.0585	0.4025	0.1923	−0.0999	0.1351	0.2053
(Jo)	Q sort 55	**0.7980**	−0.0752	−0.0278	0.1590	−0.0228	0.1188	−0.0042	0.0506	0.0514
(Je)	Q sort 56	−0.0841	−0.0231	**0.8633**	0.0537	0.0720	0.1687	0.0002	0.0800	−0.0142
(E)	Q sort 57	−0.1823	**0.6379**	−0.0218	0.1931	0.2695	0.0723	−0.1915	−0.1041	0.0293
(L)	Q sort 58	**0.6829**	−0.2542	−0.1078	−0.1323	0.1208	−0.1291	0.2447	−0.1098	0.3172
(Jo)	Q sort 59	**0.8539**	−0.1517	−0.0185	−0.0969	0.0464	−0.1650	−0.0367	0.0672	0.0279
(Je)	Q sort 60	0.0484	0.4198	**0.6162**	0.0919	0.3575	0.1193	−0.0994	0.0951	0.0807

Part III

Examples of mixed method research

7   Valuing the "value of life"

A case of constructed preferences?

Susan Chilton, Judith Covey, Lorraine Hopkins, Michael Jones-Lee, Graham Loomes, Nick Pidgeon*, Angela Robinson, and Anne Spencer

Introduction: mixing it with methods, economics and psychology

In this chapter we describe the conceptual background to, and some research findings from, a policy-oriented research project concerned with the valuation of the benefits to people of improved health and safety controls. This project is doubly unusual since not only has it involved the combined use of qualitative with quantitative methods, but at the same time a collaboration between psychologists and economists in a single research programme. Accordingly, the chapter aims to describe some of the theoretical and methodological challenges involved when mixing both methods and intellectual disciplines in a single research programme.

In the domain of health and safety an increasingly important policy question concerns the relative benefits of safety controls designed to reduce an individual's risk of death or serious injury (for example, improvements in roadway or cyclists' infrastructure, personal safety equipment, or railway safety investments). Given that not all safety improvements can be implemented, and that the actual costs of a given level of protection vary widely in different areas of life (Tengs et al., 1995), cost–benefit analysis seeks to demonstrate whether in any particular circumstance the cumulative benefits outweigh the costs or vice versa.

In principle one can evaluate the benefits of implementing safety controls to a specified population in terms of the likely injuries and deaths that will be prevented over a given period of time. But this does not in itself resolve the policy question: whether the benefits that might be obtained outweigh the costs of implementing any specific programme or level of safety investment. Costs are typically represented in monetary terms while deaths and injuries

---

*   Because a large team of people contributed to different aspects of the research reported here we have adopted the convention of listing authors in alphabetical order. All correspondence should be addressed to Nick Pidgeon.

are not. Accordingly, if the two are to be directly compared a means of placing both on a common metric (usually although not necessarily money) is needed. The paradigm we discuss in this chapter is the contingent valuation (or CV) method, which is one of the techniques that economists have devised for placing an economic value upon amenities, services, or other benefits such as safety which are not routinely priced or traded through a "market".

The chapter is structured in eight sections. In the first we outline the basic contingent valuation paradigm. We then go on to note why there has been increasing interest in the CV technique amongst psychologists. Indeed debates about this method are now a key point of interface between environmental and experimental economists on the one hand, and psychologists interested in judgement and decision making on the other. At the root of most recent contestation is the interpretation to be placed upon a variety of anomalies and inconsistencies in people's preferences that have been revealed by numerous recent CV studies. In the third section the case for mixing quantitative and qualitative approaches, as in the current study, is outlined. Not only are we interested in using the qualitative *outputs* (i.e. data) of the study for exploring the meaning to be placed upon the quantitative data, but also in using more qualitative-based *designs*, such as focus groups, to provide participants with information that they might find useful in forming a quantitative judgement and to allow opportunity for reflection upon the questions being posed *prior* to eliciting any quantitative responses. The next two sections describe the policy context of the study (and in particular so-called "value of statistical life"), and the three-step study design respectively. We then go on to describe first some of the quantitative results, and then the qualitative data and its interpretation in relation to the quantitative results. The chapter concludes with some theoretical conclusions and methodological reflections that arise from the work.

The contingent valuation paradigm

The broad philosophy of contingent valuation (or CV) was first elaborated by behavioural economists[1] in the mid-1970s (see e.g. Jones-Lee, 1976; Mitchell & Carson, 1989) as a means of placing an explicit monetary value on goods or public services which are not directly (or only imperfectly) traded in a market. Such "goods" might include libraries, fire services provision, safety, or individual or community health. Increasingly CV has also been adopted as a means to "value" a wide variety of intangible environmental impacts or resources; such things as air quality, natural habitats, or threatened species (Arrow, Solow, Portney, Leamer, Radner, & Schuman, 1993; Cummings, Brookshire, & Schulze, 1986; Dixon, Fallon-Scura, Carpenter, & Sherman, 1994). Valuation of such environmental resources can be used as one input to environmental impact and policy assessments.

As an example, consider fire service provision. It is relatively easy for policy makers to gauge the costs of a given provision of fire service infrastructure, in terms of equipment bought, personnel employed and levels of training provided. However, the *benefits* to society of having a fire service are far more diverse, difficult to measure, and at times intangible. The physical impacts of having, or not having, a certain level of provision can be both estimated and costed – as prevention of material damage to buildings or motor vehicles – and other monetary benefits will include the savings made in reduced insurance premiums, or the avoided costs to the uninsured. However, the more intangible benefits (which in this case probably outweigh the direct physical damage as a justification for social provision of fire services) include the prevention of a certain proportion of the injuries and deaths that would otherwise occur in fires,[2] along with avoidance of general community disruption, individual and family pain and suffering, as well as any long-term psychological impacts on those involved. In the absence of other social decision rules (such as all communities should maintain a fire service as a matter of principle, and no matter what the costs and risks) the policy maker is faced with the difficult question of whether a given level of provision is in line with the benefits obtained.

In conventional economic terms the value to people of a good is defined by the maximum amount they are *willing-to-pay for it*. But a public provision such as the fire service is not bought and sold in any conventional sense in a "market" where the actual costs people might directly pay for receiving the benefits the service gives them, and hence its direct monetary value to them, could be observed. In addition to this, some of the benefits are strictly non-monetary – avoided injuries and deaths would be a good example – in the sense that they are rarely represented, in lay discourses at least, in financial terms at all and there may even be strong and explicit social conventions against doing so.

Accordingly, CV is one of the indirect techniques devised to estimate the value of intangible (sometimes called non-market) benefits. The basis of the technique is surprisingly simple: a quantitative survey method which elicits participants' hypothetical[3] preferences for (that is contingent upon) the non-monetary good in question. For example, one might ask participants how much they would be willing to pay in extra taxes to have a fire service in their community, for a safety feature fitted to their car that would reduce the chances of a certain injury, to fund a forestry conservation scheme in their area, or to facilitate higher air quality in the city where they live. By aggregating across a representatively sampled group of individuals a mean value for the resource or good in question can, in theory at least, be obtained. So suppose that from a representative survey we estimate that each of a population of one million people was willing to pay on average £5 for fire service provision, that scheme would be "worth" £5,000,000 to them as a community.

Biases, inconsistencies and constructed preferences

Psychologists have become interested in the CV technique for two interrelated reasons. First, because it represents an important application of social science research which until quite recently has relied almost exclusively upon the use of standard questionnaire methodology. The use of such methods has been critiqued, and in some cases improvements suggested, when viewed from the perspective of traditional psychometric and survey methodology (see e.g. Fischhoff & Furby, 1988). Second, and more significantly, a number of recent studies have demonstrated various anomalies and inconsistencies (in relation to the predictions from standard economic theories) in the judgements people make when responding to CV questions. There is now a long tradition of experimental psychological research within the field of behavioural decision making on inconsistencies and biases of judgement (e.g. Kahneman, Slovic, & Tversky, 1982). This work aims to demonstrate the cognitive heuristics (shortcuts and rules of thumb) that people use when simplifying probabilistic or other quantitative tasks. While such strategies are argued to be generally useful (Jungermann, 1986) they can also lead to severe and systematic errors of judgement in relation to standard normative models. Hence, bringing to bear the theoretical insights from this line of empirical work might help to explain some of the problems economists have encountered with CV tasks, as well as to take forward application and theory in both disciplinary domains.

In the CV field one can identify two broad classes of inconsistency:

(a) *Oversensitivity to theoretically irrelevant aspects of the good and/or task.* Oversensitivity arises from a number of factors, primarily dependent upon the researcher's selection of a particular response scale or elicitation paradigm. For example, in a study of anchoring and range effects Duborg, Jones-Lee and Loomes (1997) asked participants whether they would pay some amount x for a given risk reduction, and depending upon their response x was increased or decreased until the range within which their willingness-to-pay lay was established. Perhaps not surprisingly, participants who were presented with an initial value of x of £75 were ultimately prepared to pay much higher values than those given £25 first.

(b) *Insensitivity to theoretically relevant information.* In standard economic terms people should (generally) be prepared to pay more for a good as the size or quantity of the benefit they receive increases. However, in the context of CV for environmental improvements Carson and Mitchell (1995) showed a part-whole bias in which respondents offered approximately the same willingness-to-pay for a "large" good as they did for a "small" one. Kahneman and Knetsch (1992) called this the "embedding effect", and by using a between groups design they found similar willingness-to-pay (i) for city environmental services (including disasters preparedness), (ii) for disaster preparedness alone, or (iii) for improved rescue equipment and personnel alone.[4]

One interpretation of these anomalies, not surprisingly taken by many of the advocates and practitioners of the CV technique, is that the trouble lies in the various elicitation procedures themselves. That is, the conceptual basis for asking people hypothetical questions to elicit their values is sound – but that very great care is needed in using the technique correctly in any specific instance (Brookshire & Coursey, 1987; Arrow et al., 1993).

A second, more radical proposal, is that the persistence and severity of the growing list of anomalies challenge CV's very theoretical basis. Put simply, when viewed from a psychological perspective people may not hold stable preferences or values for environmental resources or public services with which they are not directly familiar, or which they do not routinely trade in a market[5] (Fischhoff, Slovic, & Lichtenstein, 1980; Fischhoff, 1991). Rather, preferences for such goods are actively *constructed* as people deploy whatever heuristics and problem solving strategies they have available to them to make sense of and structure the task, to reduce the cognitive demands placed upon them (Gregory, Lichtenstein, & Slovic, 1993; Slovic, 1995), and to bringing to bear whatever general value commitments that they do hold. The notion of constructed preferences is one that has only recently emerged from behavioural decision research (e.g. Curley, Browne, Smith, & Benson, 1995; Payne, Bettman, & Johnson, 1992), and implies that judgements and decisions regarding unfamiliar goods will be extremely sensitive to characteristics of the task and wider issues that frame the context of judgement.

The case for mixing methods

Our own research combines a qualitative approach to data generation and analysis with the traditional quantitative CV elicitation survey. There were three principal reasons for this.

First, one very valid criticism of CV is that people may not possess the information they need to accurately conceptualise the benefits of unfamiliar goods (Arrow et al., 1993; Carson & Mitchell, 1995). This is probably as true in health and safety valuation as it is in the environmental field, and we wished to provide in advance of eliciting any quantitative judgements, relevant *knowledge and information* that people might not routinely hold (on such things as level of risk, the absolute numbers of fatalities, age distribution of victims, etc.). This in itself necessitates a more interactive and flexible process of *dialogue* between researcher and participants, than is adopted in the traditional forms of psychology or behavioural economics study, where what is said and presented to "subjects" is tightly controlled by the canons of experimental method. Accordingly, the first part of the three-stage design, to be described more fully below, involves bringing together participants in focus groups to discuss and debate the issues involved (for an example of the use of focus groups in presenting risk information see Desvousges & Smith, 1988).

Second, and in part following on from the above, our basic theoretical orientation (also Fischhoff, 1991) is that the values which people might attach to intangible benefits such as safety are rarely pre-formed or available for immediate articulation, either in terms of their consistency or completeness. Accordingly the study was designed to allow participants sufficient time to deliberate upon both their own prior beliefs (such as their own household's level of exposure to the risk) and the information provided by the researcher. The time available also allowed us to explain in some detail the quantitative elicitation techniques to be used. In this way it was hoped that the quantitative values elicited would be more complete, well thought-out, and stable than those obtained solely via a traditional one-off questionnaire survey.[6]

Finally we were, of course, also interested in collecting concurrent qualitative data to help us interpret people's reasons and rationalisations, including preference construction processes which might underlie the quantitative responses. There have been very few attempts to do this, in part because economists (even more so than psychologists) have traditionally viewed qualitative data with an extreme degree of both scepticism and hostility. A particular focus in the current study then is the qualitative responses underlying preference patterns in line with normative standards of economic theory, comparing these with the qualitative responses where preference patterns contradict such theory (as with insensitivity to the quantity of the benefit). In this way we hoped to be able to account for anomalies and inconsistencies in psychological terms, rather than merely treat them as outliers or "aberrant" responses. It is important to emphasise then, that in our study "mixing methods" is viewed as much more than just an attempt to combine and interpret qualitative and quantitative data (important as that is in and of itself). Mixing methods is also an essential part of the *process* by which participants arrive at the judgements we wish them to make.

The "value of statistical life" and road safety policy

The conventional way to proceed with CV in the health and safety domain has been to translate the benefits (in this case aggregate lives saved) into an individual reduction in the risk of death across the exposed population.[7] By asking for people's personal willingness-to-pay for that small reduction in risk, both the individual and aggregate benefits of the safety improvement can be estimated in monetary terms. For example, if people are on average willing to pay up to £20 to reduce their annual risk of death by 4 in 100,000 then for every four fatalities prevented there will be 100,000 people willing between them to pay a total of £20 × 100,000 = £2m, which implies that the value of preventing each statistical fatality is £500,000. This aggregate value can then be interpreted as the "value of a statistical life" (VoSL),[8] for direct use in cost–benefit analyses. Jones-Lee (1998) has conducted a meta-analysis of 28 CV surveys for safety benefits and reports a typical VoSL in 1994 prices of between £1 million and £10 million. There was, however, a very wide variation in the estimates he reviewed (£60,000 as the lowest value and £44 million the highest), a point to which the discussion returns later.

In the United Kingdom one of the first national CV studies of road safety risk was conducted for the Department of Transport in the early 1980s (see Jones-Lee, Hammerton, & Phillips, 1985), and in terms of practical decision making road planners have for a number of years now used a VoSL figure at the lower end of the ranges from published surveys such as this. After updating for inflation and the growth in real gross domestic product per capita this figure now stands at £903,000 in 1997 prices. This also provides a monetary "standard" against which cost–benefit decisions in other areas of government safety regulation and investment are commonly judged, sometimes with weightings applied to reflect the different risk regulation context.[9] Perhaps not surprisingly, however, the VoSL concept has attracted criticism on both philosophical and practical grounds (see e.g. Adams, 1995, Ch. 6; Broome, 1985).

Study design

The study that we report here is one part of a much larger programme of work looking at the possible differential valuation of health and safety controls across a number of contexts, including the roads and other public transport modes, fires in the home and in public places. In the current chapter we focus solely upon road transportation risks.[10]

As noted above there is growing evidence that responses to CV questions are subject to a range of anomalies and inconsistencies (one of the most serious being an insensitivity to the quantity of the good being valued). The basic elicitation paradigm used in the current study presented participants with a prespecified number of deaths in a given population, and asked for their willingness-to-pay to prevent them. Although previous evidence indicates that presenting risk information in this way does not in itself eliminate insensitivity to quantity (Desaigues and Rabl, 1995), it seemed plausible that when used with the intensive study design outlined below, we would encourage sensitivity of responses. Also, by varying the numbers of deaths to be prevented in a repeated measures design, it was anticipated that the inappropriateness of giving the same willingness-to-pay responses for the prevention of two different numbers of fatalities would be much more evident (a transparent test of sensitivity to quantity: see also the comments made earlier in note 4).

A total of 52 participants – broadly representative in terms of age, gender and household income – were recruited by professional market research agencies on a quota sample basis from the Newcastle, Bangor and York areas. A three-stage procedure was adopted, to facilitate both preference construction and value elicitation, as follows.

(i) Participants were recruited to focus groups of 5 or 6 participants. In these focus groups (moderated by members of the research team) various safety issues were discussed and participants were introduced to the stimuli and concepts that were to be used in the individual interviews in the second stage.

(ii) One-to-one interviews were then conducted (typically within a few days of the initial focus group meetings) in which respondents completed a specially designed structured interview containing a variety of CV and indirect valuation questions. All interviews were carried out by members of the research team.

(iii) Feedback meetings were then arranged (again typically involving 5 or 6 participants) in order to show respondents the patterns of results they had collectively generated and to invite their reaction and comments. These meetings also provided participants with the opportunity for further reflection and comment upon the reasons underlying their responses in the interview.

The initial focus group discussions, which lasted about one hour, were used largely to take participants through the types of questions they would be presented with during the individual interview. In particular, it was made clear that they would be asked to consider the "worth" to their household of a safety programme which would prevent a certain number of deaths in the area in which they lived and another which would prevent three times that number of road deaths. This was done in order to give every opportunity to consider the relative worth of the two programmes well in advance of the individual interview. At this stage participants were also asked whether they considered a safety improvement that would prevent the larger number of road deaths to be "better" than the one that would prevent fewer, the overwhelming response being that it was. They were also encouraged to reflect upon how much the safety improvements were worth to their household in whichever way they felt most comfortable with.

During the subsequent individual interviews participants were first encouraged to consider the benefits of the road safety improvement to their household relative to the other households in their area. They were then asked to imagine that there was a programme of road safety improvements affecting the area in which they lived (e.g. for Bangor the area encompassing North and Mid/West Wales), with a population of 1 million people, or roughly 400,000 households.

Participants were then presented with the programme having the largest benefit (R3), with the sample also divided into two further sub-groups A and F. Respondents in sub-group A (or Annual) were told that the safety programme was expected to prevent 15 deaths on the roads in this area in the next year and asked to consider what this improvement would be worth to their household *over the next year*. Those in group F (Five Yearly) were told that the programme was expected to prevent 75 deaths on the roads *over the next five years* and asked to consider what this improvement would be worth *in total* to their household. The A versus F framing represents a further (but between groups, or non-transparent) check on participants' sensitivity to quantity. Participants were then asked to state: (a) an amount such that they were sure the safety programme would *definitely be worth* at least that much to their household; (b) an amount at which they would start to *become uncertain* whether or not the safety programme was worth that much; and (c) the amount at which they were sure it would *definitely not be worth* that much to their household.

Having answered these questions participants were then presented with CV questions for the programme with the lesser benefit (R1). These were respectively 5 road fatalities for sub-group A (Annual) and 25 for sub-group F (Five Yearly). Once again judgements were made for "definitely worth", "uncertain", and "definitely not worth".

The quantitative results

The quantitative results shown in Table 7.1 are based upon the revised "start to become uncertain" responses and are on an annual equivalent basis (i.e. the raw responses for group F have been divided by 5).

There are two features of note regarding Table 7.1 (see also Beattie et al., 1998). The first concerns the *repeated measures* test of sensitivity to the quantity of the good, shown as the differences between R1 and R3 for every column in the table. Although the actual ratio of deaths in the two consecutive questions (R3 then R1) presented to participants was 3, the mean responses comparing rows of Table 7.1 show that the willingness-to-pay for the larger risk reduction (R3) was not anything like three times as much as for the smaller (R1). Taking the means for the whole sample there was a CVR3/CVR1 ratio of 1.33 indicating marked insensitivity to the size of the risk reduction. What is more, a breakdown of the CV ratios at the individual level (column 1 of Table 7.2) shows that of the full sample of 52 respondents 22 gave *identical* non-zero willingness-to-pay amounts for both road safety improvements, and that this was despite provision of an explicit prompt that R3 might be seen as "worth three times as much" as R1 (see also below), and an opportunity to give revisions.

Second, the *between-groups* test was designed as a further consistency check, and here we can compare responses to the Annual (Version A) and Five

Table 7.1 Contingent valuation responses for prevention of road fatalities

	Group A Annual (n=26)		Group F Five Year (n=26)		Sample N=52	
	Mean (s.d.)	Median	Mean (s.d.)	Median	Mean (s.d.)	Median
R1	79.3 (131.3)	30	138.3 (166.7)	90	108.8 (151.5)	55
R3	95.8 (131.3)	45	196.1 (242.4)	115	145.1 (199.6)	77.5

Table 7.2 Individual CVR3/CVR1 ratios

	Full sample N=52	Transcribed sub-sample (n=21)
= 1	22	7
> 1	30	14

Year (Version F) framing of the question. Looking across row R3 in Table 7.1, in the annual framing condition, where participants were asked to pay for a safety programme that would prevent 15 deaths in one year, mean willingness-to-pay is £96. In the five year framing they were asked to pay (yearly or in aggregate) to prevent 75 deaths over 5 years, which is *effectively the same number of deaths per year* as in the annual framing. Hence if people are basing their annual willingness-to-pay solely on the size of the annual benefit (15 deaths prevented per year) they should give similar amounts. From Table 7.1 it is clear that participants given the 5 year framing were prepared to pay far more *per year* (on average £196 compared to the £96)[11] to prevent the same number of deaths per year, and to go on paying that amount for a full 5 years.

In order to calculate the "value of statistical life" (VoSL) from these figures we multiply the mean household willingness-to-pay per annum by the number of households in the area affected (i.e. the 400,000) and then divide by the number of fatalities per annum prevented by the safety program concerned. Thus, in the case of R3 for group A the VoSL would be computed as £(95.83 × 400,000) ÷ 15 = £2.56 million. In the case of R1 for group A the VoSL comes out at £6.3 million, or almost 3 times as much. See Table 7.3 for a summary.

If the analysis were to stop merely with the quantitative results we would be left with an apparent contradiction. Based upon the within-groups consistency check, where the quantity of the benefit in terms of lives saved was varied transparently, respondents were *undersensitive* (and in some cases completely insensitive) to that change. On the other hand viewing the results

Table 7.3 VoSL estimates based upon CV responses reported in Table 7.1 (£ million)

	Version A (Annual) Mean (Median)	Version F (Five years) Mean (Median)
R1	£6.3m (£2.4m)	£11.7m (£7.2m)
R3	£2.6m (£1.2m)	£5.2m (£3.1m)

from the perspective of the between-groups design (a framing which should, in theory at least, have had no effect on responses) there is a consistent *difference* in willingness-to-pay between the two groups of participants. Paradoxically, the undersensitivity to the R3/R1 manipulation and the larger willingness-to-pay in the F framing, *both* serve to increase the final VoSL estimates. Table 7.3 demonstrates this, showing the VoSLs calculated from both R3 and R1 responses under both versions A and F. The final amounts vary between £2.6m and £11.7m.

As we have noted earlier, such results raise a serious policy dilemma, as there is no practical way of deciding, without some well-founded method-ological or theoretical reason, which of these figures better represents people's "true" preferences and therefore which should be used to guide safety policy! From a theoretical perspective we are also left with the problem of accounting for the pattern of results if the willingness-to-pay responses are not, as seems the case here, tapping some underlying and well-behaved meas-ure of subjective worth. We now go on to show how analysis of the qualita-tive data helps us to interpret this puzzling pattern of results in terms of preference construction processes and discourse theory.

The qualitative results

All of the individual interviews were tape recorded,[12] and it is the data from these that we present here. However, since many of the interviews were exten-sive the decision was taken to transcribe only a subset of these (21 of the full 52 – or seven selected from each of the three interviewers working at Bangor, Newcastle and York respectively) primarily on practical grounds.[13] As shown in Table 7.2, of these 21 transcribed tapes, 7 were from individuals who had given identical responses to the R3 and R1 questions (as compared to 22 in the full sample).

The analytic approach used was that of grounded theory (for introductory overviews see Pidgeon & Henwood, 1996). The researcher works through the transcribed material systematically assigning codes to significant themes and instances as they emerge from the data, developing an account by comparing similarities and differences between cases and themes (the method of con-stant comparison) and in relation to the research question at hand. This procedure is both iterative and flexible, allowing coding to develop in a gen-erative way as the researcher's understanding of the data corpus emerges, while at the same time providing a degree of both systematisation and public documentation of the analysis (Henwood & Pidgeon, 1992). The aim is to build an account that is both theoretically rich and grounded in the data.

To facilitate analysis the interview transcripts were stored in electronic format. Initial thematic coding was then conducted using the HyperResearch 1.56 qualitative data analysis program. This program allows flexible open-coding of text, and subsequent retrieval for further analysis of the codes and coded material. There are, of course, a number of persuasive arguments *against* the use of Computer Aided Qualitative Data Analysis (CAQDAS); including a lack of flexibility (particularly if the emerging analysis has to be forced to fit the capabilities of the computer program rather than the needs of the researcher) and a distancing of the researcher from her research material. However, in the present case CAQDAS held several clear advantages.

First, the corpus of transcribed data, even using the reduced sub-set of interviews, was relatively large and unwieldy. Hence the program permitted very rapid retrieval and initial "sift and sort" of significant material and the associated coded concepts. Second, since the structured interview took participants through a set of predefined questions, an initial organization of the data (prior to thematic coding) could be made by assigning "tag" codes to each blocked sub-section of the interview, again allowing easy retrieval of the appropriate text(s) for any particular question. Third, since the work was being conducted in a large team both the interviews and the thematic codings as they developed could be readily transferred from one member to another (in this instance between Lorraine Hopkins and Nick Pidgeon) in the form of a HyperResearch "study" for both further analysis and independent verification. In this latter case, the ease of transfer between desktop machines allowed the computer codings to function as a part of the public "audit trail", often used by grounded theorists to check the credibility of the emerging analysis (see Lincoln and Guba, 1985; Henwood, this volume).

The detailed qualitative analysis can be broken down into three phases: (a) justifications for willingness-to-pay (b) the R3/R1 difference and (c) the F versus A framing. Throughout we were concerned to relate the qualitative interpretations to the pattern of quantitative data.

(a) Justifications for willingness-to-pay

We wished to examine first the ways in which our participants generated the basic amounts that they were prepared to pay for the safety programmes. From the quantitative results in the final column of Table 7.1 we see that the median[14] willingness-to-pay for R3 in response to the question "at what point do you become uncertain?" was £77 per annum, or a little over £1 per week. For the smaller programme R1 it was £55. As with many CV studies there was very wide variation in individual willingness-to-pay evident by the large standard deviations shown. The qualitative data illustrate how, in the absence of an obvious framework for equating money with lives, participants relied upon a range of strategies for generating an amount that they were comfortable with. Many of the transcripts commenced with comments or questions that likened the proposed payments to a local tax (and what would be viewed as an acceptable increase in current taxes), or to the 400,000 households in the area under consideration.

"I mean the council tax I pay now is £60 a month and if that was increased to £70 a month that's £120 a year isn't it and if that was going to generate X millions of pounds I think yes I would be agreeable to a figure of about £100 per year."

JC13[15]

A tax contribution can form the basis of the total generated by the whole community of 400,000 households. By translating an individual contribution into an aggregate total, that contribution is both constructed *and justified as sufficient*, sometimes in relation to the imagined costs of the proposed scale of roads safety programme. That is, an initial contribution could be deemed sufficient when the total collected met the imagined costs (even though the individual contribution might in itself be described as only "small").

> "I was thinking about this catchment area of about 400,000 so I was thinking how much do these road things start to cost and I thought if everybody contributed £5 now this would be like what? £2 million?"
>
> JC04

Irrespective of whether the overall income from a particular level of individual contribution is seen as sufficient to fund the scheme, the money still has to be found from somewhere. Not surprisingly then, and arising in most of the transcripts, were subsequent references to *where* the payment would come from. This was discussed in relation to such things as wages, general household income, and in particular being able to *afford* the payment.

> "I know I shouldn't be thinking that but earnings in this area aren't very good and you've got enough to pay out but I think you wouldn't miss a pound or two pounds a month to help road safety or to help improve the area."
>
> LH07

> "At the moment I'm training and not earning very much money at all so perhaps I'm being a bit mean but I suppose if money was no object I would go a bit higher maybe a lot higher if you are Richard Branson."
>
> LH13

Such references to income and what can be afforded again serve both to construct *and to justify* a particular level of contribution. They can also be interpreted, by the standards of conventional economic theory, as evidence of "rational" reasoning in that people are trying to judge the worth of the safety improvement in relation to income and other consumption. However, in many cases the potential payment is constrained to a relatively narrow range. For example, there were many references to giving up "unnecessary" consumption, "spare" weekly money that would not be missed, or "insignificant" amounts. Conversely, mention of expenditure on more expensive but essential items like basic food, housing or lighting was absent. Participants appeared to be using relatively restricted "mental accounts" to find a realistic level of payment which would not make a major impact upon household budgets, and with the recognition that if income were higher a larger contribution might then be possible.

> "All I've done is taken something out of the family budget that doesn't really need to be there. . . . that was worked out of the lottery money [laughter] that's just in case you wondered how we did it you know . . . it's an expense we don't have to have so I'd put the money that we would spend in that onto road safety."
>
> LH04

Note that with a restricted range of potentially affordable payments (or where an affordable amount is viewed in an all or nothing way) and a focus upon the total collected or the costs of the programme rather than the level of the benefit, there may be very little latitude for the payment to vary, and certainly not in a one-to-one manner, with benefit. In one of the few other CV studies to collect systematic qualitative data, Schkade and Payne (1994) find identical willingness-to-pay for different levels of environmental improvement (saving 2000, 20,000 or 200,000 wild birds respectively). Their qualitative analysis shows considerable overlap with our own: many references to tax contributions, the total amount generated by a small contribution, and what could be afforded from family budgets. They interpret this, as we do for our own data, in terms of preference construction processes. That is, people generate willingness-to-pay responses through a variety of context dependent strategies that are only loosely related (if at all) to the direct trade-off between monetary value and level of benefit being asked for in the CV question.

A further striking feature of the qualitative data from the present study was the many references, either spontaneously or in response to the interviewer's prompting, to the *difficulty of the task*.

> "It's very emotive you know how much is this worth to you even though I came up with this figure of £10 it is negligible really because I was going through my bills and my water rate bills and I was thinking that I pay this much for water and then I thought this £10 figure it's nonsense it's really difficult."
>
> JC04

This difficulty did not appear to stem from unfamiliarity with the valuation task per se – recall the broad issues underlying valuation, and the specific interview questions, had been introduced in the initial focus group sessions, and many participants spontaneously reported that they had been thinking over their possible responses in the meantime. Some comments suggest that there were difficulties in conceptualising the detailed *impacts of the programme*: how would the lives be saved, who would die, would all of the money really be spent on safety, would the programme benefit the respondent and their family? For some participants absence of such contextual information meant that the programme's worth was ambiguous or could not be judged directly.

"I've been trying to think about it the last two days, its murder trying to put a figure on what you are prepared to pay for without actually knowing what the programme would involve or what the deaths were."

AR09

However, the principal difficulty – and in some cases extreme reluctance to pay – appears to stem from an unwillingness to trade-off lives with money. This was expressed both in terms of a reluctance to *put a price on life*, together with the recognition that the direct *comparison of lives with money* was of itself an intrinsically problematic thing to do, as the following quotes illustrate.

"Really what price do you put on one life if it was one person do you just turn round and say then they're only worth a couple of pound it's difficult you can't put a price on a life because if it was someone who was very close to you you would put everything you have got."

AR01

"Extremely difficult . . . would you like to put that it's a very hard question to definitely put an answer on."
Interviewer: "Yes this is why we have the boxes [showing different amounts]"   – "It's not the amounts it's the comparisons."

AR03

In some instances having generated an amount that could be afforded to prevent anonymous deaths this then seemed incongruous (or *negligible*) in relation to the importance of the issue. However, as noted above, by relating this back to the total to be generated across the population, or what could be personally afforded, even very small amounts could still be justified. As the quotes above also illustrate, perhaps not surprisingly, there is a big difference between being asked to pay to prevent the death of an unidentified "statistical" individual and that of somebody known to you. All of the above suggests that participants were often unwilling (rather than merely unable) to explicitly trade-off the amount of money and the absolute number of lives saved. And where comments did place the two in direct relationship, it was often to *reject* such an explicit comparison. One interpretation is that the difficulty, and sometimes outright rejection, of this aspect of willingness-to-pay stems from the inherently *dilemmatic* (Billig, Condor, Edwards, Gane, Middleton, & Radley, 1988) nature of the question being asked. This is best illustrated in the discourse generated by the R3/R1 sensitivity check, where this dilemma is brought squarely to the fore, and which we turn to next.

(b) Sensitivity to quantity: R3 / R1

Recall that the interview structure presented participants with the higher risk reduction first (R3) followed by the lower risk reduction (R1) in a repeated measures test of participants' sensitivity to the level (or quantity) of the safety benefit. The questionnaire design explicitly afforded participants the opportunity to revise their initial responses. In addition we wished to focus attention explicitly on the relative magnitudes of the two reductions in road fatalities. Accordingly, immediately after completing the two road fatality questions, respondents were presented with their "start to become uncertain" responses and prompted:

> In the past we've found that some people say that preventing 15(75) deaths on the roads is worth three times as much to them as preventing 5(25) deaths on the roads: but other people don't give this answer. Can you say a bit more about why you gave the answers you did?

As illustrated above (Tables 7.1 and 7.2) the quantitative responses from the full sample indicate that participants were often highly insensitive to the differences in benefit. That is, some people were prepared to explicitly reject the proposition that 1/3 of the number of lives was only worth 1/3 in willingness-to-pay terms. We can analyse the qualitative responses to this issue by looking at the particular participants who gave different patterns of quantitative response to these questions.

A very small minority of participants (3 of the 21 transcribed interviews) *did* give an amount for R1 that was exactly 1/3 of their R3 response. Dividing by 3 is, of course, a very straightforward heuristic to use in these circumstances. There was reference to the need to be rational or "logical", although even here participants expressed concern that this was putting a monetary value on individual lives.

> "Some people might think any lives worth saving perhaps you'd be the same or more I mean a life's a life and you can't put a value to life obviously but the reason I went for this sort of way 'cause if you talk about . . . [inaudible] . . . spending money you've got to think this way I can't see any other way really if you've got to be rational about using money."
>
> LH06

At the other end of the spectrum in 7 of the 21 transcribed interviews (and 22 of the full sample) participants gave exactly the same amount for R1 as for R3 (see Table 7.2), and this was despite the explicit prompt given above. Arguments here centred explicitly around a rejection of equating number of lives with cost, in that "saving life was saving life". Baron (1997) describes such values in theoretical terms as "protected", in the sense that they are regarded as infinitely more important than other economic goods or money. Saving one life or saving 75 still achieves the (infinitely) valued objective of saving life. Protected values also serve as statements of general principle to guide practical action, although as Baron correctly points out the problem with them is that they are unlikely to apply to every conceivable circumstance. The notion of a protected value would also be compatible with our earlier comments about the difficulty of putting an explicit price on life.

"It's very difficult isn't it to equate cost on something like this I think anything that's going to prevent whether you prevent 5 or you prevent 30 or whatever I'm going to stay with the same figures actually anything that would justify the saving in any way on road deaths in the area by getting rid of accident black spots."

JC13

"Because it's 75 lives or 25 lives it's lives saved I mean one life is important I feel 25 lives are as important as 75 in the terms of each life."
Interviewer: "Yes but if it's just as beneficial to prevent 75 as prevent 25 there's no sort of value for the extra 50 people?"
"No I realise that but from my point of view £1 a month is the amount that I would be prepared to pay."

AR08

The general argument, exemplified in the next quotation, seems to be that saving lives through the road safety programme would be a *good thing* in and of itself irrespective of the actual size of the good, or what can be afforded as a contribution (itself decided primarily by the range of heuristics discussed earlier).

"When I've worked in nursing and what not and behind all these figures there are little crumpled bodies and I don't think that it matters you can't multiply by x amount and say well this is worth that and that is worth this anything that is going to save lives is going to be worth it and to me I don't think that it matters whether you save 5 lives or 15 lives *if you are saving lives then it is good and it is worth it I mean obviously it would be better to save 15 but 5 is good.*"

JC04 (Emphasis added. Note also that this participant did nevertheless eventually give less for R1 than for R3)

There are two closely related theoretical interpretations that can be placed upon this view of saving life as a good thing, and the consequent insensitivity to quantity that it produces. The first of these concerns the "warm glow" or *moral satisfaction* obtained from giving a certain amount, as if to a charity (Andreoni, 1990; Kahneman & Knetsch, 1992). Baron (1997) argues that while warm glow does not depend upon the level of benefit obtained, it will depend upon the level of contribution. An alternative interpretation according to Baron is that such judgements are driven by the *importance* of the value addressed (a judgement obtained in our particular case from its protected status), which in turn does not depend upon either the quantity of contribution or the level of benefit. The fact that some of our participants expressed unease at the "small" or negligible amounts that they could afford (in relation to the significance of the issue as they saw it), along with references to the "all or nothing" nature of the question would be compatible with this notion of importance.

Note that many of the above quotes, irrespective of what the person eventually did contribute, are inherently *argumentative*. In particular they imply (and in many cases recognise explicitly) the dilemma raised by the mutual incompatibility of viewing saving life as a protected value and the need to value benefits when making willingness-to-pay judgements (that is, "everything has its price"). Billig et al. (1988) point out that such dilemmas are commonplace, forming an important part of everyday reasoning and argument – which will often centre around inherently contradictory themes. For example, we can all readily agree that "many hands make light work" while at the same time recognising that "too many cooks spoil the broth". Such oppositional statements of principle not only form the basis of the dilemmas around which everyday cognition and debate are structured, but also very often implicitly contain their own antithesis.

The important point to recognise here is that one can *simultaneously* both agree that "saving 15 lives is better than saving 5" and that "saving lives is a good thing irrespective of cost". From the perspective of standard economic theory to hold both beliefs as preferences would be viewed as inconsistent at best. One can, of course, resolve this by attaching more weight to one belief and then opting for this over the other (as appears to have occurred in many of the examples where people either gave 1/3 or an equal amount for R1). But, as Billig et al. (1988) also point out, the debate which surrounds such dilemmas often concerns *which particular principle to apply (and which to ignore) in the particular circumstances under consideration*, and many of the quotes given above also involve attempts to justify a choice through elaboration of the wider context of judgement (e.g. "behind these figures are little crumpled bodies" or "getting rid of accident black spots" or "spending money you've got to think this way"). We might term this the "rhetoric of preference construction", and it points once again to the critical importance of context (both as actively generated by participants and as framed by the question supplied) in influencing willingness-to-pay judgements.

Perhaps not surprisingly, then, many of the remaining participants (who neither divided the R3 amount by 3 nor opted to give equal amounts) appear to arrive at a compromise to resolve their dilemma; typically by adjusting the R3 figure downward in some proportion, *but not going as far as dividing by 3*. This might involve giving a little less, or the simple heuristic of dividing by 2. That is, the quantity of benefit is acknowledged as important by people, even when other aspects of the situation (family budgets and beliefs about protected values) ran counter to this.

> "We're saying we want a third of them basically there aren't we as I said I am a person who tends to deal with things in black and white rather because we are saving 25 lives so I am going to halve my previous figures basically on the amount of lives saved if I could save 20 I'd still be willing to pay £50 a year I could afford that amount of money."
>
> LH03

(c) F versus A framing

The final aspect of the quantitative data that we wished to explore relates to the question framing in terms of an annual or a five yearly benefit. Although the number of lives saved *per year* was the same in both questions the willingness-to-pay per year was significantly larger in the five yearly framing. We suspect that this may have been due to a failure to discriminate the temporal scale of the five yearly payment (a possibility also raised by Kahneman & Knetsch, 1992) coupled with some influence of the absolute numbers saved in each case (particularly if 75 is viewed as a close fraction of 100, and 15 as one of 10). Although the qualitative data is not fully conclusive on this point, as illustrated earlier what people could afford to pay was anchored primarily upon weekly or monthly outgoings which may have then set a dominant temporal framing for both the annual and five year groups. Furthermore, several participants in the annual framing group did remark that 15 (or 5) lives was *not many to save* and that they might have been prepared to give more if 50 or 100 lives had been involved.

> "There again I find it very difficult . . . the main reason is as I said 5 really isn't very many and I wouldn't want to pay very much because I wouldn't think that it was going to be me even 15 out of 400,000 isn't a lot."
>
> JC14

These remarks should also be interpreted in relation to other aspects of the design, which set the overall context for the willingness-to-pay judgements. Frederick and Fischhoff (1998) argue that CV responses will be sensitive to their relative position within a range, and in the preliminary focus groups we had introduced the total numbers of people affected (1,000,000), households (400,000), and the average numbers killed on the roads in this area per year (60) in the A framing or over 5 years (300) in the F. Although we do not have direct evidence (because the A and F framings were given to different groups of participants) if we take this as setting an implied range for judgements, 15(5) lives saved may well have seemed a much smaller number than did the 75(25).

Concluding comments

The chapter has demonstrated how different methods can be successfully combined in a single research design; perhaps best described as a qualitative–quantitative–qualitative hybrid. While the contingent valuation paradigm has for many years relied solely upon quantitative methods, our incorporation of a qualitative approach serves both as an essential precursor to the elicitation of the quantitative data *and* as a means of developing a more complete theoretical interpretation of those data. Perhaps more significantly, mixing methods has facilitated a critical evaluation of the particular CV paradigm described here, and its usefulness in relation to the policy goals of the research project (to advise on whether an appropriate figure for VoSL can be reliably based upon people's expressed preferences).

In theoretical terms we believe we can indeed account for the differing degrees of sensitivity to quantity observed in the quantitative findings in terms of the underlying qualitative arguments deployed by participants. We take the qualitative data to be strong evidence of the forms of preference construction process reported in other studies from the judgement and decision making literature (e.g. Schkade & Payne, 1994). However, our account also steps out of the framework offered by that literature, which tends still to be dominated by traditional information processing concerns from cognitive psychology and cognitive science, in illustrating how rhetorical arguments can also inform people's preference construction. Our participants both generate arguments (about tax, what can be afforded in weekly or monthly terms, the costs of the programme) that help to first constrain the range of payments, and then relate them, often as justifications, to the wider rhetorical dilemma of whether lives saved is a protected value or not in the context of the particular question being asked. Note that this should not be taken to imply that the number of lives saved and their cost was either absent or irrelevant. It is both implicit in the very notion of a protected value, and also formed an important part of the explicit arguments offered by participants even where it was ultimately rejected by them.

Whether the notion of preference construction is compatible with the assumptions made about human values and cognition made in CV, and more widely in standard micro-economic theory, is a point of considerable current theoretical debate. For example, some critical commentators do nevertheless believe that with proper care and attention to the preference construction process these two theoretical perspectives might yet be resolved (see e.g. Gregory, Lichtenstein, & Slovic, 1993; Baron, 1997), although this has yet to be empirically demonstrated. Our own critique of CV, grounded in the present findings and discussion, has led us in turn to propose a new approach to preference elicitation for safety valuation, taking into account some of the insights gained from the present study (see Carthy et al., 1999). What is clear, however, and as the results in Table 7.3 above aptly demonstrate, is that constructed preferences may severely limit the usefulness of CV surveys for policy: for if small changes in task or question wording can prompt wide and systematic variations in elicited values and their implications, the dilemma remains where should the "true" value for policy lie?

There is also a final methodological point that arises from the qualitative data analysis. The rapidly developing field of "qualitative research" and qualitative psychology now comprises a healthy diversity of traditions and perspectives, sometimes with very different epistemological and methodological foundations (see Henwood, this volume; Henwood & Pidgeon, 1994). The present analysis commenced from the perspective of grounded theory, which puts its primary emphasis upon the *content* of talk, or more precisely the interpretation of meanings derived from lived worlds and accounts. The developing analytic framework has suggested to us, however, the need to approach the data simultaneously from the perspective of rhetorical or discursive analysis (e.g. Potter & Wetherell, 1987), where the emphasis lies more upon the contradictions and structure of talk. From the researchers' perspective this was unexpected, and it suggests that "mixing methods" can mean far more than just crossing disciplines or the quantity/quality divide.

Acknowledgements

The work reported in this chapter was commissioned by the UK Health and Safety Executive, Department of Environment Transport and the Regions, Home Office, and HM Treasury, grant No 3271/R73.04. However, the opinions and conclusions expressed here are solely those of the authors alone, and do not necessarily reflect the views of the project's sponsors. We are grateful to Jonathan Baron, Baruch Fischhoff, George Lowenstein and Paul Slovic, as well as members of the project steering committee, for very helpful comments and suggestions.

Notes

1 For the reader with a psychology background, the use here of the term "behavioural" should not be confused with behaviourism. It merely signifies a commitment amongst such economists to empirical observation of individuals' actual choices and decisions under uncertainty and risk, typically in experimental or survey design settings.

2 In Great Britain and Northern Ireland there were 594 deaths in domestic fires and 29 deaths in fires in public places (such as cinemas or nursing homes) in 1996.

3 Although *hypothetical*, the questions used in contingent valuation must of necessity have at least some *relevance* to people and their lives.

4 There is an important methodological point here regarding the possibility of false positives and negatives in different designs (see also Fischhoff, Slovic, & Lichtenstein, 1979). Using a repeated measures design as part of the same study Kahneman and Knetsch (1992) *did* find a marked difference in willingness-to-pay for these three levels of provision. This is most probably because the first judgement in a repeated measures design provides an anchor against which the relative worth of the item presented second can be judged. In the between groups design

however only one question is asked and other strategies, which may in themselves be insensitive to the size of the good (e.g. I'll pay what can be afforded out of current income), will be used to construct an amount. Arrow et al. (1993) criticise repeated measures designs as tests of sensitivity, on the grounds that they may suffer from demand characteristics (and accordingly more chance, in comparison to the between groups design, of yielding false positive results). Responding to this point, Frederick and Fischhoff (1998) note that individuals do on the whole have a fair idea of the *relative* worth of goods, and that accordingly if they show sensitivity to quantity in a repeated measures design this may be telling more about their underlying tastes and preferences than Arrow et al. allow. We might also add that if participants are *not* responsive to the quantity of a good despite having this transparently varied in a repeated measures CV design, as occurs in the study reported in the present chapter, this would be a strong demonstration of *in*sensitivity (in that people are more likely to be explicitly endorsing a "true" negative, that reflects what they really do feel).

5 This also means that contingent valuation may be least useful in precisely the circumstances where it is needed most.

6 We did not conduct a formal completeness check, although many of the participants did remark that they had indeed taken the opportunity to reflect carefully upon the questions and issues throughout the three-step procedure. Also, a particular problem with traditional CV surveys is a refusal to answer the question at all. At worst such responses (often subsequently ignored in data analysis) can comprise up to 40 or 50 per cent of the total data collected. We avoided this situation (in fact there were *no* such refusals in the present study) by introducing the study rationale, the survey questions, their context and meaning in considerable depth first.

7 For example, in the case of road safety the risk reduction would be taken to be some fraction of 6 in 100,000, the latter being close to the average annual risk of death on the roads faced by car drivers and passengers in Great Britain.

8 In the technical literature it is often argued that the concept of VoSL is greatly misunderstood, in that it should *not* be taken to mean the value of *a life* (with the term VPF – or Value of Preventing a Statistical Fatality – sometimes preferred). It is difficult to see how such an inference could be avoided in lay discourse, however, and hence the title of the current chapter.

9 For example, for major railway accidents an equivalent risk reduction may be given a weighting of up to ×3 or more (and the VoSL used in analysis becomes of the order of £2.5 million or higher). This extra multiplier reflects, as a heuristic device, a number of diverse elements: the higher costs that large scale accidents inevitably bring (reconstruction, litigation, and inquiry), the potential inequity in distribution of harm, as well as presumed public aversion to taking on risks over which people have little responsibility or personal control (see Jones-Lee & Loomes, 1995; Pidgeon, 1998).

10 There were questions in the current study involving a reduction in fatalities in domestic fires. The analysis of this data is not reported here (see Beattie et al., 1998).

11 Although this difference, while large, just failed to be statistically significant in either the R1 ($p = .09$, Mann-Whitney, two-tailed) or the R3 ($p = .08$) case.

12 All of the initial focus groups and feedback meetings were also recorded, but we do not discuss the results of these here.

13 What is to be considered a "sufficient quantity" of material from a sample of interviews is very much a matter of judgement. It depends also upon the purposes and epistemological stance of the researcher. For example, for the purposes of discourse analysis one might only wish to analyse a single transcript. From a grounded theory perspective, as has been adopted here, one requirement is to have

enough material to arrive at *theoretical saturation* of key concepts (a state of closure, where no new insights are emerging as one works through the data corpus; see Glaser & Strauss, 1967; Turner, 1981). This will in turn depend upon the richness of the material, and could occur after analysing ten, after fifty, or perhaps only five interviews. In part, then, sufficiency (and in particular the decisions either to stop coding or add further material to the transcribed data corpus) can only be properly judged during the process of data analysis. In the present example, the twenty-one interviews were eventually deemed to be sufficient in this respect.

14 In contingent valuation studies medians are often preferred to the theoretically more appropriate means as an indicator of central tendency in willingness-to-pay because the sample distribution is often heavily right skewed.

15 The identifier at the end of each data snippet refers to the interviewer and interview number.

References

Adams, J. (1995). *Risk*. London: University College London Press.

Andreoni, J. (1990). Impure altruism and donations to public goods: A theory of warm glow giving. *Economic Journal, 100*, 464–477.

Arrow, K., Solow, R., Portney, P., Leamer, E., Radner, R., & Schuman, H. (1993). Report of the NOAA panel on contingent valuation. *Federal Register, 58*, 4602–4614.

Baron, J. (1997). Biases in the quantitative measurement of values for public decisions. *Psychological Bulletin, 122*, 72–88.

Beattie, J., Covey, J., Dolan, P., Hopkins, L., Jones-Lee, M. W., Loomes, G., Pidgeon, N. F., Robinson, A., & Spencer, A. (1998). On the contingent valuation of safety and the safety of contingent valuation: Part 1 – caveat investigator. *Journal of Risk and Uncertainty, 17*, 5–25.

Billig, M., Condor, S., Edwards, D., Gane, M., Middleton, D., & Radley, A. (1988). *Ideological dilemmas: A social psychology of everyday thinking*. London: Sage.

Brookshire, D., & Coursey, D. (1987). Measuring the value of a public good: An empirical comparison of elicitation procedures. *American Economic Review, 77*, 554–566.

Broome, J. (1985). The economic value of life. *Economica, 52*, 281–294.

Carson, R. T., & Mitchell, R. C. (1995). Sequencing and nesting in contingent valuation surveys. *Journal of Environmental Economics and Management, 28*, 155–173.

Carthy, T., Chilton, S., Covey, J., Hopkins, L., Jones-Lee, M. W., Loomes, G., Pidgeon, N. F., & Spencer, A. (1999). On the contingent valuation of safety and the safety of contingent valuation: Part 2 – the CV/SG chained approach. *Journal of Risk and Uncertainty, 17*, 187–213.

Cummings, R. G., Brookshire, D. S., & Schulze, W. D. (1986). *Valuing environmental goods: A state of art assessment of the contingent valuation method*. Totowa, NJ: Rowan & Allenheld.

Curley, S. P., Browne, G. J., Smith, G. F., & Benson, P. G. (1995). Arguments in the practical reasoning underlying constructed probability responses. *Journal of Behavioral Decision Making, 8*, 1–20.

Desaigues, B., & Rabl, A. (1995). Reference values for human life. In N. G. Schwab-Christe, & N. C. Soguel (Eds.), *Contingent valuation, transport safety and the value of life* (pp. 85–112). Boston, MA: Kluwer.

Desvousges, W. H., & Smith, V. K. (1988). Focus grous and risk communication: The "science" of listening to data. *Risk Analysis, 8*, 479–484.

Dixon, J. A., Fallon-Scura, L., Carpenter, R. A., & Sherman, P. B. (1994). *Economic analysis of environmental impacts.* London: Earthscan.

Duborg, W. R., Jones-Lee, M. W., & Loomes, G. (1997). Imprecise preferences and survey design. *Economica, 64*, 681–702.

Fischhoff, B. (1991). Value elicitation: Is there anything in there? *American Psychologist, 46*, 835–847.

Fischhoff, B., & Furby, L. (1988). Measuring values: A conceptual framework for interpreting transactions with special reference to contingent valuation of visibility. *Journal of Risk and Uncertainty, 1*, 147–184.

Fischhoff, B., Slovic, P., & Lichtenstein, S. (1979). Subjective sensitivity analysis. *Organizational Behavior and Human Performance, 23*, 339–359.

Fischhoff, B., Slovic, P., & Lichtenstein, S. (1980). Knowing what you want: Measuring labile values. In T. Wallsten (Ed.), *Cognitive processes in choice and decision behavior* (pp. 117–141). Hillsdale, NJ: Erlbaum.

Frederick, S., & Fischhoff, B. (1998). Scope (in)sensitivity in elicited valuations. *Risk Decision and Policy, 3*, 109–124.

Glaser, B., & Strauss, A. (1967). *The discovery of grounded theory.* Chicago: Aldine.

Gregory, R., Lichtenstein, S., & Slovic, P. (1993). Valuing environmental resources: A constructive approach. *Journal of Risk and Uncertainty, 7*, 177–197.

Henwood, K. L., & Pidgeon, N. F. (1992). Qualitative research and psychological theorizing. *British Journal of Psychology, 83*, 97–111.

Henwood, K. L., & Pidgeon, N. F. (1994). Beyond the qualitative paradigm: A framework for introducing diversity in qualitative psychology. *Journal of Community and Applied Social Psychology, 4*, 225–238.

Jones-Lee, M. W. (1976). *The value of life: An economic analysis.* London: Martin Robertson.

Jones-Lee, M. W. (1998). Appendix A: Summaries of selected publications on contingent valuation and other direct preference-elicitation methods in the fields of health and safety. In J. Beattie, S. Chilton, R. Cookson, J. Covey, L. Hopkins, M. W. Jones-Lee, G. Loomes, N. F. Pidgeon, A. Robinson, & A. Spencer, *Valuing health and safety controls: A literature review* (pp. 59–135). London: Health and Safety Executive Books.

Jones-Lee, M. W., Hammerton, M., & Phillips, P. R. (1985). The value of safety: results of a national survey. *Economic Journal, 95*, 49–72.

Jones-Lee, M. W., & Loomes, G. (1995). Scale and context effects in the valuation of transport safety. *Journal of Risk and Uncertainty, 11*, 183–203.

Jungermann, H. (1986). The two camps on rationality. In H. R. Arkes, & K. R. Hammond (Eds.), *Judgement and decision making* (pp. 627–641). Cambridge: Cambridge University Press.

Kahneman, D., & Knetsch, J. L. (1992). Valuing public goods: The purchase of moral satisfaction. *Journal of Environmental Economics and Management, 22*, 57–70.

Kahneman, D., Slovic, P., & Tversky, A. (1982). *Judgement under uncertainty: Heuristics and biases.* Cambridge: Cambridge University Press.

Lincoln, Y. S., & Guba, E. G. (1985). *Naturalistic inquiry.* Beverly Hills: Sage.

Mitchell, R., & Carson, R. (1989). *Using surveys to value public goods: The contingent valuation method.* Washington, DC: Resources for the Future.

Payne, J. W., Bettman, J. R., & Johnson, E. J. (1992). Behavioural decision research: A constructive processing perspective. *Annual Review of Psychology*, *43*, 87–131.

Pidgeon, N. F. (1998). Risk assessment, risk values and the social science programme: Why we do need risk perception research. *Reliability Engineering and System Safety*, *59*, 5–15.

Pidgeon, N. F., & Henwood, K. L. (1996). Grounded theory: Theoretical background/ practical implementation. In J. T. E. Richardson (Ed.), *Handbook of qualitative research methods for psychology and the social sciences* (pp. 75–101). Leicester: British Psychological Society Books.

Potter, J., & Wetherell, M. (1987). *Discourse and social psychology*. London: Sage.

Schkade, D. A., & Payne, J. W. (1994). How people respond to contingent valuation questions: A verbal protocol analysis of willingness-to-pay for an environmental regulation. *Journal of Environmental Economics and Management*, *26*, 88–109.

Slovic, P. (1995). The construction of preference. *American Psychologist*, *50*, 364–371.

Tengs, T. O., Adams, M. E., Pliskin, J. S., Safran, D. G., Siegel, J. E., Weinstein, M. C., & Graham, J. D. (1995). Five-hundred life-saving interventions and their cost effectiveness. *Risk Analysis*, *15*, 369–390.

Turner, B. A. (1981). Some practical aspects of qualitative data analysis: One way of organizing the cognitive processes associated with the generation of grounded theory. *Quality and Quantity*, *15*, 225–247.

8 Method and methodology in interpretive studies of cognitive life

Katie Vann and Michael Cole

The purpose of our chapter is to contribute to understandings of "mixed methods" in psychology by considering cases in which quantitative representations of cognitive life are used as methodological strategies of interpretive cultural psychology. Although quantification may seem to be at odds with principles of interpretive studies, these studies urge us to think about a different possibility: that such "odds" may derive from ways in which quantification, as a mode of representation, is mapped onto social and cognitive phenomena rather than from any inherent attribute of quantitative methods in general. We discuss two related research projects that suggest that quantification may enable the tasks of interpretive studies of cognitive life when cognitive phenomena are conceived of and juxtaposed in particular ways. We focus on the design and uses of experimental tasks and quantitative comparison – as parts of an overall cultural-historical research methodology – to illustrate moments in which fruitful meshing of qualitative and quantitative approaches has been attempted.

I Method and methodology

Fred Erickson, an anthropologist who makes wide use of qualitative methods, once suggested that he prefers the term "interpretive methods" because "it avoids the connotation of defining these approaches as essentially non-quantitative". The key feature of "interpretive methods", he wrote, "is the central research interest in human meaning in social life and its elucidation and exposition by the researcher" (Erickson, 1986).

There are two analytically different theoretical assumptions that underlie this view. The first is that in their interactions with the world, human beings draw on cultural/conceptual resources, which they use to construct the meaning of their circumstances. The second assumption is that the resources upon which such constructed meanings are based are themselves constitutive of that individual's material, socio-cultural context. Thus the two-fold notion that meanings are constructed and material as well as situated and conceptual comes to play an important role in guiding research (Cole, 1996).

In Erickson's view, "a crucial analytic distinction in interpretive research is that between behavior, the physical act, and action, which is the physical behavior plus the meaning interpretations held by the actor and those with whom the actor is engaged in interaction" (Erickson, 1986: 126–127). The study of action does not in principle preclude the use of quantitative techniques.

However, some scholars who share Erickson's view that individual human development and behavior are constructive and situated by nature believe that it is therefore inappropriate to understand cognitive life using quantitative modes of representation. According to this line of reasoning, through acts of quantification, numbers are substituted for the dynamic nature of situated action, which always requires a degree of creative deviance. As a consequence, the "it" produced by quantification is no longer strictly reducible to the "it" produced by qualitative analysis of a dynamic, emergent process (Mehan and Wood, 1975; Schütz, 1962). On such readings, techniques exemplified by classical experimentation and quantification become problematic in so far as they tend to strip away from inquiry the very blood and organizational complexity that give cognitive functioning its dynamism.

Goethe precisely captures this reductionist tendency of quantitative approaches in *Faust*. In the scene where Mephistopheles advises an eager student on his future career, he describes the consequences of following the path of science. The conversation begins with Mephistopheles admiring the work of weavers, who create patterns, a process in which "A single treadle governs many a thread, And at a stroke a thousand strands are wed". Quite different is the scientist's approach, and quite different the result. In light of the discussion to this point, it would not be amiss to think of the scientist as a quantitative psychologist and the weaver as the qualitative psychologist.

> And so philosophers step in
> To weave a proof that things begin,
> Past question, with an origin.
> With first and second well rehearsed,
> Our third and fourth can be deduced.
> And if no second were or first,
> No third or fourth could be produced.
> As weavers though, they don't amount to much.
> To docket living things past any doubt
> You cancel first the living spirit out;
> The parts lie in the hollow of your hand,
> You only lack the living link you banned.
> (Goethe, 1988: 95)

It is crucial to recall that quantification as a mode of representation has given special meaning to psychological research historically, as has been noted by Danziger.

Such sacred and unquestioned emblems of scientific status included features like quantification, experimentation, and the search for universal (i.e., ahistorical) laws. A discipline that demonstrated its devotion to such emblems could at least establish a serious claim to be counted among the august ranks of the sciences.

(Danziger, 1990: 120)

Danziger continues,

The contribution of investigative practices to the professional project of psychology involved two sets of problems with often diverging implications. On the one hand, there was the need to develop practices whose products would answer to the immediate needs of socially important markets. But on the other hand, there was a need to establish, maintain, and strengthen the claim that what psychologists practiced was indeed to be counted as science. These two requirements could not always be reconciled, and so it was inevitable that there was conflict within the discipline with some of its members placing relatively more emphasis on one or another of these directions. But in the long run the two factions depended on one another, rather like two bickering partners in a basically satisfactory marriage. For the very term "applied psychology" reflected the myth that what psychologists used to put outside universities was based on a genuine science, much as engineers based themselves on physics. Without this myth the claims of practitioners to scientific expertise must collapse. But at the same time, the pure scientist in the laboratory could often command much better support for his work if it was seen as linked to practical applications by a society for which utilitarian considerations were paramount.

(Danziger, 1990: 120)

Notwithstanding the risk associated with the use of quantitative representational practices, we would like to call attention to a strand of interpretive studies that use them. Like Erickson, such studies suggest that calls for the use of qualitative description *in place of* quantitative description are unwarranted. Though non-quantitative (qua "qualitative") data have increasingly been associated with constructivist and contextualist theorizing, the studies we wish to point to provide examples for thinking about ways in which qualitative approaches do not necessarily exclude quantification.

Social studies of cognitive life all rely on representational strategies. Some of these strategies use natural language and others use the language of numbers. These languages construct different kinds of knowledge because they are different modes of representation, but each of them performs a reduction with respect to the phenomena that they purport to represent. Quantification has been and can be used as a form of reductionism that supports highly problematic social and political projects. It is both a mode of representation and a tool, a cultural resource that enables researchers, as much as our "subjects", to construct meanings. The question is whether natural language and quantification can be used together and complement each other in ways that give fuller meaning to interpretive approaches.

One way of specifying useful ways of overcoming approaches that pit quantitative against qualitative research is to differentiate between the terms *method* and *methodology* that are often used as synonyms for each other in North American psychological research.

We will use the term *method* here in a two-fold sense, as "a systematic procedure, technique or mode of inquiry employed by or proper to a particular science, art, or discipline" and as "a particular way of viewing, organizing, and giving shape and significance to artistic materials" (Webster's 3rd International Dictionary, unabridged, 1966.). By contrast, we refer to *methodology* as the logic by which theoretical principles are linked to data through *combinations of methods*. Just as methods mediate the relations between empirical phenomena and data, methodologies mediate the relations between methods and theories. Our differentiation of these concepts roughly corresponds to Erickson's distinction between "method" and "technique". The question before us is *how one might combine quantitative and qualitative methods as elements of an interpretive methodology*.

We will consider these issues in the context of two research efforts that sought to create synthetic interpretive methodologies by integrating quantitative and qualitative methods: Scribner and Cole's (1981) research on the cognitive consequences of literacy among the Vai of Liberia, and Scribner's study of the cognitive consequences of the structure of work carried out by dairy workers (1984, 1986). Although these two lines of work have been commented upon separately (see Goody, 1987; Ratner, 1997), we want to focus on commonalities in the ways they designed cognitive tasks on the basis of field studies and how quantitative data were mapped to performances on these tasks. These methodologies serve as lenses through which better to understand the interpretive uses of quantitative description in conjunction with qualitative field methods.

II Understanding the cognitive consequences of Vai literacy

The Scribner–Cole study of literacy among the Vai hinged on the intriguing opportunity provided by a society that had developed its own system of writing, which was in use by a significant number of adults, but which was acquired and used almost entirely outside of the formal structures of schooling. Their prior research had shown that performance on a wide range of cognitive tasks widely used at the time to assess the sophistication of cognitive processes such as deliberate remembering, reasoning, and inference, was markedly influenced by attendance at schools modeled on an Euro-American curriculum. At the same time, it had revealed that when the performances required by their cognitive tasks drew upon areas of local cultural practice, Liberian rice farmers could out-perform American undergraduates (Cole, Gay, Glick, & Sharp, 1971; Gay and Cole, 1967). This combination of results made them curious about what features of schooling might be responsible for the changes in tested performance. One obvious candidate was literacy. According to various theorists in vogue when they began this work, the acquisition of literacy changes one's orientation to language and the functional systems of thought that guide action. So, the most simple-minded question posed by this research was "Does literacy substitute for schooling" in boosting performance on a variety of cognitive tasks where schooling has been shown to produce performance increases?

Although it was clear at the outset that research on literacy among the Vai would allow them to separate literacy and schooling, they had little idea of what connections there might be between literacy in Vai or in English, the "lingua franca" of Liberia and the language of schooling, between Vai literacy and Qur'anic literacy, the "lingua franca" of religion, or between Vai literacy and a variety of social conditions that could also be expected to influence cognitive performance: extensive travel, knowledge of other spoken languages, etc. Consequently, a major component in the first round of research was a massive quantitative survey of the precursors, concomitant variations, and performance differences associated with different past experiences, including different forms of literacy experience, to be found in the Vai population. In parallel, one member of the team, Mike Smith, conducted a detailed ethnography of the genealogy and everyday practice of Vai literacy, and another, Stephen Reder, conducted a detailed study of spoken and written Vai (Reder, 1981).

The short answer to their question about literacy versus schooling was that being literate in Vai had very little impact on cognitive performances that were markedly influenced by years of schooling. Only in one case, an ability to categorize pictures of geometric shapes varying in form and number, did people literate in Vai outperform non-literates, although not to the extent of those who had attended school.

Having conducted the main line of research thus far based upon tasks whose structure derives from methods used to study cognitive development in the United States, Scribner and Cole turned to the study of the practices where the Vai script was actually used, and constructed cognitive tasks modeled on those practices. Several examples are contained in the monograph. We have selected for discussion just one task because it illustrates the central logic of the approach with particular clarity.

Once they began to focus on the specific skills that are promoted by the way in which the Vai script entered into script-mediated practices, Scribner and Cole believed that one of the most straightforward questions one could ask about the cognitive consequences of Vai literacy was whether knowing how to read Vai makes it easier to read another unfamiliar system of graphic symbols. If so, what specific skills do Vai literates bring to bear on tasks requiring that they make sense out of graphic symbols but which non-literate Vai do not?

The starting point for answering this question depended upon the use of what are often termed qualitative methods. These included analysis of the characteristics of the Vai script as a means of representing oral Vai and extensive observations of people reading Vai in a variety of circumstances.

With respect to the script, Scribner and Cole found that the Vai language is represented in a syllabary consisting of approximately 210 symbols that map onto consonant–vowel or consonant–vowel–vowel combinations. Tone, which is important to the pronunciation of the syllables of spoken Vai, is not represented in the script. Furthermore, the Vai (like the ancient Greeks) do not place spaces between lexical units English literates identify as words (soreadingrequiresonetoparsetheflowofsymbols). The result of these characteristics is that reading Vai requires the reader to cope with a good deal of ambiguity when compared to English texts on the same topics.

Ethnographic observation revealed that reading was often done aloud, with, and sometimes for, others. Consequently, it was possible to note how literate Vai dealt with the ambiguities resident in their system of writing. Scribner and Cole referred to the reading they observed as a process of "semantic integration". They illustrate this process with a transcription of an audio recording of a person reading a family history that he himself had written. Despite his familiarity with the text, he nonetheless needed to work through parts of it by sounding out individual characters as if seeking for word boundaries and testing out possible integrations of text fragments that made sense in the context of the passage. For example, a sentence that (using alphabetic characters) began *Dudu ata ba kpaloee* . . . (*Dudu's mother came from* . . .) was initially sounded out as *Dudu a ta ba kpa lo ee* where only the proper name (which repeats the same syllable twice) is integrated, while all of the remaining initial guesses remain at the level of individual syllables corresponding to individual graphic characters.

They observed that people first sound out syllables and then integrate them into meaningful sentences. Such practice, Scribner and Cole reasoned, ought to result in skilled use relating syllables of spoken Vai to the syllable-level graphic symbols of written Vai in order to come up with interpretations. Note that this is a question about process (How do Vai literates go about reading?) and about transfer (Is it possible for Vai literates to bring resources developed and drawn on in reading Vai to the process of reading another graphic system?) In short, compared to non-literates, or those literate in English or Arabic, which use phonetic/alphabetic representations of the spoken language, Vai literates ought to make special use of syllables when interpreting an unfamiliar graphic system.

With these observations as a foundation, the next step was to devise a task that could be given to literate and non-literate people alike (and to people literate in alphabetic as well as syllabic writing systems.) That is, on one level, the task needed to call upon interpretive resources that all groups could bring to the task in order for the performance of people with differing literacy backgrounds to be comparable in a meaningful way. On a second level, the task had to provide an opportunity to assess whether the specific cultural practices of one of the groups, in this case, those literate in Vai, enable them to perform the task in a distinctive way associated with the characteristics of their writing system. It is the ability to specify the links between practices and skills brought to the particular task that is the focus of interest.

The notion that task materials must "call upon" the interpretive, culture-specific resources of a group is based in the idea that a skill is not a general entity that one "has", but rather is a set of component processes that work together in a functional system to accomplish certain cognitive ends in particular circumstances (see Hutchins, 1995). The set of component processes (the content and organization of the person's particular functional cognitive system) is, on this view, thought to be intimately bound with the character of the practices within which the functional cognitive system develops, including the representational features of, in this case, the writing system. Vai country provided a potential set of such subjects in the sense that there were institutional practices sustaining three distinguishable literacy groups, each of which was proficient in spoken Vai, in addition to non-literate Vai speakers.

But the differences and commonalities would become salient only in the context of the structure and content of the tasks in terms of which they could be expressed. The design of the task materials thus entails a tremendous burden. These are best understood by considering the content and rationale of a specific, concrete, task design.

The solution was to present people with a symbol-decoding task, using pictures of objects familiar to their Vai subjects, regardless of their literacy experiences. A typical rebus task was a possible candidate for this.

Whereas the rebus task shown in Figure 8.1 is often thought to be able to identify reading skills *in general*, it is important to note how much it assumes about the "subjects" to whom it will be presented. Specifically, it assumes

Figure 8.1 A typical rebus puzzle.

literacy in a phonetic writing system; it assumes that subjects speak *and* read English; it assumes that subjects speak and read numeric script; it assumes that the principle of homonymity works at the level of the word. Many of these assumptions do not obtain for non-English reading populations of Vailand, so Scribner and Cole figured that it would be better to transform the rebus to reflect the reading practices suspected to be associated with the special features of Vai language.

So, for example, they presented people with a picture of a chicken *(tiye)*, a picture of a canoe paddle *(laa)* and other similar items (see Figure 8.2 below), which they asked people to name aloud. Once assured that everyone could name each of the items each subject was told, "I am going to put these pictures down so that their names tell something in Vai. Name each of the pictures as I put it down." To make sure that everyone could also carry out the task of integrating symbols to create a new meaning that was derived from the sounds of the words they spoke aloud, all subjects were given a practice example that created a single word, different in meaning from the names of the two pictures, but derivable from integrating their sounds. The chicken *(tiye)*-paddle *(laa)* pair was used for practice. When spoken one right after the other in an integrated fashion, *tiye* and *laa* are pronounced *tiye la*, which means "waterside". Note that as part of the integration process, it is necessary for the "reader" to change one feature of the original – by shortening the vowel sound of the second element.

After subjects had demonstrated their ability to "read" waterside (by responding correctly to the question, "What place is this?" they were given seven pictographically represented sentences to read and answer questions about. Figure 8.2 provides a rebus-like representation of the sentence, "The man cooked a big chicken."

Scribner and Cole described in qualitative terms what they believed to be involved in the performance of this task:

> The sentence displayed . . . illustrates some of the processes involved in going from picture naming to "reading" with these materials. The first picture – "hoe" *(kai)* – stands for "the man" *(kai")*. [Note that] the Vai words for "hoe" and "the man" are not pure homonyms. "Hoe" requires one

	(a) Picture name	kái	làà	tíyé	bá	tá
	(b) Sentence	kálĕ	lá	tíyé	bà	táă

Figure 8.2 Reading task, "The man cooked a big chicken".

tonal and one vowel change to become "the man". *Ta* ("fire") – requires elongation of the vowel to become *taa*, "cooked" and so on. . . . All sentences required feature changes of this sort in a manner analogous to the feature changes involved in translating the written page into spoken Vai.

(Scribner & Cole, 1981: 168)

Based on their fieldwork and analysis of the processes required by Vai speakers to perform this task successfully, Scribner and Cole used two methods to quantify the relative skill levels of the different groups. First, they noted whether the person read off the pictures in an integrated way, or pronounced them one by one as discrete units. Second, they counted the number of correct responses to the comprehension questions following each sentence. (In the case of "The man cooked the big chicken" they asked what happened to the chicken, for example). Of the many findings associated with this research, the following are the most salient:

1   Despite the unfamiliarity of the task, non-literate Vai speakers read and comprehended approximately 50% of the rebus-like "sentences" that were read to them.
2   Vai literates significantly outperformed non-literates by reading and comprehending approximately 80% of the time.
3   Reading aloud the pictures in an integrated manner did not guarantee comprehension, even for Vai literates.
4   The more feature changes needed to create a meaningful sentence from the pictures, the greater the difference in performance between literate and non-literates in Vai.
5   Literacy in English had an effect roughly equivalent to literacy in Vai, but Qur'anic literacy did not, even for people who could comprehend Arabic. However, on a companion task where people were asked to *create* ("write") sentences using the pictures as constituents, all three literate groups outperformed non-literate participants to a similar degree.

A particularly telling feature of the results were repeated observations that subjects engaged in a process that mimicked the processes observed in naturally occurring uses of the Vai script: People often began by saying the names of the objects in the pictures as discrete units and then varied their pronunciation of these units until a meaningful sentence emerged.

Here we see a microcosm of a reading process that embodies the notion of reading as the simultaneous operation of, and integration of, "top-down" and "bottom-up" reading processes: People appeared to be engaged in the following sequence of processes: from visual examination of the graphic symbol → sound of lower-order semantic unit → recycle vis-à-vis other lower-order units given in the task → alter pronunciation until lower-order units "click" into meaningful higher-order units.

Following a replication of these results, Scribner and Cole, satisfied that they had created a useful model of one aspect of Vai literacy, sought to determine if life experiences other than literacy might also influence people's abilities to read the rebus/pictogram sentences using multiple regression analysis to partial out the effects of various possible contributory factors. Knowledge of Vai consistently "appeared" as an independent contribution to performance, but performance was also enhanced by knowledge of other Liberian tribal languages, and by advanced knowledge of written Arabic or English. Other experiential factors (occupation, extent of travel, etc.) did not influence performance.

Although we have treated this research project only briefly, we hope that we have directed readers to an interpretive methodological effort that combines several different methods: some qualitative, some quantitative, some based on observation of naturally occurring cultural practices, some based on contrived tasks modeled on those cultural practices. The combined effect of the different methods used in conjunction with each other is to provide evidence of quite specific "cognitive consequences of literac(ies)" conceived of as cultural practices mediated by specific representational technologies.

III Understanding workplace cognition

Following the research on Vai literacy, Scribner undertook a new research program that drew on and elaborated both its theoretical underpinnings and its methodology in order to study workplace literacy and cognition in the United States (Scribner, 1984, 1986). Her specific topic was a form of cognition that she called "practical thinking", which she referred to as thinking that is embedded in larger purposive activities that functions to carry out the goals of those activities. Although practical thinking might entail either mental or physical products (calculating a delivery cost or moving boxes of dairy products) Scribner explicitly contrasted it to the kinds of thinking that she, following Bartlett, called "closed system thinking, ordinarily studied in psychological experiments" (Bartlett, 1958; Scribner, 1984). The closed system thinking model imagines cognitive life as occurring in isolated mental space "having no transactions with the external environment or other people". Accordingly, the model conceives cognitive performance as an end in itself, and analyzes mental functions (e.g. memory, perception, reasoning) in isolation from one another and as separated from the sphere of action. Scribner noted that

> it seems clear that psychologists have long been preoccupied with intellectual achievements which, by rule of thumb, qualify as theoretical: logical operations (Piaget, 1950) scientific concepts (Vygotsky, 1962) and problem-solving in closed symbolic domains (Newell and Simon, 1972). Practical knowledge and thought for action have been under-examined and theoretically neglected topics in psychology.
>
> (Scribner, 1984: 2).

So construed, this "theoretical thinking" model is eschewed in favor of a model of "practical thinking" recognizable only through a consideration of the socially meaningful, purposive activities of subjects, and the goals to whose achievement their practical thinking is instrumental. The practical thinking model therefore sought to create a space for a different kind of psychological research.

Scribner's dairy studies drew upon three classes of methods for the study of practical thinking in activity. The first depended on empirical description based on observation of people performing tasks under actual working conditions, informal chats, and formal interviews, which served, as in the Vai research, to provide hypotheses about the factors that might influence the ways in which the workers performed their tasks (in this case, tasks that seemed to require practical thinking).

The second method was to create simulations of selected tasks in order to provide a format for testing hypotheses about factors regulating skilled cognitive performance (for example, effects of knowledge or changes in goals) and for studying the acquisition of problem solving skills. This simulation method is analogous to the rebus-reading study in the Vai work discussed above.

The third method was experimentation, which was intended to provide more detailed knowledge concerning, for example, workers' changing representations of the objects that they used in their work activity as they gained more experience on the job.

Scribner emphasized that these methods need not, and ideally should not, be used serially in a rigid manner, although the work typically begins with observations and interviews. Accordingly, as in the Vai research, she sought to create and analyze data sets by proceeding on the basis of an inclusion of those features of the concrete context on which and through which mind is theoretically posited to occur.

An important step in the cultural comparisons reported in both our examples is the identification of groups that differ on specific, hypothetically relevant variables that "naturally" occur, but that are nonetheless able to perform on the task. The construction of "groups" as such is an issue we will return to in the discussion section of this chapter. For now we want to note, however, that whereas in the rebus task discussed above the groups could vary in their successes on the task, in the dairy product assembly task, subjects are only compared on the routes they construct to accomplish the "correct" answer. These "accurate" performances serve as the constant, which enables the other variables – task solution strategy and institutional/group identity of subjects – to be compared.

As in the Vai research, Scribner's research on the cognitive life of working people maintained a commitment to the principle of embedded intellectual development and performance in cultural practices. However, her theoretical approach had expanded. Now cultural practices were interpreted as *activities* within the framework of activity theory. Drawing upon the writings of A. N. Leontiev and his students, she wrote that an activity:

is a system of goal-directed actions integrated around a common motive and directed toward specific objects. Activities represent a synthesis of mental and behavioral processes and can be analyzed psychologically on a number of levels: on the molar level of activities as such; or in terms of the goal-directed actions which comprise them; or the specific operations by which actions are carried out.

(Scribner, 1984: 3)

In the particular study we will use to highlight the way in which Scribner integrated "quantitative" and "qualitative" methods as elements of her activity theory methodology, she concentrated on work activities involving manual components, in a highly structured occupation with tasks whose goals were predetermined and explicit. The advantage of this choice, she reasoned, is that such activities are organised within and by the institution in which people are working so that the investigator needn't bring a priori definitions of activity or goal-directed actions to the site in hopes of finding some version of them in naturally occurring behavior; they were supplied by the institutional arrangements themselves. The activities were identified institutionally as different categories of occupations and the goal directed actions were the locally meaningful categories of work tasks (loading dairy products into crates for delivery, for example). Note, however, that this does not mean that such institutionally defined activities and goal directed actions – as institutionally recognised descriptions of behaviors – may be taken at face value. Indeed, "it is possible to start with behavioral descriptions and classifications already existing in the workplace *and allow the evolving research to test their adequacy*" (Scribner, 1984: 3; our emphasis).

In an early observational phase of this study, Scribner developed a set of hunches about the practical thinking of product assemblers, all of which focused on how to characterise and explain the cognitive contributions of so-called low-skilled, manual workers engaged in this occupation/activity. A production process mediating the production and distribution of dairy products, "product assembly" (activity) involved locating and sending precise amounts of products to the loading platform. It wasn't difficult to see that this "manual job" required intellectual operations in a symbol system of some complexity. Of that set of component tasks comprising the activity of "product assembly" Scribner focused on the task (goal-directed action) referred to as "filling an order".

As in most activity theoretic approaches, tool analysis figures prominently in the fieldwork. In this case, the "load-out order form" was found not only to be a key medium of communication between product assembly and other activities in the dairy, but also a primary tool structuring the assemblers' own activity.

For the drivers, an assembly consists of a specified number of units. Their order is expressed accordingly, showing, for example, number of gallons, number of quarts, etc. This order then is converted into case equivalencies by a computer program. "If the leftover amount equals half a case or less, the order is expressed as number of cases *plus* number of units; if the leftover amount is more than half a case, the order is expressed as number of cases *minus* number of units" (p. 11). For example, 16 quarts equals 1 case; 18 quarts equals "1 + 2"; 10 quarts equals "1 – 6". Moreover, a case is a virtual quantity, since the number of "units" per case varies according to the product (e.g., 1 case equals 16 quarts, or four gallons, or eight half-gallons, and so on.) Scribner reasoned that filling an order is a succession of moves that transforms an initial problem state, the given physical array of products stacked in the storeroom, into a final problem state, a case containing the number of units specified in symbolic form on the order. The task is an embedded formal problem, then, in the sense that 1) it proceeds within a rule-regulated number representation system in a determinate universe of admissible problems (orders), and according to fixed criteria for (accurate) solutions; 2) it proceeds in relation to a concrete environment ("the actual product arrays in the icebox"); and 3) it proceeds within the context of the general work goals of the problem solver (ibid.: 11).

Field observation of assemblers solving such embedded problems revealed that different "modes of solution" were employed.

> The order "1 – 6 quarts" (i.e., 10 quarts) recurred six times during the observation. On two occasions, assemblers filled the order by removing 6 quarts from a full case. Their behavioral moves were isomorphic to the symbolic moves in the problem presentation (subtract six quarts from one case.). We refer to these as literal solutions. On two occasions, assemblers took advantage of partial full cases in the area to modify the numbers in the subtraction problem: they removed four quarts from a partial case of 14, one from a case of 11. On the two remaining occasions, they behaviorally transformed the subtraction problem to an addition problem: they made up the required case of 10 by adding two quarts to a partial case of eight and four quarts to a partial of six. We refer to these as non-literal solutions.
>
> (Scribner, 1984: 12)

Notice that the modes of solution do not strictly correspond to the numerical properties of the orders. In some cases, "identical orders received different modes of solution on different occasions" (a and b in Figure 8.3). This solution variability interested the researchers, because the variability itself is not necessary to satisfy the job requirements (i.e., there is no formal institutional rule dictating how the problem ought to be solved, so the strategies are interpretable as worker innovations and contributions). Moreover, non-literal strategies (on a prima facie basis) suggest the use of increasingly complex cognitive requirements. For example, they "require additional manipulation of the original properties of different physical arrays".

One of Scribner's working hypotheses concerned the workers' goal in solving the order-filling problem. First, the choice of solution mode "is regulated

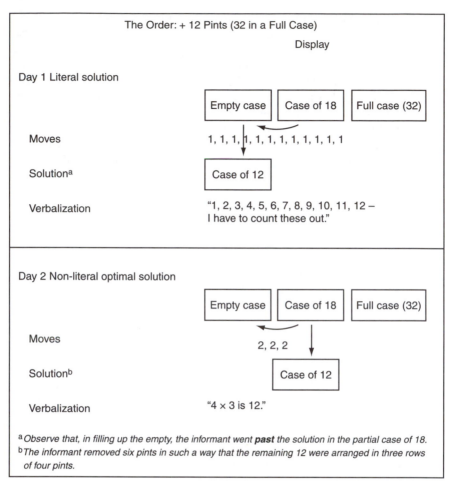

The Order: + 12 Pints (32 in a Full Case)

Display

Day 1 Literal solution

| Empty case | Case of 18 | Full case (32) |

Moves   1, 1, 1, 1, 1, 1, 1, 1, 1, 1, 1, 1

Solution[a] | Case of 12 |

Verbalization "1, 2, 3, 4, 5, 6, 7, 8, 9, 10, 11, 12 –
               I have to count these out."

Day 2 Non-literal optimal solution

| Empty case | Case of 18 | Full case (32) |

Moves   2, 2, 2

Solution[b] | Case of 12 |

Verbalization "4 × 3 is 12."

[a] *Observe that, in filling up the empty, the informant went **past** the solution in the partial case of 18.*
[b] *The informant removed six pints in such a way that the remaining 12 were arranged in three rows of four pints.*

Figure 8.3 Product assembly simulation learning study. Example of a student's change in solution mode.

by a criterion of least physical effort"; and, second, "extra mental effort may be expended to satisfy this criterion".

> In this view, problem-solving skill in product assembly consists of choosing just that path to solution which requires the least number of moves to fill a particular order in a given set of circumstances.
>
> (Scribner, 1984: 12)

This description of the phenomenon of "variable solutions to 'identical problems'" immediately provides a means for quantitative comparison of subjects' performance on the task. In some situations, a literal solution saves physical effort, while in other situations, a non-literal solution does. What stood out in the field observations of product assemblers filling orders was their flexibility in deploying both literal and non-literal strategies relative to the physical effort they reduced respectively, within particular problem states. The researchers therefore identified "number of moves" with "number of unit containers transferred from one case to another". Field observers reported that 83% of the product assemblers' literal solutions were "optimal" meaning that they used least physical effort while getting the order filled. All of their non-literal solutions were optimal. Their flexibility in utilizing both literal and non-literal solutions, according to the nature of the problem, was most intriguing. Scribner called this "higher-order" skill – selectively adapting solution modes to reduce physical effort – "an optimizing strategy". She suspected that the development of this strategy was a special feature of the activity called "product assembly" in the dairy.

A simulation of the order-filling task was devised in order to compare four institutionally defined subject populations on their respective solution strategies, and the extent to which they used the "optimizing strategy". Three of the four subject populations were drawn from the dairy, according to their occupations, or the activity by which they were designated institutionally: 1) experienced product assemblers; 2) inventory men and wholesale drivers; and 3) office workers. The fourth was built from ninth grade students at a nearby high school, none of whom had any knowledge of the dairy business or dairy product assembly.

With the three-level activity structure in mind, one way to understand the comparative logic of the simulation is as follows: the task – filling an order – is a goal-directed action within the activity of product assembly. Modeling this goal-directed action in the simulation, then, one can compare different ways through which this task is successfully fulfilled by other subjects who typically participate in activities other than that of which this goal-directed action is a part.

The order-filling task simulation was constructed with facsimile order forms in an assembly area that held cases and empty paper containers (simulating quart units and pint units only). In each display were a full, an empty, and a partial case whose number of units varied from trial to trial. Each subject went to the assembly area, received an order form, and was asked to fill the order. Each subject solved ninety order-filling problems over two sessions.

A coding scheme was derived from the "least physical effort" hypothesis so that it would be possible to count the "operations hypothetically required to convert literal to non-literal optimal solutions [those that require least physical effort]" (p. 12). The greater the number of such operations, the greater the mental difficulty. In most cases, the optimal strategy was non-literal; however, there were some problems in which the literal solution was the most optimal. In all cases where optimal solutions were literal, product assemblers used optimal solutions. In 72% of the cases where the optimal solution was non-literal, they used optimal solutions. Inventory workers and wholesale drivers were less consistent, using an optimal solution in only 65% of those problems in which the non-literal solution was optimal. Office workers used non-literal solutions only 45% of the time on problems where these were optimal. High school students by contrast used non-literal solutions only on 25% of those problems for which non-literal solutions were optimal. In fact, their consistent use of literal strategies suggested to Scribner that a higher-order strategy – always use the literal solution – was at work in their performance, and, in the context of this particular task, does not bear out the least physical effort hypothesis.

The comparison of groups that were differentiated on the basis of the task environments with which they normally participated, enabled Scribner to draw connections between the material properties of the simulation task and the intellectual strategies the product assemblers brought to it. Insofar as product assemblers used certain solution strategies to a greater degree than other groups in the context of the simulation, and since the simulation modeled concrete features of the product assembly task environment, a case could be made that these solution strategies, and the higher-order strategy which compelled their varied uses, arise on the basis of the product assemblers' practice in such environments. The "hallmark of expert problem-solving", Scribner wrote, "lay in the fact that the experienced worker was able to use specific dairy and job-related knowledge to generate flexible and economical solution procedures. Expert problem-solving procedures were content-infused, not content-free" (p. 39). While the least physical effort principle structures the solution strategies developed by workers, and, in that sense the product assemblers' expertise was adaptive in nature, such expertise is best construed as both adaptive and creative. Adaptation is manifested in workers' creations of new solutions and strategies. That such creations speak to institutionally given functional job requirements and resources makes it possible to characterise the trajectory of product assemblers' problem-solving as a path from the identification of a solution to the creation of a problem.

IV   Discussion: interpretive studies of cognitive life

We began with the aim of pointing to studies whose methodological strategies suggest ways of mapping quantitative modes of representation onto social and cognitive phenomena – ways that pursue rather than preempt principles of interpretive studies of cognitive life. The comparison of literacy groups solving a rebus task (in the Vai study) and the comparison of occupational groups solving an order-filling task (in the dairy study) were our examples. In these cases, the relation between simulation, comparison, and theory has a significant place in the methodology, and quantification serves as a useful tool. This relation is the focus of our attention in this concluding section.

The researchers both on Vai literacy and on the product assembly task drew heavily on the theoretical foundations of Vygotsky, particularly his mediational theory of mind and his application of historical materialism to problems of psychology. Explicit references to Vygotskian theory in each research report suggest that this Vygotskian framework drew heavily on very particular features of Marx's writings. Instances where Marx and/or Engels focused on species reproduction or the transformation of human nature through labor appear to have been particularly strong influences on Vygotsky's views on the substantive organization of mind. Perhaps these particular features of Marxist thought seemed most relevant to the concerns of psychology, such as it was in Vygotsky's day. For example, in *Mind in Society* (an important point of departure for both studies considered here) it is noted that Vygotsky followed Engels' emphasis on the "critical role of labor and tools in transforming the relation between human beings and their environment". (John-Steiner & Souberman, 1978) Along this line of reasoning, Vygotsky

> argued that the effect of tool use upon humans is fundamental not only because it has helped them relate more effectively to their external environment but also because tool use has had important effects upon internal and functional relationships within the human brain.
>
> (Ibid.: 132–133)

This perspective provided a starting point from which many contemporary researchers who have drawn on Vygotsky frame interpretive studies of cognitive life. Thus, we note these passages not only to situate the examples of "mixed methods" provided here in a particular theoretical trajectory, but also to note that this trajectory derives from specific understandings of Marxian theory as it was transformed by Vygotsky into a basis from which to articulate the direction of psychological theory.

An implicit hypothesis and an explanatory burden flow from such a Vygotskian project. The hypothesis concerns the substantive consequences of the psychological subject's participation in historically specific social activities. The burden is to bear out this hypothesis empirically and to specify the logic of the subject's participation and consequent transformation ("development"), so construed.

In this Vygotskian framework, "tool" is a relational construct in the sense that an object becomes a tool in virtue of the kind and degree of its instrumentality vis-à-vis any goal or objective. In this sense, all manner of "things" can serve as tools – from literacy to the representational features of script, and from the organization of milk bottles to the concept of "a case". Within this framework of understanding, tools as such may be framed as cultural resources and, effectively, as levers of transformation (or development.) Thus, when we have suggested that researchers in the two studies observed "naturally occurring" phenomena (e.g., naturally occurring uses of the Vai script; naturally occurring order-filling strategies in the dairy) the meaning of "natural" has been quite peculiar. It is to refer to the practices predicated on subjects' ongoing construction of their situations, situations that have been made over time (see also Lave, 1988). The idea is that these practices are not induced by, but found by, the researcher at a particular point in history. Having come upon these practices, the researcher then aims to represent their cultural-historical integrity.

In both studies considered here, simulation was adopted as a method through which to answer specific questions about the relations between cultural resources and the research subjects' cognitive development. However, while each of these efforts highlights transformation or development, the scoring of performances on simulation tasks serves to characterize subjects at a given point in time – the time of the simulation. This snapshot of the subjects in time implicitly assumes that particular developmental processes have occurred prior to the time of the simulation, on the basis of that subject group's appropriation of the cultural resources bound to particular activities (known via field studies to characterize certain subject groups' practices.) The simulation, in each case, models those activities, and their concomitant cultural resources, and attempts to specify whether certain cultural resources have had developmental consequences for the subjects whose practices they have typically characterized outside the context of the simulation. In this sense, while in each case at least four subject groups are compared, the researchers can be said to have been directly targeting the performances on simulated tasks of only one group: Vai literates, in one case, and product assemblers, in the other. The performances of the other groups serve as foils insofar as they may mark the kinds of performances brought to the simulated task by persons whose typical cultural resources are *different* from those of the targeted group and that are modeled in the simulation. In each case, quantification turns on a common-sense assumption that frequency and regularity in performances or behaviors indicate something. Note that this assumption can be manifested in both quantitative descriptions and descriptions by natural language. What ultimately gives meaning to such frequency and regularity, however, is the logic of the relations between performances and the conditions under which they occur. It is this relation that takes different forms and is structured by the theoretical principles that the methodology utilizing quantification (or natural languages) aims to reflect. In this sense, the snapshot of development garnered through comparison of groups on simulation tasks serves as a *medium for asking questions about the consequences of history for cognitive life*. The role of history, and the relation between history and cultural resources modeled in simulations is, we believe, what most characterize these approaches as interpretive.

References

Bartlett, Sir F. (1958). *Thinking*. New York: Basic Books.
Cole, M. (1996). *Cultural psychology a once and future discipline*. Cambridge, MA: The Belknap Press of Harvard University Press.
Cole, M., Gay, J., Glick, J. A., & Sharp, D. W. (1971). *The cultural context of learning and thinking*. New York: Basic Books.

Danzinger, K. (1990). *Constructing the subject: The historical origins of psychological research*. Cambridge: Cambridge University Press.

Erickson, F. (1986). Qualitative methods in research on teaching. *Handbook of research on teaching* (3rd ed., M. C. Wittrock, Ed., pp. 119–161). New York: Macmillan Publishing Company.

Gay, J., & Cole, M. (1967). *The new mathematics and old culture*. New York: Holt, Rinehart & Winston.

Goethe, J. W. von (1988). *Faust: Part I* (P. Wayne, Trans.). London: Penguin.

Goody, J. (1987). *The interface between the oral and the written*. Cambridge: Cambridge University Press.

Hutchins, E. (1995). *Cognition in the wild*. Cambridge, MA: MIT Press.

John-Steiner, V., & Souberman, E. (1978). Afterward. In M. Cole, S. Scribner, E. Souberman, & V. John-Steiner (Eds.), *Mind in society* (pp. 121–133). Cambridge, MA: Harvard University Press.

Lave, J. (1988). *Cognition in practice*. Cambridge: Cambridge University Press.

Mehan, H., & Wood, H. (1975). *The reality of ethnomethodology*. New York: Wiley.

Newell, A. & Simon, H. A. (1972). *Human problem solving*. Englewood Cliffs, NJ: Prentice-Hall.

Piaget, J. (1950). *The psychology of intelligence*. New York: Harcourt, Brace & Jovanovich.

Ratner, C. (1997). *Cultural psychology and qualitative methodology: Theoretical and empirical considerations*. New York: Plenum.

Reder, S. (1981). The written and the spoken word. In S. Scribner, & M. Cole, *The psychology of literacy*. Cambridge, MA: Harvard University Press.

Schütz, A. (1962). *Collected papers I: The problem of social reality*. The Hague: Martinus-Nijhoff.

Scribner, S. (1984). Cognitive studies of work. *Quarterly Newsletter of the Laboratory of Comparative Human Cognition*. January/April, 6, Nos 1 and 2, pp. 1–50.

Scribner, S. (1986). Thinking in action: Some characteristics of practical thought. In R. J. Sternberg, & R. K. Wagner (Eds.), *Practical intelligence: The nature and origins of competence in the everyday world*. Cambridge: Cambridge University Press.

Scribner, S., & Cole, M. (1981). *The psychology of literacy*. Cambridge, MA: Harvard University Press.

Vygotsky, L. (1962). *Thought and language*. Cambridge, MA: MIT Press.

Vygotsky, L. (1978). *Mind in society* (Ed. M. Cole, S. Scribner, E. Souberman, & V. John-Steiner). Cambridge, MA: Harvard University Press.

Webster (1966). 3rd International Dictionary (unabridged).

9 Integrating survey and focus group research

A case study of attitudes of English and German language learners

Zazie Todd and Margarita Lobeck

One reason for using different methods in the same study can be to provide triangulation of your results. The use of multiple methods is only one form of triangulation, but is perhaps the most commonly used. If you arrive at the same results with both of your methods, then it gives increased confidence that the results you have found are genuine, and reflect something real about the topic under study, rather than an artefact of the method chosen. The different methods used could be any, but often involve one qualitative and one quantitative method. What do you do, then, if you design two studies using different methodologies to look at the same question, and they apparently produce quite different results? This chapter is a study of just such a case. The topic under investigation was the effects of second language acquisition on attitudes and stereotypes, and involved asking learners and non-learners of English and German a batch of questions about their views of Britain and Germany.

First, some background to the case. British attitudes towards Germans appear very much to be rooted in our recent cultural history, with frequent reference to the Second World War. A report in *Psychologie Heute* (Kerber, 1998) finds that the British think of Germans as aggressive and humourless, and have stuck with stereotypes which have no validity (such as ideas about Germans being as industrious as ants). On the other hand, Kerber says German attitudes to the British are more positive, with the Brits being seen as "polite, conservative and chaotic". There is no shortage of stereotypes of Germans in the British media. The *Fawlty Towers* sketch in which Basil Fawlty repeatedly reminds himself "don't mention the war" (and fails) is still current today, and Cumberbatch (1992) found that the war is a frequently used theme in the British media. Husemann (1992) found similar tendencies of nostalgia for a time when Britain was seen as a powerful and united nation in his investigation into the Colditz war escape story. This study was designed to investigate whether language learning and exposure to the other nation would have an effect on Anglo-German stereotyping and attitudes.

Living in a foreign culture involves not just learning the other language, but also adapting to a new environment. It is not just the language per se that is different, but the cultural rules which govern interactions. Furnham (1994) argues that anyone who encounters a new culture undergoes a culture shock which Oberg (1960: 176) describes as ". . . reaction of loss of familiar social environment with all its rules and routines. . . . For example to know how to apologise, when to shake hands, etc. . . . in short, the loss to talk to people that make sense". Furnham (1993) compared people who are new to a culture to people who are socially unskilled. They are individuals who are unsatisfactory in expressing attitudes, feelings and emotions appropriately, making errors in ritualised routines such as greetings, self-disclosure, and making or refusing requests. Since most of these individuals are highly skilled in their own cultures, they find this sudden incompetence in the new culture particularly frustrating.

There are individual differences in adapting to a new culture, and while some people will identify with the new culture and language very quickly, others might never overcome these language and culture barriers (Cleveland, Margone, & Adams, 1963). The integration may also depend on the person's attitude towards the new culture and language. Gardner (1980) found that positive attitudes and a high level of motivation facilitate second language acquisition. It is probably a two-way relationship with attitudes and motivation influencing second language acquisition, and vice versa.

Few studies have compared Britain and Germany on the basis of culture and language. Cooper and Kirkcaldy's (1995) study of stereotyping between German and British managers suggests there are some perceived unique characteristics. Germans were perceived as being more industrious, meticulous, structured, workaholic and threatening, and less accepting, open and humorous, than their British colleagues. While these attitudes will to some extent reflect in-group favouritism, it has been shown that social reality also plays a role in determining stereotypes of other nations (Poppe & Linssen, 1999).

Politeness appears to be an important stumbling block for Anglo-German relations. Göldner (1988) examined the phenomenon of "politeness" in the English language, and found that Germans seemed to have particular difficulties in the appropriate use of linguistic features such as politeness and indirectness. The most common mistakes were being too direct in a request situation, misuse of standardised phrases such as greetings, and ignoring politeness markers such as "please". This last mistake in particular could make the learner appear to be abrupt and unfriendly. This is supported by Stubbs (1983) who found that native speakers may not realise that a linguistic mistake has been made by the foreigner, but instead perceive it as the speaker being impolite or blunt. This helps to explain the difficulty or even impossibility of mapping one language frame onto the other. The language learner has to understand that speaking another language is also speaking another culture. Therefore s/he has to learn that, for example, the words "please" and "sorry" have different cultural meanings compared to the German "bitte" and "Entschuldigung"/"tut mir leid".

This study aimed to investigate contemporary Anglo-German attitudes, both amongst those who had some experience of the other language and culture, and those who had none. It was hypothesised that British attitudes towards Germany would reflect stereotypes of Germans as more aggressive and industrious, whereas the Germans would see Britons as conservative and polite. It was also expected that ability in the second language and length of time spent in the other country would improve attitudes and reduce stereotyping. It was a mixed method study, with an initial quantitative component followed by a focus group with a sub-set of the participants.

Study One: Quantitative

The survey approach

We briefly describe this work in the following sections.

Participants

The participants were 146 adults (59 British, 87 German) who agreed, when approached, to take part in the study. All were born after the Second World War, and the mean age was 23. In order to avoid a student-only population, participants were recruited from a range of backgrounds. Overall, 79 were female and 67 male.

Apparatus and material

A questionnaire was first designed in English and then translated into German, so that it could be presented to participants in their mother tongue. The translated version was proofread by two native speakers of German to check its suitability in both languages. The questionnaire was in three parts. Part I concerned personal details and second language acquisition. The questions about motivation and language anxiety were mainly obtained from Gardner (1985). Part II dealt with topics such as culture, integration process, and attitude towards the host country and its inhabitants. The 30 adjectives used to describe people and nation were mainly obtained from Linssen and Hagendoorn (1994). The added adjectives were: class-oriented, conservative, progressive, dominant, ecological, emotional, pro-European, anti-European, funny, polite, serious, and xenophobic. Participants were asked to respond, depending on the question, either by ticking the appropriate box or by indicating their position on a Likert-scale from 1 to 5, with 1 meaning "strongly agree", "very similar", or "regular contact", and 5 meaning the opposite. Part III was concerned with participants' attitudes to their own countries, and largely mirrored Part II.

Design

Participants were divided into four groups, depending on their nationality and place of residency at the time of the study: Group I was 30 Britons living in Britain; Group II was 29 British people who were staying in Germany at the time of the study; Group III was 50 German people living in Germany; Group IV was 37 German people who were staying in Britain at the time of the study (in each case, staying means for a length of time of at least six months).

Procedure

A total of 120 questionnaires were sent out to Germany (60 in English and 60 in German, for British and German participants respectively) and 120 distributed in Britain (again, for both British and German participants). Out of the 240 questionnaires, 146 (61%) were returned. Participants were assured of the anonymity and confidentiality of their responses. A short introduction to the questionnaire stated that the project was looking at Anglo-German attitudes, and a paragraph at the end thanked them for their time and asked for volunteers to take part in a follow-up interview.

Results

The data from all the questionaires was amalgamated, with own and foreign country answers being considered as separate for the first part of the analysis. This led to N = 292 responses (2 × 146), considering nationality/country of residence as not important for this part of the analysis.

Table 9.1 shows the mean response and standard deviation for British attitudes to Germany and German attitudes to Britain.

Tests for homogeneity of variance (<7.7), skew (<±3) and kurtosis (<±14) of the variables showed no violations. A principal components factor analysis was performed using SPSSx. Five factors were extracted from the data after a varimax rotation. Table 9.2 shows the loadings for each factor extracted in the analysis.

The first factor (t = 13.37, df = 139, p) was named **"Nation"** and included "economical and political powerful", "prosperous", "pro-European", "industrialised", "progressive", "directed at equality between women and men", "clean and orderly", "ecological", "democratic", "rich" (eigenvalue 7.63; factor loadings from .77 to .42).

The second factor (t = 6.73, df = 140, p<0.01) was titled **"Dominance"** and included "dominant", "aggressive", "egoistic", "competitive", "independent", "xenophobic" (eigenvalue 3.21; factor loadings from .79 to .44).

Factor 3 (t = 6.74, df = 140, p<0.01) was named **"Courtesy"** and clustered the following items: "polite", "conservative", "friendly", "proud", "class oriented" (eigenvalue 2.53; factor loadings ranging from .66 to .53).

Factor 4 (t = −3.61, df=139, p<0.01) was named **"Emotion"** and included

Table 9.1 Means and standard deviations for the variables

Variables	British perceptions of Germans		German perception of British	
	Means	SD	Means	SD
aggressive	2.71	1.12	3.39	0.99
class oriented	3.42	1.02	2.31	1.07
competitive	2.05	0.93	2.93	0.81
conservative	2.63	0.85	2.11	0.80
democratic	2.12	0.74	2.72	0.84
dominant	2.30	0.95	3.28	0.80
economical and political powerful	1.56	0.77	2.83	0.86
ecological	2.05	1.02	4.02	0.81
egoistic	2.70	1.04	3.26	0.81
emotional	3.45	0.93	3.15	0.87
enjoy life	2.86	1.13	2.55	0.92
directed at equality between women and men	2.66	1.01	3.00	0.90
pro-European	1.78	0.79	3.89	0.81
friendly	2.54	0.76	2.01	0.83
funny	3.43	1.13	2.64	0.78
honest	2.51	0.79	2.73	0.82
independent	2.40	0.95	2.73	0.90
industrialised	1.78	0.87	1.92	0.75
intelligent	2.41	0.71	2.83	0.71
orderly and clean	1.81	0.78	2.90	1.00
polite	3.02	1.11	1.78	0.81
progressive	2.07	0.87	3.10	0.85
prosperous	1.69	0.84	2.99	0.93
proud	2.14	0.90	2.12	0.99
religious	3.21	0.84	3.20	0.91
rich	2.64	0.75	3.54	0.86
scientific	2.40	0.73	3.15	0.79
serious	2.00	0.91	3.14	0.80
xenophobic	2.95	1.01	3.25	0.97

the items "enjoying life", "funny", "emotional" (eigenvalue 1.49; factor loadings ranging from .72 to .62).

The fifth factor ($t = 6.49$, df = 137, p<0.01) was named **"Intellect"** and included the items "serious", "honest", "religious", "scientific" and "intelligent" (eigenvalue 1.32; factor loadings ranging from .58 to .45). A total of 53.9% of the variance was explained (KMO = .87; Bartlett = .01).

Means and standard deviations for each factor are shown in Table 9.2. Since the investigation was focusing on what participants thought of the other country, two-tailed t-tests were carried out for each factor on these views. The Germans perceived the British as lower on the Nation factor than the British perceived the Germans ($t = 13.37$, df=139, p<.01). This means that Britain

Table 9.2 Means and standard deviations for the five factors

	Britain	Germany
Factor 1: Nation		
British participants	22.62 (4.17)	28.55 (4.61)
German participants	22.86 (3.52)	29.15 (3.92)
Factor 2: Dominance		
British participants	15.05 (4.13)	17.21 (3.30)
German participants	13.96 (3.33)	18.94 (2.87)
Factor 3: Courtesy		
British participants	13.70 (2.31)	11.13 (2.59)
German participants	14.45 (2.72)	10.34 (3.16)
Factor 4 (Emotion)		
British participants	7.70 (2.50)	9.24 (3.33)
German participants	8.22 (2.20)	9.07 (1.72)
Factor 5: Intellect		
British participants	14.93 (3.88)	11.98 (3.20)
German participants	14.71 (2.98)	13.75 (2.58)

was perceived as less "economical and powerful", "prosperous", "pro-European", "industrialised", "progressive", "directed at equality between women and men", "clean and orderly", "ecological", "rich", and "democratic" than Germany. Similarly, the Germans perceived the British significantly lower than the British perceived the Germans on the Dominance factor ("dominant", "aggressive", "egoistic", "competitive", "independent", "xenophobic") (t = 6.73, df = 140, p<.01). Britain was also ranked significantly lower than Germany on the Intellect dimension ("serious", "honest", "religious", "scientific" and "intelligent"). However, Britain was rated significantly higher than Germany on the Courtesy dimension ("polite", "conservative", "friendly", "proud" and "class-oriented") (t = 6.74, df = 140, p<.01). Britain was also rated significantly higher than Germany on the Emotion dimension ("enjoying life", "funny" and "emotional") (t = −3.61, df = 139, p<.01).

A multiple stepwise regression was performed to examine the effect of the variables "duration of longest visit", "there now", "level of contact with native speakers", "standard of language ability" and "country of origin" on ratings of the other country. The five factors were combined to one factor ("total") as the dependent variable, and the participants' autocorrelations were not included in the regression. The regression equation showed only "country of origin" to be a significant predictor of the dependent variable (Multiple R = 0.74, r^2 = 0.54, adjusted r = 0.54, beta = −0.74. Country of origin ($F_{(1,133)}$ = 157.43, p<.01) accounted for 54% of the variance.

Study Two: Qualitative

The focus group approach

Participants

Ten participants (six German and four English) from the questionnaire study also took part in a follow-up focus group interview. The participants were chosen because they were experienced in their second language ability and in their knowledge of the other country. The interview took place in England, and so the group only included participants who were resident in England at the time of the study.

Apparatus and materials

The interview was both video and audio taped and later transcribed. Analysis was carried out using NUD•IST software.

Design

The group was selected so that all participants were experienced in the other language and other culture. The Germans had all lived in Britain for at least five months prior to the group interview, and all had regular contact with English-speaking people. The British people had all spent at least a month in Germany in the recent past. The interview was carried out by a German bilingual (ML), and participants were told they could speak in either language, although in practice most of the time the conversation was conducted in English.

Procedure

All participants signed a consent form prior to the start of the discussion, which was both audio and video taped. The interviewer gave a short introductory speech telling participants about some of the findings of the questionnaires and explaining the procedure for the focus group. The discussion was opened with a question about stereotypes. Other topics discussed were ecology, politeness vs. bluntness, learning about the other culture, Europe, East- and West-Germans, change of attitude, family life, student culture, friendship, living in the other country, housing, humour, class system and education. The interview lasted 1 hr 50 mins. The interview was then transcribed for a content analysis, along with the many written comments on the questionnaire.

Results

In this section, rather than present the results in full, we will concentrate on those aspects that are linked to the quantitative results. We will also focus on the interview with experienced language learners, as many of the comments written on the questionnaires are outside the scope of this chapter. The main finding was that participants in the group expressed the opinion that spending time in the other country and getting to know the language and people had made a big difference to their attitudes and opinions about that country. They described the stereotypes they had before they went (the nationality of the participant is denoted by B – British and D – German):

> "When I went to Germany the stereotype I had was lots of beer and people in Lederhosen, and that's what I expected. And I saw lots of beer but I didn't see any Lederhosen unfortunately."
>
> (B; 59–61)

> "German people who expect them, English men, [to] look like bowler hat and umbrella."
>
> (D; 77–78)

It was suggested that participants' views had changed as a result of time spent in the other country, not just time in the classroom:

> "You can't really teach another nation about another nation . . . you have to live there."
>
> (D; 27–271)

> "You get definitely more open-minded that's for sure . . . yeah definitely it broadens your mind and you understand things better (. . .) you know more about different countries and cultures and you get a lot more tolerant as well I think."
>
> (D; 436–442).

Participants are describing not just how learning another language and living in that country affected their views of that country, but also how it broadened their minds in general. The implication is that as well as changing their feelings and attitudes towards the country whose language they have learnt, it has also changed their views on other countries in general. Thus, the change in behaviour is global, and not related only to the country they have spent time in.

As well as discussing this in general terms, the changes that language learning led to in their own behaviour were also highlighted:

> "I would agree (. . .) I got more open-minded (. . .) and also my, my own behaviour maybe changed that I became a little bit more restrained (. . .) to be more careful and polite I think."
>
> (D; 504–508)

The importance of face-to-face contact in (assisting) this change was stressed:

> "and it's only when you actually go and speak to German people or whatever nationality that is (. . .) you realise that you're actually all talking about the same things but might just be approaching them (.) in a slightly different way."
>
> (B; 519–523)

Participants also expressed the view that the changes in their outlook were a result of their own behaviour when they were in the other country; in other words, that they had sought out natives and made an effort to join in with local activities:

> "before when I saw erm foreign students who come to Germany and ah they all they they stayed together, they didn't, I mean they all said "Uh, all the Germans, they they don't want to be friendly with us". But they didn't really make the effort."
>
> (D; 547–551)

Here a participant is describing how he has seen foreign language-students visiting his own town in Germany and sticking closely together, and not really trying to get to know the locals. Although he says the visitors put the blame on the Germans, he is putting it down to their attitude and saying it is because they didn't really try. He then contrasts this with his own behaviour:

> "When I went to England, came over here for a year (.) I mean (. . .) obviously all the foreign people stayed together quite a bit but er, we we also had lots of English friends because we, we all experience it before from the other foreigners (. . .) so, I don't know if it's because we made the effort to do it."
>
> (D; 552–555).

Here he says that although he did stay with his own nationality to some extent, he also made lots of friends amongst the local people, and made the effort to do this. It was seen that this made quite a big difference to the kind of experience that learners had.

It would be expected that people who have become experienced in another language are so because they have put a lot of effort into it, and have persisted at making contact with the other language group. This does not mean that this group of learners have had an easy time of it; in fact they all described situations when they had felt awkward because of their lack of language ability:

> "Sometimes I feel here like a child between adults, I cannot understand what they are talking to each other."
>
> (D; 618–619)

An English participant described a similar experience in which:

"you felt really clumsy and awkward and (.) weird."

(B; 625–626)

This had wider implications beyond the actual language production and comprehension. For example,

"It's not only that that not being able to but it's also the sort of way you come across. If you're not fluent in a language, then your personality will not come through as much."

(B; 647–649)

In other words, limited ability in the language, as well as restricting what you can say, will affect your self-presentation. The language learner's personality will not come across the same way in their second language, and they may come across as lacking in humour or politeness, for example, when it is really their language that is deficient.

The concept of courtesy was raised by the interviewer, since it had featured as one of the factors in the quantitative analysis. Participants discussed differences in courtesy between the Germans and British, often linked to specific experiences that participants had had. One British participant illustrated this when she said:

"I had a friend who used to say (.) you look awful in that, your bum is too fat and no English person would ever really say that. They might say well (.) maybe you should wear something else kind of thing and they say a few things but she comes right out with it and obviously it has some good points and you know (.) that (.) you shouldn't really wear this. But it is quite upsetting this business I find."

(B; 248–252)

In contrast a German participant said:

"I knew [if] we asked somebody in Germany, in Germany "How are you?", we expect that you want to have small talk, but not simply "fine, how are you?". This kind of conversation is very very ritual . . . at the beginning you you start and you [question from other participant omitted] you expect to have some conversation or something like that. But the other person doesn't expect this (. . .) and this is very confusing."

(D; 168–178)

There seemed to be a general consensus amongst the participants that the British were more superficially polite, and the Germans more frank, but there were differences of opinion as to which was the best way to be. These comments are interesting because they relate to the quantitative results on "courtesy", in which the British were rated as more polite than the Germans. In the context of these comments, it would seem that there are different cultural norms, whereby the British use more politeness markers and try to remain polite on the surface, but that the Germans are more honest in their manner of expression and perhaps more sincere in their expression of sentiment. This is, of course, not the same thing as saying that one group is more polite than the other.

Discussion

The results of the quantitative analysis showed that there was no effect of language ability or time spent in the country on attitudes towards the other people/nation. On the other hand, participants in the group interview, who were all experienced speakers of the other language, strongly expressed a feeling that learning the language and visiting the country had had an impact on their beliefs and attitudes about that country/people. In particular, they said that it had made them more open-minded and culturally aware. They described stereotypes they had had before visiting the country, and said that these had changed. Interestingly, they said that they became more open-minded not just in their beliefs about the other country, but about other countries and peoples in general. In other words, the effect (as they described it) was not specific to the country they had experienced and learned about, but was much more general and applied in global terms to other countries and nationalities. Their experiences of feeling clumsy in the other language, and feeling that it affected them in terms of expression of personality as well as linguistically, are in line with previous research on second language acquisition (Furnham, 1993, 1994).

There is clearly a direct contrast between the results of the quantitative survey and the views expressed by participants in the interview: on the one hand, there is no evidence that ratings improved as language ability and cultural experience increased, but participants with high levels of ability and experience felt that their own opinions had changed considerably. This is interesting because the results of focus groups have often been described as comparable in many ways to those of surveys; indeed, this is one form of triangulation. Triangulation is supposed to increase confidence in results when studies using two methods have led to the same findings. Does that mean, then, that the results of one of these studies is wrong? And if so, how does one know whether to place one's confidence in the quantitative or qualitative data? In this section we will explore some of the possible reasons for the difference in findings and their implications.

It is of course the case that the quantitative survey captured a wide range of language abilities, whereas only those who were highly experienced were included in the interview procedure. It is theoretically possible that this group of experienced language users had changed their opinions over time, but that they were unusual in this respect and it isn't the case for language learners in general. However, there is nothing to indicate that, as far as experienced language learners go, there is anything unusual about this group. The manner in which they have learnt the language and the periods of time that they had spent abroad would appear to be typical for people who have gone on to study the language at university. Hence, this does not appear to be a likely explanation for the difference between the quantitative and qualitative results in this case. It does suggest, however, that it would be interesting to carry out longitudinal studies of language learners, following them through their language classes and periodically sampling their views to see if they change over time.

Another possibility might be that the experienced language learners had started with quite different views about the country and people from the rest of society, and then, as their language experience had increased, their views had moved to be more in line with those of people with no language experience. Since they said that their attitudes had improved, if this possibility were correct it would mean they had started off with unusually negative attitudes towards the country. This does not seem plausible, however, as such negative attitudes do not seem likely to lead people to learn a language

It is also possible that the measures used were too crude to show any differences in opinions. However, again there is no evidence to suggest this. The scales were adapted from previous studies by Linssen and Hagendoorn (1994), and Gardner (1985), and so have been used successfully before. Not only that, but differences were found in the quantitative results, showing that participants did have different impressions of the two countries; it was just that their language experience was not linked to these differences. So again, this is not a likely explanation for why the two sets of results did not appear to match up.

Another explanation could be that one method is preferable to the other, and leads to more honest responses from participants. How can this be assessed? In practice it is very difficult to investigate this possibility – short of asking participants in which study were they more honest, but if you have to ask that question, you cannot trust the response. The demand characteristics of the two studies can be considered. In the questionnaire study, participants completed the questionnaire in private. They did not have to tell anyone else what they had put, and they did not have to give their name unless they were willing to take part in a follow-up study; even then, the sheet of paper with their name was detached from the questionnaire by participants, and they were clearly informed that it would not be linked up with the quantitative results at all. So it would seem that the survey was conducted in such a way as to encourage participants to give honest responses.

In the interview, on the other hand, it was necessary for participants to speak their views in front of other people; although they were all asked to keep what was said in the interview confidential, they did have to voice their opinions in front of other participants. Not only that, but both nationalities were present in the interview. Hence, it is possible that participants modified their opinions in front of the other nationality, and that they felt they had to be polite about the other nation. Again, this is not backed up by the evidence. Participants were on occasion impolite about the other nationality and differences of opinion were expressed. Also, regardless of the opinions they expressed about the other nation itself, there would be no pressure on them to say that their opinions had improved as a result of language experience. Finally, participants of each nationality were present in sufficient number to give some feeling of safety in numbers. So there do not appear to be any reasons why participants would be more or less honest in the interview than in the questionnaire.

While the issue of self-presentational biases in responses to questionnaires has received considerable attention in psychology, far less attention has been paid to this issue in relation to interviews, and in particular to focus groups. An empirical comparison of individual interviews with focus groups (Kaplowitz, 2000) found that sensitive topics are much more likely to be raised in individual rather than group interviews. Kidd and Parshall (2000) make a number of helpful recommendations for enhancing the rigour of focus group research, but few comments on the data acquisition aspects. Further research on presentational issues in focus group research would be welcomed.

There is evidence from this study that participants have responded to questions in the survey and interview in different ways. The questions on the survey were general questions, and explicitly stated that they were talking about the other nation or other people *in general terms*. We know that participants have responded to them in this way, because a number of them wrote comments on the form that it was difficult to generalise, because there were always individual differences. A couple of participants expressed this view very strongly, saying that it was wrong to ask for general impressions because it only encouraged stereotyping. On the other hand, in the interview, although some general responses were given, it is also clear that participants have been talking about specific examples and specific people. Rather than just giving a general overview of the other country/people, they were thinking about specific experiences they had had, and linking their views to particular occurrences. Thus, in the part of the discussion relating to courtesy, we saw that as well as general comments (for example, the German participant who discussed the different implications of "how are you" in both countries), there are very specific comments about individual people (e.g. the friend who said "your bum is too fat"). Even in the discussion of "how are you", it seems that the generalisation is being drawn direct from personal experience, and of particular "how are you?" conversations with other people. This is not necessarily the case for survey responses, since it is possible they are drawn from general cultural viewpoints rather than generalisations of personal experience.

It would seem, then, that there is a difference in the way participants have responded in the two parts of the study. This could be explained by developments in social psychology, in which it has been argued that the idea of fixed attitudes is outdated; people's opinions and beliefs alter depending on the situation they are in and the context in which they are expressing themselves (e.g. Potter and Wetherell, 1987). Although we were not trying to tap into something fixed with the attitude scale, since we were expecting to find differences based on language experience, it is possible that it was nevertheless too fixed to show changes over time. It is also possible that when thinking in general terms, people fall back on cultural ideas and stereotypes more than when discussing individual cases. Cultural ideas and stereotypes were discussed in the interview, but they were usually identified as such and distinguished from personal experience. Although we have no way of knowing what participants were thinking when completing the survey, it is highly likely that it did not tap into personal experience in the same way. Although participants were asked to respond with their personal opinion, they will have completed the questionnaire relatively quickly, and not had time to reflect on their own experiences or remember particular instances. Some of these issues have also been considered in relation to research on distress by Massé (2000), whose findings led him to conclude that "qualitative and quantitative methodologies are incommensurable at the level of the finalities of the research but not on the basis of the methods as such" (p. 422).

In the interview, participants had to justify their opinions, which they didn't have to do with the questionnaire (although they were invited to write comments). Some people gave quite long descriptions of incidents or other things that they remembered, and accounts from one person often triggered off stories from another. This all took place in a friendly atmosphere, and so people were often encouraged by other participants to expand on their stories. Accounts from a participant in one country also often led to similar or related stories from a participant from the other, as when a reminiscence about the German countryside led into discussion of the English countryside. Thus, the discursive nature of the interview meant that participants were encouraged to talk about their own specific experiences.

In fact, the importance of these personal experiences can be seen in the discussion of courtesy. Here, the interview can be seen to explicate the quantitative results. Although the questionnaire would imply that there is a simple distinction between levels of politeness across the two countries, this is seen from the interview to be a *qualitative* difference, which reflects differing cultural norms. This ties in with previous research into differences in Anglo-German politeness (Göldner, 1988) and is not apparent at all from the questionnaire.

Another possibility that arises from this is that the interview could be used to devise a new questionnaire that, rather than focusing on general attributes of the two nations (useful those these may be in other circumstances), was tailored more specifically to the language learner's experience. Given the difference between experienced participants' perceptions of changes in their behaviour and views, of which they were able to give specific examples, it may be that language learning has changed their views in more subtle ways than can be found by focusing on general attributes. In other words, it may be that being a poor or beginning language learner is enough to experience apparent differences in politeness, and that it is only with more experience that these can be put into the context of differing cultural norms. Thus, the quantitative difference that was found may be experienced by poor and experienced learners alike, but the qualitative differences may only become apparent with greater exposure and cultural sensitivity. Further research, with a greater number of language learners, would be needed to investigate this hypothesis.

In conclusion, then, the questionnaire study showed that five factors, relating to Nation, Dominance, Courtesy, Emotion and Intellect, accounted for participants' views on the two nations. Although differences were found on some of these factors, they were related only to participants' nationality, and their level of language experience and time spent in the other country did not have an effect. However, in the interview, experienced language learners said that their views had changed as a result of the language experience, and in particular that they had become more open-minded towards other countries and peoples in general as a result. This appears to set the qualitative and quantitative results in opposition. However, as the discussion of the results relating to "courtesy" has shown, it is possible to explain the quantitative differences in terms of a qualitative one. It would be possible to use this (and further) qualitative interviews to develop more specific hypotheses about the effects of language learning on the self. Thus, greater integration of quantitative and qualitative methods could lead to better development of theory and of specific applications of the findings to language learning.

References

Cleveland, H., Margone, C., & Adams, J. (1963). *The overseas Americans*. New York: McGraw-Hill.

Cooper, C., & Kirkcaldy, B. D. (1995). Executive stereotyping between cultures: The British vs. German manager. *Journal of Managerial Psychology*, *10*, (1), 3–6.

Cumberbatch, G. (1992). The portrayal of Germany in the media. In D. Balance (Ed.), *Anglo-German attitudes – how do we see each other?* London: Goethe-Institute.

Furnham, A. (1993). Communication in foreign lands: the cause, consequence and cures of culture shock. *Language, Culture and Curriculum*, *6*, 11–17.

Furnham, A. (1994). Communicating in foreign lands. In M. Byran (Ed.), *Culture and language learning in higher education* (pp. 91–109), Cleveland: Multilingual Matters.

Gardner, R. C. (1980). On the validity of affective variables in second language acquisition: Conceptual, contextual and statistical implications. *Language Learning*, *30*, 255–270.

Gardner, R. C. (1985). *Social psychology and second language learning: The role of attitudes and motivation*. London: Edward Arnold.

Göldner, B. (1988). *Höflichkeit im englischsprachigen Dialog (Untersuchungen zu Ausdrucksmitteln und Lerndefiziten)*. Unpublished PhD thesis, University of Potsdam.

Husemann, H. (1992). The Colditz industry. In D. Balance (Ed.), *Anglo-German attitudes – how do we see each other?* London: Goethe-Institute.

Kaplowitz, M. D. (2000). Statistical analysis of sensitive topics in group and individual interviews. *Quality and Quantity, 34*: 419–431.

Kerber, W. (1998). Hitler, Klinsman, Mataus. Don't know any other footballer. *Psychologie Heute* 2/1998, 30–35.

Kidd, P. S., & Parshall, M. B. (2000). Getting the focus and getting the group: Enhancing analytical rigor in focus group research. *Qualitative Health Research, 10*: 293–308.

Linssen, H., & Hagendoorn, L. (1994). Social and geographical factors in the explanation of the content of European nationality stereotypes. *British Journal of Social Psychology, 33*, 165–182.

Massé, R. (2000). Qualitative and quantitative analyses of psychological distress: Methodological complementarity and ontological incommensurability. *Qualitative Health Research, 10*: 411–423.

Oberg, K. (1960). Culture shock: Adjustment to new cultural environments. *Practical Anthropology, 7*, 177–182.

Poppe, E., & Linssen, H. (1999). In-group favouritism and the reflection of realistic dimensions of difference between national states in Central and Eastern European nationality stereotypes. *British Journal of Social Psychology, 38*, 85–102.

Potter, J. & Wetherell, M. (1987). *Discourse and Social Psychology*, London: Sage.

Stubbs, M. (1983). *Discourse analysis: The sociolinguistic analysis of natural language.* Oxford: Blackwell.

Part IV
Mixing methods within the discipline

10 Educational psychology and difficult pupil behaviour

Qualitative, quantitative or mixed methods?

Andy Miller

Introduction

A topic of recurring public concern is the behaviour of children and young people in schools. Although historical studies (e.g. Humphries, 1981) suggest that this may not be the recent phenomenon that current accounts suggest, media headlines and pronouncements from various political sources certainly create an impression of a problem which is contemporary, escalating and resistant to solution.

Various psychological (and other) perspectives have informed research efforts in this area, from the highly constructionist view of "deviance" as a negotiated entity within educational institutions, which also reflect a wider stratified society (Sharp and Green, 1975), through to surveys which treat pupil "behaviours" as discrete and quantifiable entities (Wheldall and Merrett, 1988). Although of central concern to professional educational psychologists (EPs), pupil behaviour in schools has not been a topic that has attracted a substantial or coherent body of research within the discipline of psychology itself. Instead, research within sociology, psychiatry, education and psychology have all contributed studies, introducing an inevitable diversity of methodologies, with no clear pattern of quantitative and qualitative studies emerging within or between different discipline boundaries.

In an attempt to clarify this diversity, this chapter will present a brief and selective review of the literature. Within the quantitative tradition, surveys, single case designs, and multi-factorial process-product designs have all been employed. Methods deriving from a qualitative perspective, on the other hand, have included ethnomethodological and ethological studies and "clinical" case studies. These various methodologies and discipline bases are illustrated in Figure 10.1, which is, in itself, an attempt to bring some coherence to the study of pupil behaviour in school.

Manicas and Secord (1983) have distinguished the task of the scientist from that of the clinician or technician in terms of the former practising science by creating at least partially closed systems, and the latter using the discoveries of science, but also employing a great deal of knowledge that extends beyond science in order to bring about changes in the everyday

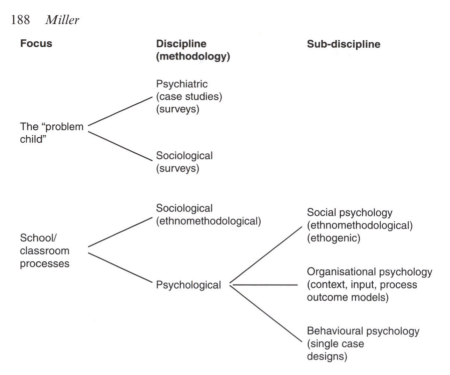

Figure 10.1 Studies of pupil behaviour in schools by focus, discipline and methodology. From Miller & Todd (2002). *Educational and Child Psychology*, *19*(3). Leicester: The British Psychological Society.

world. These authors are at pains to point out that this principle defines respective roles more clearly, but certainly has no unfavourable connotations for either side.

Within the "technician" or "clinical" role, EPs, alongside teachers, pupils, parents and policy makers, are engaged in the daily tasks of educational realities, including making sense of, and responding to a proportion of pupils whose behaviour is considered by others to be challenging and unacceptable. It is in these contexts that EPs attempt to act as scientist-practitioners, bridging the gap between educational policies and practices and the research community. This chapter is therefore particularly concerned with research across this divide – the contribution to educational practice that psychology as a discipline is able to make, the potential "sticking points" in these applications, and the richness of research possibilities that this area of work offers.

Following the review of illustrative studies, the author's own research into successful consultations between EPs and teachers is presented. This study employed a quantitative, followed by a qualitative approach, reversing what Rosenthal and Rosnow (1991) saw as the "empirical snobbishness" sometimes implicit in the qualitative–quantitative sequence of studies. In such a sequence, one approach may be seen as being preparatory for the other, usually a qualitative approach, with its more exploratory nature, being seen as suited to unearthing leads and hunches that can then be more methodically and rigorously followed up via a subsequent experimental study. The problem with the qualitative–quantitative sequence, argues Bryman (1984), is that it places qualitative approaches on a "lower rung of the epistemological ladder", serving only to provide "fodder for quantitative researchers".

In the author's study, an attempt was made to investigate successful professional collaborations involving the application of behavioural psychology by means of a survey of EPs. Frequencies and correlational data were extracted from the questionnaire returns – in essence, a quantitative methodology applied to an area of practice with its own firmly positivist theoretical roots. However, for practitioners, this research not only failed to answer the most intriguing questions around successful practice but also, in fact, seemed to add to the research agenda by providing tantalising glimpses of further, less explored and central features of effective professional collaboration.

Manicas and Secord (1983) have criticised the social sciences, and psychology in particular, not for attaching themselves to science per se, but for drawing on a philosophy of science that is outmoded and mistaken. Manicas and Secord (1983) have argued that social sciences, unlike physical sciences, operate in an open system and, therefore, explanations, to be complete, need to range across a range of theories from the physiological to the socioeconomic. Similarly, Scarr (1985) has argued that hierarchical models of nested theories are required to understand fully behavioural phenomena – "Different levels of analysis do not compete. Each lower level is a constituent of the next higher, and in no sense can one account for the others." She goes on to argue that theoretical development is likely to be enhanced through research that deliberately crosses layers of stratification – "pitting proximal and distal variables against each other in competing models can enrich our theoretical lives".

Given the wide range of levels of analysis to which "problem pupil behaviour in schools" has been subjected (see Figure 10.1), and the insubstantial nature of the results from the survey, a method for "nesting" the investigation of successful professional practice more within psychological, sociological and educational theoretical formulations, appeared to be required. Because of its capacity to incorporate a wide range of theoretical constructs and because the survey had drawn attention to social complexities surrounding consultations between EPs and teachers, a grounded theory approach was selected as a means of extending the investigation. It was judged that such an approach would be capable of addressing this complexity whilst at the same time employing methods and results open to scrutiny. The outcome satisfied the criteria for a quality grounded theory (Strauss & Corbin, 1998) and provided new insights with implications for practitioners, thus justifying the adoption of the *quantitative–qualitative* sequence employed.

In the light of the findings, new questions inevitably arise for both researchers and practitioners, and the chapter concludes by clarifying the focus for future research in this area – research that should profit from the application of deliberately mixed methods.

The role of professional educational psychologists

Currently around 2500 professionally qualified EPs are employed by local education authorities in the United Kingdom, with a much smaller number operating in a private capacity. Training as an educational psychologist currently requires psychology graduates to work for at least two years as qualified teachers and to complete a recognised professional training course at Masters level. Within a local authority employment base, educational psychologists carry out a range of tasks, predominantly acting as consultants to schools in respect of pupils who, for a variety of reasons, have difficulty in easily accessing the opportunities for academic, social and emotional development afforded by schools.

Recent legislation has consolidated for educational psychologists a long-standing trend in practice away from clinic-based work and towards co-operative endeavours with teachers in schools. In particular, a major set of statutory duties (Department for Education and Skills, 2001) require schools to identify and attempt to meet the special educational needs of particular pupils. If unsuccessful, schools are required to seek advice from educational psychologists, either in terms of developing further "psycho-educational" strategies or in making multi-professional assessments of the needs of pupils.

Pupils whose behaviour is perceived by school staff to be challenging or unmanageable, represent a considerable proportion of the "caseload" of many educational psychologists and it is to psychological and educational research that these professionals look in order to support their collaborative activities with schools.

Within this taxonomy, a primary distinction is made between studies and approaches that basically focus upon the "problem child" or the "difficult pupil" and those that concern themselves with school and classroom processes, including wider societal issues that are represented within schools. Of course, some of the latter, which are located within sociological and social psychological paradigms, view the construct of "difficult behaviour" as being problematic in itself. Whilst recognising the validity of constructionist approaches to "deviance" within schools, this chapter will, solely for ease of exposition, discuss "problem behaviour" in most sections as though an "entity" located in the external world.

Studies focused upon the "problem child"

Psychiatric perspectives

A classic case study account within a psychoanalytic paradigm was provided by Axline (1964) in *Dibs: In search of self*. Although strictly outside the concerns of this chapter because the young person "Dibs" was displaying autistic behaviour, rather than more common forms of unmanageable school behaviour, this study is particularly important in that its account of therapeutic work exemplifies such practice and was widely read by a generation of teachers in training, leading to a common perception – many would argue a misperception – among the teaching profession of the possible contribution of psychology to educational concerns.

Another major contribution from the psychiatric perspective came in the form of the *Isle of Wight study*, carried out by Rutter, Tizard, and Whitmore (1970). In these cross-sectional studies of children's health, behaviour and scholastic attainments and adjustment across whole geographical areas, surveys were combined with psychiatric interviews for a smaller subsample. Many important relationships between the variables investigated were established in these studies, and the incidence findings for a range of childhood problems continue to form one of the bases for current legal and policy formulations covering the extent of provision for pupils with special educational needs.

A third study (Kolvin, Garside, Nicol, Macmillan, Wolstenholme, & Leitch, 1981), originating within a psychiatric tradition and widely considered the largest and most ambitious British study of its type – involving around 4300 children in 12 schools – examined the relative effectiveness of three forms of intervention with "maladjusted" children attending mainstream schools. One treatment approach was psychodynamic in orientation, while the second derived from a behavioural approach. The third consisted of parent counselling and teacher consultation. Pupils were randomly assigned to the three treatments and a no-contact control group. The results for this study were complex, as might be expected from the nature of the interventions, the design and size of the sample. However, it was possible to demonstrate that therapeutic interventions in schools achieved more positive outcomes than none on at least some measures. The more direct interventions (nurture work and play group for juniors; group therapy and behavioural approaches with secondary age pupils) were generally more effective than indirect approaches

Sociological perspectives

Major debates within sociology have centred around the opposing philosophical perspectives of positivism and constructionism, with an earlier and greater movement towards the latter occurring in the sociology of education than in the psychology of education. Comte has generally been identified as the nineteenth century's most forceful proponent of a positivist sociology, this being reflected most clearly in his call for a "science of society". Sharp and Green (1975) criticised this approach within sociology for having engaged in "a series of 'fact finding' and 'head counting' missions, producing a great deal of statistical information . . . but offering little by way of explicit or conceptual breakthroughs for interpreting such data".

Nevertheless, within this tradition major investigations have been carried out, two of the most prominent being longitudinal cohort studies. The first, by Douglas, Ross, and Simpson (1968), pursued a cohort of 5386 children born in the first week of March 1946 and the second, the National Child Development Study is based on a cohort of 16,000 children born in the first week of March 1958 (Fogelman, 1983). Both groups have been followed through their primary and secondary school careers and data collected by means of educational tests, questionnaires, medical examinations, and interviews with parents. Such studies generate a multitude of correlational and between groups findings, with these researchers being particularly interested in differential treatment of, and outcomes for children from different social class backgrounds. For example, at a time when streaming was the norm within schools, Douglas (1964) highlighted the over-representation of pupils from lower socio-economic backgrounds in the lower "streams" of schools, and the lower expectations that teachers had of these pupils in terms not only of their academic attainments, but also of their behaviour.

Studies focused upon school and classroom processes

Sociological perspectives

In contrast to empiricist approaches within the sociology of education, Sharp and Green (1975) studied the "micro-sociological" contexts of classrooms in what was then termed a "progressive primary school". Although the methods of investigation were primarily participant observation in classes and interviews with key actors, Sharp and Green were also concerned with investigating "macro-sociological" concerns, in particular, the ways in which social control in a stratified society was translated into school and classroom life, even within a school with a professed ideology of "child-centredness".

The particular contribution made by this study for understanding pupil behaviour judged to be difficult, lies in the researchers' theory building, in the linking of economic power structures outside of the school to the control exercised by the teachers. This control was seen to include not only the familiar creation of order within school, but also the ability "to define reality" and the "parameters of negotiability" for others (i.e. pupils). The major technique employed in generating this theory was the analysis of conflicts between teachers' accounts of the rationale for various of their specific actions and the *in situ* observational evidence of the nature and effects of these same actions.

Social psychology

A classic study from a social psychology background is that conducted by Hargreaves (1967) and reported in his book *Social relations in a secondary school*. Adopting an ethnographic approach, Hargreaves spent one year in what was then a "secondary modern school" studying fourth-year pupils and collecting data by means of multiple choice questionnaires, sociometric techniques and informal interviews with all pupils in the age group, teacher questionnaires and direct observations. In addition, numerical data from school such as attendance rates and house point allocations, and from home, such as socio-economic class, family size and housing conditions, were also assembled. Pupil tastes and preferences were even investigated as to the extent to which they preferred "long-haired" or "other" pop groups – a measure of rebellious dissent now quaintly assigned to the time capsule!

A major outcome from Hargreaves' study was his description of an anti-school sub-culture which he attributed to the school's streaming system and the creation of a group of pupils rejected as public examination candidates. The description of the structure and membership of various cliques among pupils, the culture within and between various friendship groups, and the relationship between these and the teaching groups into which these pupils were organised, enlivened as they are by pupil quotes, bring a vividness to the social complexity of school life which is still pertinent and worthy of study today.

Straddling both sociological and social psychological perspectives is the ethogenic study of young football fans, seen by others as "hooligans", and, to a lesser extent, these young men's experiences of "fooling around" while at school (Marsh, Rosser, & Harré, 1978). An ethogenic approach is characterised by these authors as being based on the idea that "human social life is a product of an interaction between sequences of actions and talk about these actions". This "intensive" study looked at the actions and accounts of a group of football fans, but only at the accounts of the school misbehaviour as the researchers were not "there when it all happened".

Nevertheless, common themes between behaviour at school and on the terraces were established. In particular, the common perception of football hooliganism as "mindless violence" was replaced by an account of rituals which were strictly rule-bound and constructed so as to confer status and dignity on members through respect for and adherence to hierarchies, reputations and symbolic contests. To a lesser extent, these same processes were detected among the accounts given by the pupils when describing their behaviour within classrooms.

Organisational psychology

Although perhaps falling outside the traditional orbit of "organisational psychology", a sequence of major studies in what has become known as "school effectiveness" has pointed to organisational factors within schools which can exert an influence, mainly on pupils' academic performance but also, in some cases, on the adjustment of pupils in school.

A major milestone in the early development of the school effectiveness literature was the study carried out by Rutter, Maughan, Mortimore, and

Ouston (1979) in 12 London comprehensive schools. Using measures of 46 "process variables" and a "pupil behaviour" scale consisting of 25 dimensions, Rutter et al. were able to demonstrate that "within-school" factors were likely to be important influences on pupils' behaviour. Process and product measures were obtained by means of pupil questionnaires, teacher and headteacher interviews, and observations in a sample of classrooms and playgrounds. Reports from primary school teachers, test scores before entry, and demographic data were used to control for variations in each secondary school's intake.

By such means, Rutter et al. were able to conclude among other things that ". . . the very considerable differences between schools in their pupils' behaviour could not simply be seen as a continuation of patterns previously established in primary schools". Further, the study linked better pupil behaviour with schools in which teachers concentrated on the topic of the lesson, interacted more with the class or groups rather than concentrating on individuals, started and finished lessons on time and required their classes to spend time working silently. On the other hand, worse behaviour tended to occur in schools in which there were frequent interruptions or reprimands by teachers and in which there was a high rate of unofficial punishment.

Ground-breaking in its time in terms of its scope and focus, the research reported in *Fifteen thousand hours* (Rutter et al., 1979) was criticised for certain methodological weaknesses, a fault that was remedied in the later study of 2000 pupils followed over four years in their 50 London primary schools by Mortimore, Sammons, Stoll, Lewis, and Ecob (1988). Once again, factors within the control of schools relating to policy, procedures and culture were shown to have an effect upon the attainments and behaviour of their pupils.

Behavioural psychology

Parallel to, and in many ways insulated from other developments, a series of studies exploring the possible contribution of behavioural psychology was set in motion in 1968 by Madsen, Becker, and Thomas. This early work, in common with developments in clinical psychology at the time, contrasted "problem child" formulations deriving from psychoanalytic perspectives with classroom management techniques emanating from behavioural psychology.

In the Madsen et al. (1968) study, carried out in American primary and kindergarten schools, the researchers were concerned to illustrate the major behavioural tenet that behaviour was learned and that pupils could thus learn more acceptable and productive behaviour. The case studies also show a concern with "clearly defined and observable behaviour" rather than assumed personality characteristics and motivations of pupils. The collection and careful recording of data, often in tabular and graphical form, was another key feature of the approach conspicuously present in their study.

Madsen et al. set out to explore the effects of training teachers in the "contingent use" of praise and ignoring and in the formulation and expression of clear classroom rules. Trained observers recorded the extent to which particular pupils who were concerning their teachers exhibited certain precisely defined "behaviours" during 10-second intervals. By comparing the incidences of these behaviours during the praise, ignoring and rules conditions, with a baseline period, the study demonstrated that the rules and ignoring phases on their own produced little change but the combination of these with praise from teachers for acceptable behaviour proved highly effective in reducing inappropriate behaviour.

Because the *Zeitgeist* within education at the time, certainly in Britain, was one of "child-centredness", behavioural approaches managed to generate a considerable degree of controversy, opposition and hostility. Winnet and Winkler (1972) warned that behavioural approaches were in danger of supporting an injunction to pupils to "be still, be quiet (and) be docile", and subsequent British developments attempted to move beyond a reliance on "reinforcers" and to focus upon strategies planned jointly with pupils and taking account of the need for appropriate and stimulating educational activities.

In terms of methodological developments, British studies have mainly been carried out from a practitioner base and have demonstrated a range of commitment towards rigour. A review of this literature suggests that the full possibilities of single-case experimental designs (Barlow & Hersen, 1984) have not yet been explored.

The Elton Report – research into policy?

Discipline in Schools, the report of the Committee of Enquiry chaired by Lord Elton, was published in 1989, having been commissioned by the Secretary for State for Education a year earlier following concerns within the teaching profession and the popular media that pupils' behaviour in schools was deteriorating. In addition to the usual course of seeking comment from a wide selection of interests, and a programme of visits, the Committee commissioned two studies. Represented within these survey and interview studies, are the methods developed in some of the earlier research already described, and revealed in the findings are a number of familiar themes.

The postal survey

A questionnaire sent to a national sample of 4400 secondary and primary schools by Gray and Sime resulted in an 82 per cent reply rate. The report authors acknowledged that earlier research by Wheldall and Merrett (1988), two leading British researchers into behavioural approaches, had contributed in several ways to the practical tasks of constructing questionnaires for the national survey. Consequently, items such as "Talking out of turn" (e.g. by making remarks, calling out, distracting others by chattering) and "Hindering other pupils" (e.g. by distracting them from work, interfering with equipment or materials) – two items which Wheldall and Merrett had discovered to be of particular concern to teachers, were included among the 14 questionnaire items sent to the teachers.

The questionnaire also examined the types of pupil behaviour that teachers most frequently encountered outside of their classrooms in the course of their general duties around the school. In addition, teachers' views of the "seriousness" of discipline problems in their school, and the strategies and sanctions that they employed, were also examined.

The Elton Report in many ways provided a reassuring message to many at the time in concluding, in contrast to more sensationalist claims, that the incidence of very violent behaviour in schools was small. The much higher degree of lesser but frequent classroom disruption that was detected was seen as a challenge for educators, but one for which effective solutions in such areas as teacher training, school policy development, and support service activity, were seen as realisable.

The interview study

Although methods developed within behavioural psychology largely informed the postal questionnaire, research commissioned for the Elton Report also attempted to draw on other traditions and "go beyond the kinds of information [that could be obtained in] . . . a national survey". To this end, 100 secondary school teachers in ten inner-city comprehensive schools were interviewed by means of a semi-structured schedule in a study by Gilborn, Nixon and Rudduck. Little detail is given concerning the actual method of analysis employed, beyond a statement that the tape recorded transcripts of all the interviews were read by each member of the team.

However, as well as providing accessible accounts through the selection of verbatim sections of the transcripts, the interviews are also able to illuminate more clearly certain of the results obtained from the survey questionnaire. For example, when discussing teachers' experiences of physical aggression, interviewees usually "qualified their answers by emphasising the need to understand pupils' actions within their situational context" so that some teachers described receiving a blow by accident when trying to break up a fight between pupils. Rating the frequency of supposedly "objective" measures, on such occasions, may give a misleading impression when reported devoid of context and intentions.

Researching successful consultations between educational psychologists and teachers

Professional educational psychologists were at the forefront of the response to the Elton Report in terms of in-service teacher training and policy development at the school and local educational authority level – in essence, the school and classroom processes focus described in Figure 10.1. Galvin,

Mercer, and Costa (1990), among others, have developed training materials for schools and emphasised that any coherent plan should ideally ensure that implementation take place in a particular order, with appropriate policy serving as a foundation for supporting the development of effective class management skills, which in turn provide a secure basis from which individual strategies may be constructed. Despite these innovations, however, the legislative requirement is for educational psychologists to be primarily involved with assessment and provision for particular individual pupils – the "problem child" focus.

Behavioural approaches had become incorporated into the practice of educational psychologists, and reported in numerous case studies following the original Madsen et al. (1968) study and subsequent British replications. However, McNamara (1988) argued that these "demonstration studies" are likely to have been carried out in highly conducive settings, whereas the usual run of professional consultative work is often done in far less favourable circumstances.

In order to understand the extent to which various forms of educational and psychological research might be of use to applied psychologists, it was necessary to carry out research that focused more directly on a broader range of consultative practice beyond selected, and possibly misrepresentative case studies. Consequently, in order to gain a clearer impression of the actual nature of the programmes educational psychologists were devising with teachers, a national survey of practice was carried out (Miller, 1996).

The postal survey

This questionnaire was circulated to all the educational psychologists in 13 randomly selected local education authorities in England and Wales. Questions were restricted to programmes designed for mainstream primary classrooms and focused particularly on children described as either restless, unsettled, completing little work, engaging in physical attacks on other children or not being compliant with teachers' requests or instructions.

Completed questionnaires were received from 68 educational psychologists, representing a response rate of 64 per cent. The questionnaire was mainly structured by listing as inclusively as possible sets of possible components of a behavioural intervention. Respondents were asked to answer each item from two separate perspectives, one with their last recommended intervention in mind, and the other in terms of their typical practice. The results from this survey provided for the first time details of the composition of strategies developed with teachers, and information concerning the nature of this professional consultation, such as the number of monitoring visits carried out by the educational psychologists, their frequency and the overall duration of the strategy.

In addition, it was also possible to examine whether the presence or absence in each strategy of each item from the questionnaire was associated with those interventions which were judged by the teachers to have resulted in "considerable improvements" in the pupils' behaviour. From more than 100 items, only one emerged as being differentially associated with successful outcomes – classroom rules being explained differently to the pupil in question.

This use of a standard tool within quantitative methods – a postal questionnaire – analysed in terms of item frequencies and inter-correlations, was able to shed some light on the nature of successful consultations between teachers and educational psychologists. However, one of the major outcomes, the positive effects of restating classroom rules, raises more questions than it answers. Also, despite including a seemingly exhaustive list of items on the questionnaire, respondents frequently selected "Other" categories where provided. These findings suggest a deeper level of complexity to the mechanisms underlying successful practice than can be determined by means of "behaviour counting" questionnaires. Consequently, an interview study with the other partners to these consultations – the teachers – was carried out using a grounded theory approach.

The teacher interviews – a grounded theory study

Turner (1992) has argued that this approach might be seen as "developing local theory", where the resulting substantive theory, if the analysis is carried out thoroughly, is likely to be a "local" variation of larger psychological or sociological theories.

Twenty four primary teachers were interviewed using a structured interview (Miller, 2003). They were identified by contacting educational psychologists in a number of local authorities and asking whether they could supply the name and address of any primary range teacher with whom they had developed an intervention deriving to a greater or lesser extent from a behavioural perspective. The pupil's behaviour had to be of a similar type to that examined by the survey questionnaire sent to the educational psychologists.

The teachers in the sample were eventually drawn from eight local education authorities spanning an area between the English Midlands and the Scottish border. The pupils were drawn from the full primary age range with a bias towards the younger group, the mean age being 7.1 years. In terms of the perceived severity of the problem behaviour, ten teachers said that the pupil was the most difficult they had ever encountered and eight said he or she was among the most difficult half-dozen. Because of the sample selection, all teachers reported success following their collaborative work with an educational psychologist – six expressed the view that the intervention had been successful but had some reservations, such as that there might be deterioration again in the future, eleven saw a definite improvement with no qualification, and seven saw such a degree of success that it made a strong emotional impact on them.

In the study, the first transcript yielded over 80 "open codes", many of these recurring a number of times. To develop "theoretical sensitivity", a number of procedures were used. First, a list of "theories, models and concepts", all of which were hypothesised as having the potential to yield codes for the data that might be found within the transcripts, was drawn up. This list was composed from within and beyond the range of theoretical perspectives represented within Figure 10.1. Then a period of reading was embarked upon, revisiting texts with a deliberately broad range of coverage.

Within a number of the interviews, discussions about teacher colleagues seemed to contain paradoxical and contradictory items and strong feelings. Within the list made during the early stages of developing theoretical sensitivity, the area of relations with colleagues had not been included and thus came to be seen as a potential category within which theorising could be extended. Consequently, for the transcripts of later interviews, open coding was carried out only on sections referring to this area. In total, 24 different open codes relating to "Other staff" were discovered within the first two-thirds of the transcripts and no further new codes then emerged within the later ones, thus generating a reasonable degree of confidence that for this category a stage of "saturation" had been reached. These "level I" codes are listed in the left hand column in Figure 10.2.

There is a marked difference between a grounded theory approach and conventional verification research in the function of the literature review. In the latter it is necessary to present a review of the literature before narrowing down the study to the research hypothesis, in order to demonstrate how the literature has led to the research and how the findings may be linked back into the relevant literature. In contrast, a grounded theory derives from the field data, "coded under conditions of theoretical sensitivity", and then, as the grounded theory emerges, the research literature is turned to in order to provide support for it. In this example, a detailed literature review in the areas of systems and their boundaries, schools as organisations, colleague relationships, teacher thinking, and sociological studies of teaching as work, was then pursued.

A major finding from this study emerged in the form of a three part pattern:

i) The pupil who was the focus of the intervention was acknowledged by most staff to have a deviant identity. Previous teachers usually described the pupil as difficult to manage as did other teaching and non-teaching staff responsible for such activities as dinner and playtime supervision.

ii) Following the classteacher's intervention, other members of staff remarked upon their perception of positive changes in the pupil.

iii) Despite this, these other staff did not enquire about the possible reasons for the improvement, nor ask about the recommendations made by the educational psychologists, and neither did the classteacher seek to inform them.

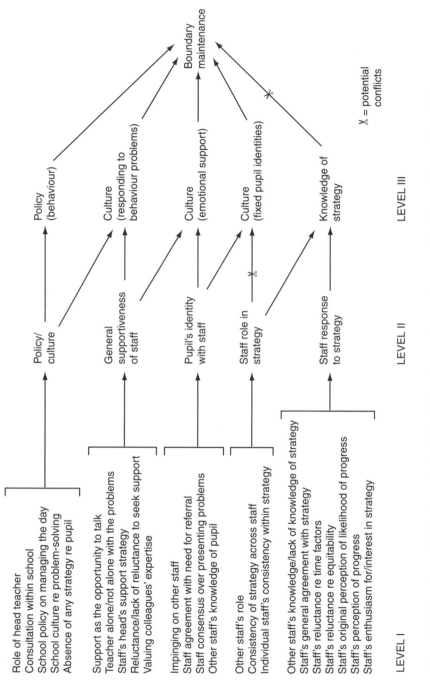

Figure 10.2 The relationship between levels I, II and III codes relating to "other staff". (Adapted from Miller, 1996.)

This pattern was distinctly present in nine of the interventions studied, and partially discernible in all the others.

Figure 10.2 shows the higher level coding and categorisation of the level I codes relating to "other staff". Developed in interaction with the theoretical literature, this process of categorisation and sorting leads to the emergence of "boundary maintenance" as a core variable or, in Glaser's (1978) terminology, a Basic Social Psychological Process. This core variable satisfies Glaser's three criteria of recurring frequently in the data (that is, the data concerning "other staff" rather than the full transcripts), linking the data together, and explaining much of the variation within the data. Figure 10.2 also illustrates that there are two areas that are likely to threaten the relationship between these codes, and hence the "boundary maintenance" variable itself: too great a role for other staff in the strategy, which would clash with the fixed identities of "deviant" pupils constructed within the staff culture; and, too much knowledge of the strategy and its effectiveness on the part of the other staff, which could lead to a tension with a range of aspects of the culture and policy in relation to managing difficult behaviour.

The grounded theory analysis – combining the three levels of coding with memoing, theoretical sampling, sorting, selective coding and the literature review – generated an explanation for this "cultural" resistance to the wider adoption of potentially successful practice in terms of the aspects of the psycho-social system boundaries of schools (Rice, 1976) and the boundaries between homes and schools (Dowling & Osborne, 1995). For example, the teachers in this study displayed a strong tendency to attribute the difficult behaviour of the pupils to the parents whilst at the same time feeling "saddled" with the responsibility to effect a solution.

These boundary uncertainties are temporarily resolved with the involvement of an educational psychologist who creates a temporary system which includes at least one member of staff, one parent, the pupil and the psychologist, and within which new norms and rules are created, in much the same way that a therapist and a family may form a "therapeutic suprasystem" (De Shazer, 1982). This new system enables participants to act towards, and construe each other in new and more positive ways, which provides the basis from which the pupil can assume a new identity. However, the need for internal stability among staff within schools encourages certain attributions and constructions of difficult pupils and their parents, and developments within the new and temporary system take place in isolation from the regular activities of the wider school – a process which enables successful individual outcomes to take place but also ensures their limited wider impact.

Evaluating the grounded theory and the suitability of the methodology for investigating the research question

The original research question had asked how interventions supposedly deriving from behavioural psychology could at times achieve their effect. This question was particularly pertinent to the researcher because of the suspicion engendered by conversations with colleagues over many years that teachers would often only tolerate "light" interventions and that these in themselves might only then be implemented by the teachers with a variable regard to rigour. Given that theoreticians with allegiance to other paradigms could also argue convincingly that classroom interaction was an immensely complex social activity and that notions of "deviance" should pay regard to a range of sociological and interpersonal processes, how could it be the case that these very light interventions, often diluted beyond their explanatory tolerance, could sometimes lead the teachers involved to experience a sense of success when all their previous best efforts had failed? And why was it only sometimes? What factors were at work in these instances?

Clearly any research that attempted to answer these questions would have to be exploratory in nature. As this was not a specific area that was developed within the research literature, a methodology concerned with hypothesis testing was not applicable and any "hunches" or beliefs that the researcher brought to the task would need to be acknowledged and controlled for at an the early stage. The grounded theory methodology was ideally suited to this task, first because it acknowledges the importance of these possible researcher effects, and then through the discipline imposed by "fracturing" the data during the lengthy process of open coding.

Given that difficult behaviour has been approached from a range of theoretical perspectives it was important not to foreclose upon possible explanatory mechanisms too early and grounded analysis, especially in the process of theoretical sensitivity, is well suited to avoiding this. Similarly, any attempt to impose a more global theoretical formulation from any particular discipline onto a puzzling practical phenomenon, would be likely to underestimate the complexity of the area under investigation and thus limit its explanatory power. Because of the emphasis on its emergent and "local" nature, grounded theory again seemed particularly suitable to the task.

Strauss and Corbin (1998) have proposed a set of questions which, they claim, are redefinitions of the "canons of good science" into a form necessary to fit the "realities of qualitative research and the complexities of social phenomena":

i) How was the original sample selected?
ii) What major categories emerged?
iii) What were some of the events, incidents, and actions that pointed to some of the major categories?
iv) On the basis of what categories did theoretical sampling take place?
v) What were some of the hypotheses pertaining to conceptual relations among categories?
vi) Were there instances when hypotheses did not hold up against what was actually seen?
vii) How and why was the core category selected?

Because the approach requires that an extensive series of "memos" be compiled through the course of the research, and these began as soon as the first interview had taken place, and eventually became the formal statement of the grounded theory (Miller, 1996), it was possible to provide full answers to each of these questions, thus increasing confidence that the grounded theory procedures had been rigorously applied.

Implications for future research – the need for mixed methods

Given the range of explanatory frameworks surrounding "problem pupil behaviour in schools", the bipolar focus of much current "policy-driven" research in this area – "problem child" or school/classroom processes – seems particularly limited. A fuller model of the context of pupil behaviour in schools is shown in Figure 10.3, a model originally developed to guide EPs in helping to maximise the effectiveness of teacher–pupil interactions (Miller and Leyden, 1999).

The framework set out in Figure 10.3 shows the key sub-systems within the psycho-social context of the school. Pupil behaviour may be, and has been,

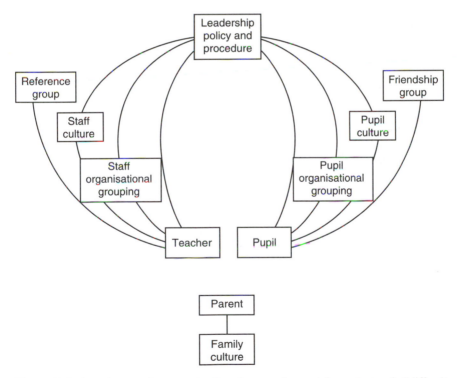

Figure 10.3 A coherent framework for the psycho-social context of "difficult pupil behaviour". From Miller and Leyden (1999). Reprinted with permission from Taylor and Francis Ltd. www.tandf.co.uk/journals/carfax/01411926.html

studied in relation to most of these sub-systems. Further advances are now likely to require a greater recognition that, because of their systemic nature, none of these sub-systems can be considered to exist independently of each other. In order to study effective practice meaningfully, a range of mixed methods will need to be employed in order to investigate the dynamic relationship between the various formal, observable factors and the hidden, "cultural" processes within a school (Miller, 2003).

Difficult pupil behaviour in schools remains a pressing problem. It is a subject area in which research psychologists and their professional cousins should be able to develop fruitful partnerships, but only if there is clarity about the focus of study and a rigorous and appropriately sensitive approach towards the necessary mixture of research methods required.

References

Aubrey, C. (1987). Training for the role of school consultant as a means of dealing effectively with behaviour problems in schools. *Educational and Child Psychology*, *4*(2), 14–29.

Axline, V. M. (1964). *Dibs. In search of self*. London: Penguin.

Barlow, D. H., & Hersen, M. (1984). *Single case experimental designs. Strategies for studying behaviour change* (2nd ed.). Oxford: Pergammon.

Bryman, A. (1984). The dabate about quantitative and qualitative research: A question of method or epistemology? *British Journal of Sociology*, *35*(1), 75–92.

Department for Education and Science (1989). *Discipline in schools. Report of the committee of enquiry chaired by Lord Elton (The Elton Report)*. London: HMSO.

Department for Education and Skills (2001). *Code of practice on the identification and assessment of special educational needs*. London: HMSO.

De Shazer, S. (1982). *Patterns of brief family therapy. An ecosystemic approach*. New York: Guildford Press.

Douglas, J. W. B. (1964). *The home and the school*. London: Panther.

Douglas, J. W. B., Ross, J. M., & Simpson, H. R. (1968). *All our future*. London: Panther.

Dowling, E., & Osborne, E. (1995). *The family and the school. A joint systems approach to problems with children* (2nd ed.). London: Routledge.

Fogelman, K. (Ed.) (1983). *Growing up in Great Britain: Papers from the national child development study*. London: Macmillan.

Galvin, P., Mercer, S., & Costa, P. (1990). *Building a better behaved school*. Harlow: Longman.

Glaser, B. (1978). *Theoretical sensitivity*. Mill Valley, CA: Sociology Press.

Hargreaves, D. H. (1967). *Social relations in a secondary school*. London: Routledge & Kegan Paul.

Humphries, S. (1981). *Hooligans or rebels? An oral history of working-class childhood and youth 1889–1939*. Oxford: Blackwell.

Kolvin, I., Garside, R. G., Nicol, A. R., Macmillan, A., Wolstenholme, F., & Leitch, I. M. (1981). *Help starts here. The maladjusted child in the ordinary school*. London: Tavistock Publications.

McNamara, E. (1988). Behavioural contracting with secondary aged pupils. *Educational Psychology in Practice*, *2*(4), 21–26.

Madsen, C. H., Becker, W. C., & Thomas, D. R. (1968). Rules, praise and ignoring: Elements of elementary classroom control. *Journal of Applied Behavioural Analysis*, *1*(2), 139–150.

Manicas, P. T., & Secord, P. F. (1983). Implications for psychology of the new philosophy of science. *American Psychologist*, *38*, 399–413.

Marsh, P., Rosser, E., & Harré, R. (1978). *The rules of disorder*. London: Routledge.

Miller, A. (1996). *Pupil behaviour and teacher culture*. London: Cassell.

Miller, A. (2003). *Teachers, parents and classroom behaviour. A psychosocial approach*. Maidenhead: Open University Press.

Miller, A., & Leyden, G. (1999). A coherent framework for the application of psychology in schools. *British Educational Research Journal*, *25*(3), 389–400.

Miller, A., & Todd, Z. (2002). Educational psychology and difficult behaviour in schools. Conceptual and methodological challenges for an evidence-based profession. *Educational and Child Psychology*, *17*(3), 82–95.

Mortimore, P., Sammons, P., Stoll, L., Lewis, D., & Ecob, R. (1988). *School matters*. Wells: Open Books.

Rice, A. K. (1976). Individual, group and inter-group processes. In E. J. Miller (Ed.), *Task and organisation*. Chichester: Wiley.

Rosenthal, R., & Rosnow, R. (1991). *Essentials of behavioural research: Method and data analysis*. New York: McGraw-Hill.

Rutter, M., Maughan, B., Mortimore, P., & Ouston, J. (1979). *Fifteen thousand hours*. Wells: Open Books.

Rutter, M., Tizard, J., & Whitmore, K. (1970). *Education, health and behaviour*. London: Longman.

Scarr, S. (1985). Constructing psychology: Making facts and fables for our times. *American Psychologist*, *40*(5) 499–512.

Sharp, R., & Green, A. (1975). *Education and social control. A study in progressive primary education*. London: Routledge & Kegan Paul.

Strauss, A. L., & Corbin, J. (1998). *Basics of qualitative research: Techniques and procedures for developing grounded theory*. London: Sage.

Turner, B. (1992). Looking closely and creating grounded theory. Paper presented at ESRC Research Seminar, University of Warwick, 5 March 1992.

Wheldall, K., & Merrett, F. (1988). Which classroom behaviours do primary school teachers say they find most troublesome? *Educational Review*, *40*(1), 13–27.

Winnet, A. R., & Winkler, R. C. (1972). Current behaviour modification in the classroom: Be still, be quiet, be docile. *Journal of Applied Behaviour Analysis*, *8*, 259–262.

11 Taking quality seriously

The case for qualitative feminist psychology in the context of quantitative clinical research on postnatal depression

Paula Nicolson

Introduction

In this chapter I re-examine the impact and role of qualitative feminist psychological research, as both a *contrast* and *complement* to quantitative studies, such as structured interviews and randomised control trials (RCTs), in research on postnatal depression (PND). Feminist analyses of the concepts and methods employed by traditional clinicians and researchers to investigate PND, led initially to qualitative research as a *critique*. Qualitative feminist psychology highlighted women's experiences and the social context of early motherhood, which was taken by the traditional clinical psychologists and medical researchers to be a radical attack, and thus dismissed or ignored (Nicolson, 1998). However, over the past ten years, to a small degree, a mutual tolerance has emerged. Thus mixing methods has become a reality, although one still tinged with caution on both sides.

Why qualitative psychology?

Psychology as a "science" takes a pride in asserting its "unbiased" approach to issues of inequality, whether about gender, ethnicity, class or disability (Morgan, 1998). Both feminist and qualitative psychologies are perceived, by the majority of traditionalists, to be discrediting rather than enhancing to the discipline. This continuous conflict has led to a polarisation and stagnation of the research agenda for psychology as a whole.

The wave of feminist psychology research which has grown in Western Europe and North America over the past fifteen years (Wilkinson, 1996) has been (mostly) qualitative. Thus criticisms levelled at qualitative researchers have directly mirrored those directed towards feminist psychologists.

Feminist psychologists are especially concerned that psychological knowledge and practice be for the benefit of women. Feminist psychology, as a discipline and as a research endeavour, seeks to attend to women's lives, behaviour, experiences and needs in an appropriate manner (Harding, 1991;

Boyle, 1997). That is, that the source and context of inequalities are identified and challenged through having been "counted in" as research data. Some commentators see this as introducing unacceptable bias into the hitherto "rigorous" nature of the discipline (McKnight, 1999). Critics see feminist psychology as rhetoric rather than scholarship and ideology rather than science (Buss, 1995).

A recent article published in *The Psychologist* (the British Psychological Society house magazine) made the following point, which illustrates the antipathy mainstream psychology profers to qualitative research including contributions qualitative psychology might make towards understanding and explaining inequalities:

> From time to time, heads of departments of psychology have to beat off determined challenges to the status of psychology as a laboratory-based subject. All this will be at risk if psychology goes down the road which qualitative researchers would like to follow. Psychology would become . . . an arts-based discipline; its funding would be in decline; and scientific psychologists would leave to take up appointments in departments of cognitive science or neuroscience.
>
> (Morgan, 1998: 481)

This short paragraph is crammed with meaning! It demonstrates the high level of anxiety directed towards preserving psychology's status as a science, which is placed above that of the status of arts. It confirms the marginal status of qualitative research within the discipline of psychology, the self-perceived fragile hold psychology has upon its own claim to be a science and the influence of funding *per se* on what counts as psychological knowledge. The emphasis upon laboratory research as the mainstay of the discipline also clearly challenges the legitimacy of "counting in" the context of human behaviour and experience (Eagley, 1987; Nicolson, 1995; Reinharz, 1992). Is this the basis from which a value free science can grow?

Feminist psychology

Feminist researchers in psychology have a primary concern with explaining women's experience and behaviour in a patriarchal context – a brief extending far beyond the narrow enterprise set by the mainstream of the discipline. Traditional psychology, on the occasions that it *has* explored matters of potential interest to feminists, has typically focused on issues that exploit *gender differences*. These frequently privilege men and male behaviour, and support the status quo in terms of power relations in the family, the health-care system and the workplace (Ussher, 1989; Nicolson, 1996). This is achieved through an overwhelming concentration upon differences, especially those which expose apparent female *deficiencies* between women and men in cognition, performance, sex-roles, sex-role stereotyping and the psychobiology of female hormonal cycles and male aggression (see for example Bem, 1993; Frieze, Parsons, Johnson, Ruble & Zellman, 1978; Sheilds, 1975). These beliefs have "inspired" research questions conducive to experimental methods (Buss, 1995).

The major research questions in these traditional inquiries have been focused around Western cultural beliefs. These have been identified as being that men and women ". . . have fundamentally different psychological and sexual natures, that men are inherently the dominant or superior sex, and that both male–female difference and male dominance are natural" (Bem, 1993: 1).

Up until the mid-1990s, *feminist research* in psychology was typically *qualitative research* (Griffin, 1995; Nicolson, 1995; Wilkinson, 1986). This situation came about as a justified and radical reaction to psychological science as an experimental, positivist discipline that claimed objectivity in relation to gender (Wilkinson, 1986). Feminist psychologists demonstrated the myth of this "objectivity" in which women were either invisible (Crawford & Maracek, 1989), intellectually deficient or pathological by virtue of their female bodies (Nicolson, 1992a, 1992b; Ussher, 1989). Thus the majority of feminist psychologists rejected positivism and quantitative approaches to psychological research altogether, in favour of different qualitative perspectives which ranged from discourse analysis (Hollway, 1989), grounded theory (Henwood & Pidgeon, 1995), thematic analysis (Tunaley, 1996) and phenomenology, to symbolic interactionism (Lewis, 1995; Nicolson, 1998). These approaches provided opportunities to inquire about a diversity and depth of female *experience* and to explore the role and content of the dominant discourses which circumscribe gendered behaviour and maintain patriarchal power relations.

The benefits achieved from over a decade of opening up alternative research questions about gender issues in psychology have led to a reclamation of useful features of traditional, quantitative methods. These may be used to best effect in association with qualitative approaches (see for example Sheilds & Crowley, 1996). Below, I discuss the way that my own research on postnatal depression benefited from a feminist and qualitative approach that itself emerged from a traditional study. I then outline how qualitative work in this area is informing current large-scale, quantitative studies.

Postnatal depression: from quantitative to qualitative psychology

Definitions of postpartum or postnatal depression seem to vary from researcher to researcher. However, it is broadly taken to be depression occurring during the 12 postpartum months. Some prefer to include only "clinically" identifiable depression, while others are happier with a broader category of any self-reported episode of depression during that time period (see Thurtle, 1995).

Postnatal depression provides an exemplary case study of feminist psychology and mixing methods. PND is something that only women can have because only women give birth. Those who treat and research this area have typically been men and the predominant research paradigm has been both clinical and quantifiable. A major point of contention for feminist psychologists, has been that the concept of PND has been used within this approach to pathologise the female body and mind, paying no regard to women's experiences of child care and the context in which that care occurs (Nicolson, 1988, 1992a, 1998; Ussher, 1989).

Postpartum depression has always been seen by many experts and lay people as distinct both from the social context of childbirth and motherhood, and from any other kind of depression (WHO, 1992). It is frequently described as an irrational, inevitable, response to the hormone fluctuations following childbirth (e.g. Dalton, 1980/1989). This conceptualisation is almost exclusively the result of the methodologies employed in the mainstream clinical tradition which assess themselves to be "scientific".

The research literature on postpartum depression is extensive and between 1980 and 1990 more than 100 studies were published (Whiffen, 1992). This has not necessarily led to the ability to predict, explain or treat PND in an effective way. Indeed the proliferation of studies brings into sharp focus the futility of pursuing this narrow band of research methods and the resulting conceptual bottleneck whereby PND is seen to be intrinsically related to the *process* of childbirth, or the woman's *failure to adjust* to motherhood. Even studies that took account of the difficulties of being isolated at home with a small baby seemed unable to ask different kinds of research questions.

The first phase: the pre-coded structured interview

The limitations of the scope of typical research in this area was brought home to me more than ten years ago when I set out to collect data on PND for my doctoral thesis. As a traditional social psychologist my expectation was that I would combine attitude scales, validated measures and pre-coded questions that I would test in advance for validity and reliability. The questionnaire included Bryce Pitt's measure of atypical depression following childbirth (Pitt, 1968), well considered at the time of this study (Figure 11.1). I was also governed by the need to control for intervening variables such as psychiatric history, marital stability, the health of woman and baby, other life events and social support. For some reason, which I cannot now remember, I also took a tape-recorder and a note-book with me. That action totally altered the way I understood my pilot data.

In this phase of the research I interviewed 40 women from two maternity units during their stay in hospital, between two and ten days following delivery of the baby. I interviewed them again at home, between ten and twelve weeks later (Nicolson, 1986, 1988). The women were frank and open about their feelings especially at the second interview and began to reveal information that I had neither asked for nor believed I could use in my

Could you please circle the answer that best describes how you feel at the present time:

Do you sleep well?	Yes	No	Don't Know
Do you easily lose your temper?	Yes	No	Don't Know
Are you worried about your looks?	Yes	No	Don't Know
Have you a good appetite?	Yes	No	Don't Know
Are you as happy as you ought to be?	Yes	No	Don't Know
Do you easily forget things?	Yes	No	Don't Know
Do you have as much interest in sex as ever?	Yes	No	Don't Know
Is everything a great effort?	Yes	No	Don't Know
Do you feel ashamed for any reason?	Yes	No	Don't Know
Can you feel the baby is really yours?	Yes	No	Don't Know
Do you want someone with you all the time?	Yes	No	Don't Know
Are you easily woken up?	Yes	No	Don't Know
Do you feel calm most of the time?	Yes	No	Don't Know
Do you feel you are in good health?	Yes	No	Don't Know
Do you cry easily?	Yes	No	Don't Know
Is your memory as good as it ever was?	Yes	No	Don't Know
Have you less desire for sex than usual?	Yes	No	Don't Know
Have you enough energy?	Yes	No	Don't Know
Are you satisfied with the way you are coping with things?	Yes	No	Don't Know
Do you worry a lot about the baby?	Yes	No	Don't Know
Do you feel unlike your normal self?	Yes	No	Don't Know
Do you have confidence in yourself?	Yes	No	Don't Know

Is there anything else you would like to add about the way you feel at the moment?

Figure 11.1 Pitt measure of atypical depression following childbirth. *Source:* Pitt (1968).

study. For instance if someone told me that they loved their husband, but felt aggrieved that he was not supportive, how was I to score that in relation to marital status or stability? What sense could I make of the young woman who claimed "isolation" but was never alone. Indeed she perceived herself as besieged by relatives offering child-care and help with her washing and shopping. She saw this as *interference*. No one met *her* needs. However, on my interview schedule it looked as if she had a good social support network, which indicated a potential element of pathology behind her morbid score.

I kept these anxieties to myself because the data from my interview schedule were the data I was planning to use. I categorised the women into those who had high or low scores on the Pitt measure at first and second interview. Women with morbid scores at the first interview (the "blues" period) explained themselves as having negative feelings about their treatment in hospital. These included insensitive staff, poor ward atmosphere, questions about their health or child care not answered, lack of nappies, too few midwives, a bad birth experience, exhaustion, pain and ill-health, worry about the baby's health and racism. Those women who achieved low scores at this stage, conversely tended to be satisfied with the care and had few problems with feeding, and with their own or the baby's health.

High scores at the second interview however were founded on a broader base including social isolation and problems with health. What was particularly important here though was the extent to which the Pitt scores counterbalanced what the women *actually said about themselves* against my observations, particularly of the non-verbal cues. Some women would apparently "contradict" their answers on the measure which not only raised issues about validity but, more importantly for what follows, clarified for me that it was important to consider meaning and the relevance of criteria used in validation.

So for women who said they were in pain and had sore nipples but responded to the question "Do you feel you are in good health?" with "yes", it seemed essential to find out what *they* meant and expected by the term "good health" at this stage of their lives.

There also appeared to be a tension between "polite" answers to the formal questions and more detailed answers, often emphasising problems which were only acknowledged when I was not using the questionnaire as a checklist (see Nicolson, 1986, 1988 for a full discussion).

Finally there were some inconsistencies between people's words, behaviours and the questionnaire answers, that were only revealed by observation of non-verbal cues. For example, one woman described herself as happy, but her words and manner suggested this was not the full picture. "What you would expect with duties towards a man and a family" and "what you have to do" were phrases she used, that did not sit neatly with happiness in my mind. She did not mention pleasure, nor did she smile at the baby, but talked in a "tight" way (see Nicolson, 1986, 1988).

From social to feminist psychology

The study that became the core of my doctoral thesis, emerged from a rejection of the overall value of this quantitative method of data collection for this particular study. I felt, although I had been guided by the pre-existing research and the expectations of the tools available to a social psychologist, that I was asking the wrong research questions. It was not important to look at what caused or correlated with PND, which is what everyone including myself had been doing. What was missing from the knowledge base were the kinds of question that addressed issues of *experience* and *meaning*. What *is* PND? Can it be identified as an objective, measurable concept? How did it feel to look after a new-born infant? What was it like going through the transition to motherhood (each time)? Why is it that women, as mothers, rather than men, as fathers, have the day to day responsibility for infant care? What impact do power relations in the family and society have upon the emotional state of women? How far do scientists impose their own (male-oriented) constructions on women's accounts of their experiences following childbirth? How do women themselves explain their experiences and feelings? These questions require both a feminist and a qualitative psychology perspective.

Postnatal depression: from "objective" psycho-biology to "subjective" social context

A major characteristic of traditional research in this area, is that almost none of the scientific papers sets out a clear operational definition of PND. This point has not escaped notice. Almost twenty years ago commentators argued that the literature has ". . . failed to distinguish among the maternity blues, postpartum affective psychoses, and mild to moderate postpartum depression" (Hopkins, Marcus, & Campbell, 1984: 498). Also, studies of PND ". . . are beset by methodological problems such as problems in the definition of depression itself" (Pollock, Blurton Jones, Evans, & Woodson, 1980: 1).

Despite the absence of operational definitions, an implicit model of PND has emerged. PND is characterised by scientists through its *temporal location*, as occurring during the first twelve months following childbirth; the *variety of its form*, which varies according to when during the postnatal period and for how long depressive episodes occur; whether it is in fact an "illness" with a physical cause, or a *response* to "stress" or a "life event"; how far it actually is *linked to childbirth itself* or simply connected to being a new mother; and finally there is interest in the *incidence* (Nicolson, 1998).

Brockington and Kumar (1982) suggested that the "precise" definition of the links between motherhood and mental illness is "elusive", which potentially raises doubts about the special and unique relationship (Brockington and Kumar, 1982: 2). They declare though that they themselves are convinced of the link – although they are going with their instincts rather than the evidence.

An early review of the psychobiology of mental disorders associated with childbearing argued that postpartum mental illness is not a unitary phenomenon and neither is the physiology of the puerperium a cause in itself of any of the symptoms (Steiner, 1979: 449). Therefore clinical problems that occur during this period are either triggered by non-biological factors or are attributable to other causes. Even so, this point continues to be almost universally ignored by researchers.

Indeed, it was not until 1992 that the World Health Organisation accorded puerperal mental disorders the status of a separate category and only then with a degree of ambivalence. "The new version of their International Classification of Diseases (ICD-10; WHO, 1992) does, however, go some way towards addressing this issue. Mental disorders occurring at this time may now be categorised as puerperal, but only if they cannot otherwise be classified" (Cox, 1994: 4).

What does this say about the quality of the 25 plus years of objective research which took the idea of PND as a distinct and definable mental disorder associated with child-bearing to be unproblematic? It seems clear that a feature of traditional clinically based research has been unreflexive and uncritical. PND as a concept has been challenged, but its "convenience" as an operational definition and diagnostic category has over-ridden any chance of extending the parameters of the concept.

Women's experiences of postnatal depression: differing with the experts?

There has been a feminist presence in psychology almost as long as there has been such an academic discipline; but the impetus for a co-ordinated feminist scholarship in the USA and UK arguably dates from the mid-1970s. Since then, feminist psychologists in the USA and Europe have identified the clear influence of gender bias, in favour of a male perspective, on psychological research and knowledge (Bem, 1993). As Gilligan (1993) makes clear, it does not matter how well a scientist believes that their methodology is objective, when it comes to the crunch, they interpret their findings through their own, gendered eyes. A man (and most scientists are either men or are involved in teams where a man is the leader) exploring data on PND, will see it as a discrete episode in the mother's life which is irrational and related in some way to the biology of birth. There has been a long tradition through which this view has taken shape (see Ehrenreich & English, 1979; Moscucci, 1993; Ussher, 1989). The acknowledgement that a lack of social support and the stress of early motherhood are important precipitants of PND, has only recently been taken seriously. However this has been treated simply as a means of *adding* the social context to the biology and does not represent a feminist perspective in which women's experiences are the focal point.

Qualitative methods: radical alternatives?

Following from my rejection of the structured interview approach the questions were re-framed. What is PND? What does it feel like to have and care for a young baby? What makes some women feel depressed? What prevents depression?

The research was redefined as a longitudinal, qualitative study, which focused upon women's accounts and explanations of their experiences of the latter part of pregnancy and the first six postpartum months. The rationale, sample characteristics, methods of data collection, analysis and the impact of the results are outlined and discussed briefly below.

The study was designed to collect in-depth verbal accounts of the transition to motherhood and the early postpartum months from a small sample of women (N = 24) through the transition to motherhood. Interviews were tape-recorded and took place during pregnancy, and one, three and six months after the birth. Interview 1 obtained detailed biographical material. Interviews 2 to 4 obtained detailed accounts of the birth and subsequent period focusing upon the respondents' explanations of their behaviour and emotional reactions as well as their social context (Nicolson, 1998 for details).

The design developed here was not conducive to systematic sampling in the traditional sense, as it was not intended to make statistical generalisations or predictions from the data. The aim was to see how a small cohort of women described and understood their own experiences in depth.

The major prerequisite, therefore, was that the women recruited were willing to make a commitment of around 10 hours of time over the research period. The respondents further needed sufficient verbal and intellectual competence to engage discursively with the topic of the transition to motherhood and emotional change. Thus inclusion criteria were that the woman was pregnant, and that within the sample there was a reasonably broad range of age, class, race, parity, source and type of maternity care services planned. As only one researcher with limited time was involved, a manageable span of delivery dates was essential. While the researcher was aware of the limitations of this "purposive" method of sampling (see Bott, 1957; Rapoport & Rapoport, 1976), it proved to be an invaluable source of rich, contextual and deep-level information otherwise unavailable in the main body of scientific knowledge on postpartum depression (see Nicolson, 1998).

The interviews

The intention had been to interview 20 women four times. Instead of the fourth interview, four women who for various reasons were unable to give the time for a face-to-face meeting, were sent a postal questionnaire in which they were asked to give detailed accounts of their emotional and behavioural responses since the previous interview. Therefore the data for 17 respondents were available for six months after delivery. Twenty-four women were recruited to accommodate attrition. Out of this original number, only one dropped out after the first interview, only two following the second and thirteen remained in the study to be interviewed for a fourth time with four additional respondents completing a questionnaire on this occasion.

The interviews took the form of a planned discussion rather than a structured interview. This was based upon the pilot study (see Nicolson, 1986) and other similar work reported (Bott, 1957; Rapoport & Rapoport, 1976) where a structured conversation was used to gather data to provide a subjective perspective on the context of the respondents' daily lives. Thus, while there was a conversation structure to aid both comparison between individuals and systematic data collection, there was also the maximum scope to pursue specific topics according to their degree of importance, mutually defined by respondent and researcher, in the course of the interview. This enabled breadth for the identification of individual differences as well as similarities while providing in-depth richness.

Respondents had been recruited in the knowledge that the researcher was interested in postpartum depression and that they would be asked about any previous experiences of depression. Although it might be argued within the traditional paradigm that this produces "bias", in this case it was considered important, working within a symbolic interaction framework, to focus on how people *understood* depression as a concept in their own lives. Further, they were told during the first meeting, that the researcher would want to discuss their personal histories at interview 1, and at each subsequent interview they would be asked to provide an account of events and feelings about the period since the last interview, including episodes of depression.

At the first meeting the respondent was shown the plan (Appendix) and asked if this was acceptable. The tape recorder was then switched on, and a brief biographical data sheet was completed on matters regarding the projected delivery date, household composition and past pregnancies. If that task stimulated discussion, which it sometimes did, the interviewer would pursue that line of inquiry, taking care to cover all the topics on the interview plan by the end of the interview. This flexibility enabled the respondent to stress the features of her life that had the most significance *for her* at the time. The interviewer's task was to keep the discussion within the specified parameters and follow up relevant areas via prompts such as: "could you say more about . . .", "how did that make you feel?" "why . . ." and similar open-ended questions. When the researcher judged that discussion of a particular topic had been completed she would say: "Is there anything else you consider to be important about 'X' " and then: "Now could we move on to talk about 'Y'?"

In the subsequent interviews, the respondents initially were asked at Interview 2 to: "Tell me about the baby's birth and what has happened/how you felt since then" and then at Interviews 3 and 4 to: "Tell me what has happened/how you felt since the last time we met." By the second interviews the respondents had begun to make it clear they had "saved up" what they wanted to say.

(It had been suggested at the end of the first interview that they kept a personal diary as an *aide memoir*.)

Analysis

In this research the main questions concerned: a) the recognition of the range of subjectively identified significant emotional experiences which occur throughout the postpartum (with a focus on negative affect); b) the meaning these experiences have in the context of the respondents' lives; and c) how that meaning and the experience were understood by the respondents over time.

The analysis of data comprised a complex, multi-faceted process which, arguably, started before the data were collected in that the parameters were set by the questions and the categories selected in the construction of the research tool. The data were analysed within a broadly symbolic interactionist framework, in that the transcripts were studied to examine the ways in which reported experiences were given a meaning by the respondents. This was carried out through initially examining the transcripts to identify "depression" and words which referred to emotion and mood such as "down", "low" or "upset" or behaviours typically associated with negative affect such as "crying", "being too tired to move/carry on", "weeping". Then the surrounding relevant paragraphs were examined to make sense of how depression was talked about and how far it was related to meaning, experience and the biographical context of the woman's life. Selected examples are quoted below.

There were three main stages identified as follows:

1   the selection of broad categories from the interview material;
2   the identification of themes and sub-themes; and
3   the exploration of these to assess what the evidence might contribute towards a conceptual analysis.

The impact of the results

The data were analysed in order to explore the meaning of the emotional responses through emergent themes, on both a descriptive and a conceptual level, with the aim of developing a framework for explaining some of the negative affect surrounding childbirth and the early months following the transition to motherhood.

A sub-theme that emerged was of "loss", derived from exploration of the themes of "the meaning of depression" and "the context of depression". I use it here as an example, because it contrasts sharply with the popular belief that childbirth is a happy event. To identify the transition to motherhood as a "loss", challenges the view that depression following childbirth is necessarily pathological.

Identification of the sub-theme "loss"

The identification of "loss" as a sub-theme emerged from examination of the extracts concerning the "meaning" and "context" of depression. It became apparent from reading many of the transcripts that a range of feelings of negative affect following childbirth were discussed in the context of what the woman felt she had lost. This frequently occurred as the woman in question moved from exploring the context and describing the experience of depression in order to giving it a meaning. For instance:

> I got really down – oh dear it's difficult to explain really – shut up knowing you can't go out even if you wanted to. I know it was cold and everything and not everyone likes to go out – but I mean it's nice to be able to pack your things and go
>
> (Jane, Interview 3) (All names represent women who volunteered to participate in this study. The names have been changed to preserve anonymity.)

Through trying to explain both to me and to herself why she felt so down on one particular occasion, when it had been snowing and she felt especially alone and isolated, she demonstrated that *there was something that would in the past have been easy that she could not do now*. This was because things had changed for her since she had become a mother. Leaving the house in inclement weather might be putting the baby's health at risk. Leaving the flat and walking in the snow was simply not practical with a pram. Independent outings, and being able to put herself first on her list of priorities were not longer possible if she were to maintain her (desired) identity as a responsible mother. Thus the change in social status led to a sense of being down or depressed when confronted with loss of time and autonomy in this way.

In a different example, Angela was concerned about getting employment and was very depressed when she had had two job interviews without success:

> I found it hard – I'm frightened I'm going to end up cleaning or stacking shelves in a supermarket because I know that's a job – but I want to use the skills I've got – I don't want to lose my typing.
>
> (Angela, Interview 3)

She accounted for her depression as emerging from her anxiety that a suitable and desired type of employment was no longer available to her. She perceived herself as having lost opportunities in the course of early motherhood (this was her second baby, and the first was still under school age). She was further fearful of losing her skills altogether if she did not manage to gain employment; implicitly she was recognising this might lead her towards a prolonged period of depression.

However, as with many of the respondents there was more than one reason for episodes of heightened depression. Angela again:

> I have had a bad spell since I saw you last which went on for a couple of weeks where I couldn't stop crying and I was very, very depressed – I think that was tied up with my weight. I hadn't lost any – and I was starting to creep up again. I then went back on a diet – the doctor said it was a bit early – but I decided to do it and I've lost nearly half a stone again.
>
> (Angela, Interview 3)

Here Angela is focusing upon the "loss" of her body and her *failure* (as she saw it) to return to her old weight. She also acknowledged that the medical expert took a different view. It may be that she went against the expert advice because she resented being identified, by someone else, as person who should accept this larger body.

Hilary demonstrated how the intensity of a particular experience (in her case recovering from extensive tearing during delivery) can seem at the time to be a permanent change (or loss) and induce a sense of panic which leads to further depression.

> My body things are over now – I was miserable but you feel you have to be all right. So I was quite miserable – not only being ill – but being depressed about it. It has gone now, although it was bad for a couple of weeks. You think you'll never get your body back together really.
>
> (Hilary, Interview 2)

It became clear that almost every woman taking part in this study had found the experience of becoming a mother, whether for the first, second or third time, changed her life in more than one way and on several levels. This extended from having to put another (or yet another) individual's needs first, to having lost a valued identity in order to incorporate that of "mother" (for the first time or mother of one more child). Some changes were permanent and some transitional, though at the time the intensity of the feeling of loss frequently meant the respondent was unlikely to be able to distinguish or predict. Any experience of change initially was described, or understood as the "loss" of what had been their previous experience. For most, in some way, this became gradually integrated into a new sense of identity as "mother". Melanie and Natasha for instance specifically expressed the view, in the later interviews, that becoming a mother made them feel that they were "growing" as people. However they acknowledged that it often took time to meet the new challenges that this altered status brought. Growth and maturity were recognised as positive but their acceptance also meant the loss of youth or at least of the "carefree" self-centred behaviours that youth sometimes represented. While not specifically discussing depression in this part of the interview, Melanie expressed a version of this kind of loss.

> I think I've calmed down a bit. I'm not so emotional as I was. I think I'm more ambitious. That comes with the responsibility. I think I must go out and earn a crust for the family.
>
> (Melanie, Interview 4)

Natasha, however, who was a relatively young respondent (aged 23 when recruited) deeply regretted some of the changes to her sense of identity and how she believed she should behave. Motherhood in her view brought with it a weight of responsibility.

> I went out the other night but she's [the baby] on my mind the whole time. I don't act any differently. I don't think – maybe a little more grown-up.
>
> Interviewer: What exactly is it?
>
> Um, well. Whereas before I'd probably be really "mad", I won't so much now. Like on Saturday – I wanted to wear my leather mini-skirt. But I had second thoughts. . . . I'm a mother now.
>
> (Natasha, Interview 3)

First time mothers appeared to experience the changes as more significant than those who were mothers already although this was not always the case. Meg (having had her third baby) said that this new baby represented a significant change for her because it meant a loss of her "expected future", especially the loss of the expectation of a return to work. The new baby's arrival further eliminated time for her and her husband to be on their own together which stretched ahead for another 18 years. She sometimes felt very depressed about this.

Loss, then, was identified as an important concept. The transcripts were therefore further explored to assess its significance as a sub-theme emerging from the themes mentioned above. This exploration provided evidence that a sense of loss pervaded respondents' thoughts about their negative or depressing experiences. Initially this had seemed counter-intuitive as, despite the pressures, a baby would be expected to represent "gain" and "optimism". However this proved to be a naïve expectation of the process, as the analysis of the women's accounts revealed. Discussion of loss itself could be sub-divided into "loss of autonomy and time", "loss of appearance", "loss of femininity/sexuality" and "loss of occupational identity" (see Nicolson, 1998, 1999 for details).

Conceptualisation surrounding the sub-theme "loss": re-integration and change

Issues connected with the range of views and accounts of experiences of the losses suffered during the postpartum period, provided the conceptual framework to explain some of the depression. Loss is an inevitable part of any change, but most human beings survive a series of losses, which if handled appropriately, lead to re-integration of the development of increased competence and strength. Poor mental health only follows when the losses are ignored or an individual's psychological history indicates that there have been unresolved difficulties surrounding loss or bereavement in the past (see for example Murray-Parkes, 1971; Marris, 1986).

Loss, however, does eventually lead to re-integration and change for most people, and in this study it was notable in the third and fourth interviews where some expressions of a deep level acceptance of change were evident.

The ways in which women changed depended very much on their personal experiences, biographical context, events surrounding the birth and early postnatal months. For instance, Francis felt split between the two children, her husband and trying to make time for herself, something which Hilary dismissed as impossible. Others, for example Isobel and Natasha, felt older but not in a particularly positive way. Norma expressed the view that she felt able to separate herself from some of the pettiness of her former life and in certain ways saw some of her friends as immature which she had not done before. Sarah said that being a mother had:

> made me feel much more adult. I always felt not properly grown up . . . I always felt as if I'd been a daughter, and a little daughter until I had a family of my own and then I could be an adult daughter.
>
> (Sarah, Interview 3)

Melanie felt the baby made her more contented.

> I think I'm much happier than I was before. It's a difficult thing to put into words. But I think I'm more content. I feel "rounded off."
>
> (Melanie, Interview 4)

Jerri felt that she no longer had to prove herself to others any more

> Now I couldn't care less what they think of me.
>
> (Jerri, Interview 4)

Having the baby gave her that extra edge of confidence. She said that she felt more "herself".

Becoming a mother may enable a greater sense of maturity.

> I feel more separate from my parents. I feel I have joined a "secret club" of
> women who have children.
>
> (Sarah, Interview 3)

Sometimes it is only having a second baby that brings this feeling:

> You feel more of a mother. More at ease. More complete.
>
> (Angela, Interview 4)

However, it was not necessarily the case that achieving motherhood and a
greater sense of maturity or adulthood made someone more secure in their
identity.

> In theory I'm the same. In practice I'm probably slightly less confident
> than I thought I'd be . . . I've changed very little – perhaps I feel a little
> more grown up now.
>
> (Francis, Interview 3)

However, some women do experience some sense of psychological *fulfil-
ment*, which is unmistakable and directly connected to motherhood.

> Fundamentally there is something about being a mum that is quite
> magical really. . . . You can say it's love, motherhood or whatever!
>
> (Meg, Interview 3)

In Sharon's example quoted here below, it is clear how the re-integration
and adaptation to motherhood are a compromise. She is able to acknowledge
what she has lost, but more importantly to recognise that loss in the context
of the gain of being a mother to her child with the positive experiences that
that status has brought to her:

> The difficulty for me is "freedom" – Not being able to go off with my
> husband. If we want to go out having to have prior notice so we can
> have a baby-sitter and then – oh yesterday I was asked to stand in as a
> Godmother – and previously I would have gone off and bought a new
> dress. But I haven't yet worked out how to go off and buy clothes with
> one like this in tow!
>
> Interviewer: How does that make you feel?
>
> Well I had a good time – because when you go out you make much more of
> it because you go out less. So I really didn't feel upset, that I was wearing
> something 5 years old! That's not the point now. I go out to see people and
> talk to them – and I think I get a lot more out of such occasions.
>
> Interviewer: That is like you were saying last time about dinner parties.

Yes – you have friends round – you haven't the time to spend getting the meal ready – you're just pleased to see them as long as the meal's passable.

(Sharon, Interview 4)

Conceptualisation to theory: the added value of qualitative psychology

That pregnancy and childbirth in themselves are potentially disruptive life events (see Elliot, 1990) has been acknowledged to some extent for over 30 years (Holmes & Rahe, 1967). However, the complex psychological issues surrounding the experience of disruption are significant in their absence from traditional psychological literature (see Nicolson, 1998).

Hart (1976) following Glaser and Strauss (1971) argued that identity and status (i.e. social position linked to a role and set of social relationships) are bound together in such a way that status changes occurring at any stage throughout the life cycle potentially involve a shift or re-interpretation of progressively larger amounts of accumulated personal data and can constitute a critical phase for individual identity. The ultimate significance of the status change relates to the importance of the status being lost or acquired, the extent to which it interconnects with other constituent statuses and the level of expectation that surrounds the transition which may have already been partially incorporated into the self (Hart, 1976: 11).

The popular and scientific conceptualisations of the transition to motherhood are characteristically different from other status changes. "Mother" is incorporated into a woman's identity from a very early stage. Its significance and associated behaviours totally define a woman regardless of the detail of her experience of becoming a mother. Paradoxically becoming a mother (on each occasion) represents both a desired change that gains a woman a recognised social position and identity, while it involves disruption and loss of her former position. The pathway from mother of one to mother of more than one child strengthens the role of "mother" but also strengthens the loss of the former self and independence and control over life.

However, while Hart (1976) in relation to divorce has argued that ". . . the life associated with the old status may never be completely discarded" (1976: 104), with the first childbirth, the old status of non-mother is annihilated because of the central importance of "mother" in relation to female identity and the ideological equilibrium between "woman" and "mother". This makes it more difficult for women to experience the loss of their old self in a way conducive to their peace of mind. They are not permitted to grieve or mourn as with other change. If they do they are treated as ill. So strong is the taboo that women themselves frequently fail to admit their sense of loss in a conscious way.

Having a baby is marked by a series of complex losses in their lives alongside the gain of the baby and role of mother. Women are actively prevented from mourning their losses because of social constraint and the unconscious acceptance of those constraints.

Marris (1986) had argued that grieving is a ". . . process of psychological re-integration, impelled by the contradictory desires at once to search for and recover the lost relationships and to escape from painful reminders of loss" (1986: vii).

For mothers, the contradictions are more severe in that the reminder of loss of an autonomous self (i.e. owing to the baby) is constantly present and also as they get to know the baby more, it increasingly becomes the focus of attachment and love (see Sluckin, Herbert, & Sluckin, 1983). Marris' research in a variety of social situations (widowhood, re-housing, pioneering new businesses) led him to identity unifying features. The important feature is that the anxieties associated with change are centred upon the struggle to defend or recover a meaningful pattern of relationships. While he does not specific-ally include childbirth among his social situations, he draws attention to "A characteristic ambivalence, which I first noticed in the reactions of the bereaved, seemed always to inhibit any straightforward adjustment" (1986: 1).

This, Marris suggests is because resistance to change is a fundamental feature of human psychology. In order to adapt to loss and change we have to have the ability to protect the assumptions of experience as well as reconsider them. The continuing viability of a structure of meaning in the face of new kinds of experience ". . . depends on whether we can formulate its principles in terms abstract enough to apply to any event we encounter, or . . . ignore or prevent experiences which could not be comprehended in terms of it" (1986: 17).

Thus an inherent psychological impulse to conservatism insists on the need for continuity of experience. When an essential thread is broken, individuals struggle to repair it – both seeking and resisting change. So a woman (and possibly her partner) might seek to have a baby and accordingly change her life. But this means disruption of her experience of continuity. A grieving process as a means of psychological re-integration is denied under the ideo-logical conditions of the transition to motherhood and is labelled as pathology.

Randomised control trials and qualitative feminist psychology: a profitable partnership?

The study I have described in detail above was relatively small-scale. Twenty-four women were interviewed four times. The original plan for the pre-coded questionnaire would have allowed for and indeed demanded a greater number – around 200 interviews and perhaps a similar number as a follow-up. The data thus would have had some claim to be generalisable to the population of new mothers.

While the final qualitative version of the study was not in itself generalis-able, there is some evidence of its validity and reliability. First, there was an internal consistency across the respondents as discussed. Second, another study of women, some of whom were self-identified as depressed and some not, demonstrated very similar phenomena (Lewis, 1995; Lewis & Nicolson, 1998). This suggests that the findings need to be taken seriously by clinicians and quantitative researchers as a contribution to knowledge, unavailable in the traditional literature. It also indicates the need for planned replication using similar methods with another group of women across the transition to motherhood.

However, in the contemporary climate of research funding and assessment this kind of research needs to ensure it gets taken seriously and must be funded, cited and influential in clinical approaches to PND and women's experiences of motherhood. The future, I believe, lies with a mixture of different approaches to research in this area. Clinical research favours a large-scale design which appears to be the antithesis to qualitative approaches. But need this be the case? There are still a number of research questions unanswered which underlie both kinds of study.

If PND is brought about because of hormone changes at the time of birth, why do significant numbers of women *not* get depressed at that stage? Why do some women suffer from psychotic episodes and others not? Are psychological problems following childbirth, from psychosis to mild depression, part of a continuum or a series of different unrelated conditions? Are there any qualitative differences between depression at this time and other times in a woman's life, or indeed between PND and depression suffered by men?

Contemporary medical research needs to see itself as ("hard") scientific, as with experimental psychology. Thus it eschews the use of subjective data. It is characterised by large-scale randomised control trials (RCTs), frequently sponsored by government agencies or multi-national drug companies, seeking to identify the effectiveness of one treatment, or form of intervention, over another (see Oakley, 1990). Thus participants in the trial will be randomly allocated to different conditions including a control group. In the case of PND the treatment or intervention could range from a particular kind of anti-depressant drug to counselling. Traditionally, a quantifiable outcome measure will be used to see whether the intervention had been effective.

There is a clear case for mixing methods in the context of the RCT for a number of reasons:

1   To decide upon *when* the outcome should be evaluated. For example I demonstrate above, that although behaviour and mood might be similar at three and six months after the birth, the construction and meaning of the experiences are different. This has a bearing on when and what is evaluated.
2   Clinical data fail to inform researchers on the complexities of the conditions of motherhood and family relationships, other than by identifying the impact of a poor marital relationship upon mood and similar variables. Qualitative research will provide rich information about the life

circumstances of each trial participant and assist the way in which the efficacy of the intervention is interpreted.

3   To collect data on the participant's experience of the trial itself including issues of informed consent (did they really understand what the trial required of them?), why in some cases they refused or agreed to take part, their views of the intervention (beyond simply the outcome measure itself) and their general level of satisfaction with services being offered in the community to assist new mothers and their children, partners and wider social networks.

4   This increased depth and richness of information eventually should lead to more effective intervention and preventative measures.

Alternative approaches in clinical research include epidemiological studies using screening instruments and other validated measures to predict the distribution of those who have morbid scores throughout the wider population and to attempt to relate the morbid score to other variables such as age, marital status, social class and so on. Observational studies collect existing data from large-scale populations and use statistical methods to adjust the data in order to predict outcomes and evaluate different models of behaviour or interventions. There is a lot to be said in favour of these kinds of studies.

Conclusions

The scientific understanding of PND has developed over the past 20 years in terms of explaining how often and in what circumstances some women experience it. However the diversity of explanations that remain current in the scientific literature appear to be treading parallel paths with little concession to understanding women's own accounts of why they feel how they do. What is missing it seems is a means and willingness to explore the complexities in the lives of women when they have babies. The transition to motherhood can never be a standardised event – everyone's life is different. Nevertheless researchers in this area appear daunted by the challenge of explaining PND in its everyday context. Equally many feminist qualitative researchers reject association with clinical and traditionally oriented researchers. Mixing methods provides the main way forward if knowledge is to be advanced from both sides of the quantitative–qualitative divide.

RCTs and other large-scale studies, despite their statistical sophistication frequently miss the complexities of context. This does not matter to traditionalists focused upon trends, but the development of concern for consumer needs in health care is gradually leading to an attention to qualitative research data as "wrap around" in clinical studies. It is qualitative data that provide the opportunity for psychological theory building (as described above). The future of feminist qualitative research in the area of women's health hinges upon willingness of both "sides" to pay attention to each other and this is done best by mixing methods and having equal interest in both types of data.

References

Bem, S. L. (1993). *The lenses of gender*. London: Yale University Press.

Bott, E. (1957). *Family and social network*. London: Tavistock.

Boyle, M. (1997). Making gender visible in clinical psychology. *Feminism and Psychology*, 7(2), 231–238.

Brockington, I. F., & Kumar, R. (1982). *Motherhood and mental illness*. London: Academic Press.

Buss, D. M. (1995). The future of evolutionary psychology. *Psychological Inquiry*, 6(1), 81–87.

Cox, J. L. (1994). Introduction and classification dilemmas. In J. Cox & J. Holden (Eds.), *Perinatal psychiatry: Use and misuse of the Edinburgh postnatal depression scale* (pp. 3–5). London: Gaskell/Royal College of Psychiatrists.

Crawford, M., & Maracek, J. (1989). Psychology reconstructs the female: 1968–1988. *Psychology of Women Quarterly*, 13, 147–166.

Dalton, K. (1989, revised edition). *Depression after childbirth*. Oxford: Oxford University Press. (Original were work published 1980)

Eagley, A. H. (1987). *Sex differences in social behaviour: A social role interpretation*. Hillsdale, NJ: Lawrence Erlbaum Associates Inc.

Ehrenreich, B., & English, D. (1979). *For her own good: 150 years of the experts' advice to women*. London: Pluto Press.

Elliot, S. A. (1990). Commentary on "Childbirth as a life event". *Journal of Reproductive and Infant Psychology*, 8, 147–159.

Frieze, I. H., Parsons, J. E., Johnson, P. B., Ruble, D. N., & Zellman, G. L. (1978). *Women and sex roles; A social psychological perspective*. New York: Norton.

Gilligan, C. (1993). *In a different voice: Psychological theory and women's development*. Cambridge, MA: Harvard University Press.

Glaser, B., & Strauss, A. (1971). *Status passage*. Chicago: Aldine.

Griffin, C. (1995). Feminism, social psychology and qualitative research. *The Psychologist*. 8(3), 119–121.

Harding, S. (1991). *Whose science? Whose knowledge?* Milton Keynes: Open University Press.

Hart, N. (1976). *When marriage ends*. London: Tavistock.

Henwood, K., & Pidgeon, N. (1995). Remaking the link: Qualitative research and feminist standpoint theory. *Feminism and Psychology*, 5(1), 7–30.

Hollway, W. (1989). *Subjectivity and method in psychology*. London: Sage.

Holmes, T. M., & Rahe, R. H. (1967). The social re-adjustment rating scale. *Journal of Psychosomatic Research*, 11, 213–218.

Hopkins, J., Marcus, M., & Campbell, S. B. (1984). Postpartum depression: A critical review. *Psychological Bulletin*, 95, 498–515.

Jarman, M., Smith, J. A., & Walsh, S. (1997). The psychological battle for control: A qualitative study of health-care professionals' understandings of the treatment of anorexia nervosa. *Journal of Community and Applied Social Psychology*, 7(2), 137–152.

Lewis, S. E. (1995). A search for meaning: Making sense of depression. *Journal of Mental Health*, 4, 369–382.

Lewis, S. E., & Nicolson, P. (1998). Talking about early motherhood: recognising loss and reconstructing depression. *Journal of Reproductive and Infant Psychology*, 16, 177–197.

McKnight, J. (1999). On the minimum standards of argument a Darwinian would expect of a socially contructed, postmodern and/or feminist gender theorist. *Psychology, Evolution and Gender, 1*(1), 81–96.

Marris, P. (1986). *Loss and change.* London: Tavistock.

Morgan, M. (1998). Qualitative research . . . science or pseudoscience? *The Psychologist, 11*(10), 481–483.

Moscucci, O. (1993). *The science of woman: Gynaecology and gender in England 1800–1929.* Cambridge: Cambridge University Press.

Murray-Parkes, C. (1971). Psychosocial transitions: A field for study. *Social Science and Medicine, 5*, 101–115.

Nicolson, P. (1986). Developing a feminist approach to depression following childbirth. In S. Wilkinson (Ed.), *Feminist social psychology: Developing theory and practice* (pp. 135–149). Milton Keynes: Open University Press.

Nicolson, P. (1988). *The social psychology of post natal depression.* Unpublished PhD thesis, University of London.

Nicolson, P. (1992a). Towards a psychology of women's health and health care. In P. Nicolson and J. M. Ussher (Eds.), *The psychology of women's health and health care* (pp. 6–29). Basingstoke: Macmillan.

Nicolson, P. (1992b). Menstrual cycle research and the construction of female psychology. In J. T. E. Richardson (Ed.), *Cognition and the menstrual cycle: Research, theory and culture* (pp. 174–179). London: Springer Verlag.

Nicolson, P. (1995). Feminism and psychology. In J. A. Smith, R. Harre, & L. van Langenhove (Eds.), *Rethinking methods in psychololgy* (pp. 122–142). London: Sage.

Nicolson, P. (1996). *Gender, power and organisation: A psychological perspective.* London: Routledge.

Nicolson, P. (1998). *Postnatal depression: Psychology, science and the transition to Motherhood.* London: Routledge.

Nicolson, P. (1999). Loss, happiness and postpartum depression: The ultimate paradox. *Canadian Psychology, 40*(2), 162–178.

Oakley, A. (1990). Who's afraid of the randomised control trial? Some dilemmas of the scientific method and "good" research practice. In H. Roberts (Ed.), *Women's health counts* (pp. 167–194). London: Routledge.

Pitt, B. (1968). "Atypical" depression following childbirth. *British Journal of Psychiatry, 122*, 431–433.

Pollock, S., Blurton Jones, N., Evans, M., & Woodson, E. (1980). Continuities in postnatal depression, Paper presented at the British Psychological Society special conference on childbirth, Leicester University.

Rapoport, R., & Rapoport, R. (1976). *Dual career families re-visited.* London: Martin Robertson.

Reinharz, S. (1992). *On becoming a social scientist.* San Francisco: Jossey-Bass.

Sheilds, S. A. (1975). Functionalism, Darwinism and the psychology of women: A study in social myth. *American Psychologist, 30*, 739–754.

Sheilds, S. A., & Crowley, J. J. (1996). Appropriating questionnaires and rating scales for a feminist psychology: A multi-method approach to gender. In S. Wilkinson (Ed.), *Feminist social psychologies* (pp. 218–232), Milton Keynes: Open University Press.

Sluckin, W., Herbert, M., & Sluckin, A. (1983). *Maternal bonding.* Oxford: Basil Blackwell.

Steiner, M. (1979). Psychobiology of mental disorders associated with childbearing: An overview. *Acta Psychiatrica Scandinavica, 60*, 449–464.

Thurtle, V. (1995). Post natal depression: The relevance of sociological approaches. *Journal of Advanced Nursing, 22*, 416–424.

Tunaley, J. R. (1996). *Body size, food and women's identity: A lifespan approach* Unpublished PhD thesis, University of Sheffield.

Ussher, J. M. (1989). *The psychology of the female body*. London: Routledge & Kegan Paul.

Whiffen, V. E. (1992). Is postnatal depression a distinct diagnosis? *Clinical Psychology Review, 12*, 485–508.

Wilkinson, S. J. (Ed.) (1986). *Feminist social psychology: Theory and method*. Milton Keynes: Open University Press.

Wilkinson, S. J. (Ed.) (1996). *Feminist social psychologies*, Milton Keynes: Open University Press.

World Health Organisation (1992). *The ICD-10 classification of mental and behavioural disorder*. Geneva: WHO.

Appendix

INTERVIEW GUIDE: INTERVIEW 1
In this interview I would like to discuss the following with you:
I *Biography*
Name
Occupation/education of both you and the baby's father
Status of relationship with the baby's father
Number of previous children/step children
Who comprises household
Financial arrangements

II *Personal History*
Parents – status of their relationship, where, ages, occupation, relationship with you
Siblings – as above
Changes/movements of family in childhood and since
Schooling/achievements
Past and future occupational details/plans
Ambitions and aspirations/past and present
What led up to this pregnancy?

III *Relationships and Identity*
Reflections on childhood – friendships, siblings, parents
Influential people/events
Evaluation of self growing up: changes
Sexual experiences
Organisation of family life/expectations of changes
Expectations of parenthood: self/partner
Expectations of personal change

IV *Self and Disposition*
Experiences of depression/what was it like/how long/why
Expectations of depression re: parenthood ideas about gender roles
Description of self: strengths and weaknesses
How much control do you want to have over your own life/expectations of changes after birth

12 Future directions

Zazie Todd and Brigitte Nerlich

The use of different methods in combination is likely to become increasingly common. In this volume, we have looked at different theoretical and practical issues around the use of mixed methods in psychology. At a pragmatic level, we argued in the introduction that it makes sense for psychologists to continue to use the most appropriate methods for the research question, and that the combination of methods could provide many advantages at different levels, from the design of individual studies to the shape of the discipline as a whole. Nerlich (this volume) has shown that psychology has traditionally used a range of methods and that the debate about methods in psychology has a long history. Based on a consideration of both the modernist and post-modernist traditions in psychology, Henwood has argued for a re-think of issues around validity, and against the traditional dualism of qualitative versus quantitative. Several chapters (Harré & Crystal; Clarke; Stenner & Stainton-Rogers, this volume) have argued in different ways for the blending of methods to create a "hybrid psychology" or "qualiquantology". Harré and Crystal considered the kinds of explanation that psychology should seek, whilst Clarke proposed ways in which "natural psychology" can find a place within the discipline. Stenner and Stainton-Rogers provided an example of the use of Q-methodology. Other chapters have looked at specific issues to do with the design of mixed method studies. Pidgeon et al. (this volume) considered the importance of interviews within a quantitative study, and Todd and Lobeck (this volume) considered issues around triangulation of focus group and questionnaire studies. Nicolson (this volume) argued for the important contribution of qualitative feminist psychology to an understanding of post-natal depression, whilst Vann and Cole (this volume) considered the importance of quantitative methods within the toolkit of cultural psychology. Finally, the benefits of both qualitative and quantitative studies in the development of theories of difficult behaviour in schools, and in developing relationships between researchers and practitioners, was described by Miller (this volume).

Each chapter has taken a particular approach to a problem with mixed method research. The complexity of these issues is reflected in the diversity of arguments proposed. In this final chapter, we want to identify several areas for future development, and sketch out some ideas as to how mixed method studies might evolve. These areas are: the need for training; the continued evolution of criteria for assessing research; re-assessing and mixing qualitative methods; the analysis of large-scale qualitative datasets; and research reviews.

Training

In some social science disciplines, it is believed that there is a high level of expertise in qualitative methods, but not enough scholars have expertise in quantitative methods. In psychology, the situation is different. Psychologists receive general training in statistics and experimental design as part of their undergraduate degrees, and this is reinforced with more advanced study at postgraduate level. Until recently most psychologists did not receive any training in qualitative methods as part of their undergraduate degrees, and current provision of training at postgraduate level is patchy, with detailed training mostly restricted to institutions with high levels of expertise. Indeed, while there is some consensus as to the quantitative methodology training that undergraduate psychologists require, there is no consensus on the extent or type of training in qualitative methods that they should receive. Recent guidelines published by the Learning and Teaching Support Network in the UK (Gough, Lawton, Madill, & Stratton, 2003) are a first step towards defining the qualitative training that undergraduate students should get, and towards improving the delivery of such teaching.

Few psychologists are experts in both quantitative and qualitative research methods. This means that, for the most part, a mixed method study will require collaboration with colleagues. Since it will usually be the case that expertise in qualitative research will be lacking, we feel that improved training provision in qualitative research methods is required. Whilst training in mixed method research would also be welcome, at the current time there is a need for more work to be done in the field before a consensus could be reached – not only into how to carry out mixed method research, but also into which aspects should then be taught. On the quantitative side, some development of methods for analysis of large scale corpus data and in mathematical modelling would also improve mixed method research.

Criteria for assessing research

The traditional criteria for assessing quantitative research in psychology are in general well established. This is not to say that they have been fixed in stone, as indeed they continue to develop (witness the increasing attention given to calculations of effect size, for example). Through the increasing use of qualitative methods in psychology and related disciplines, it has become apparent that different criteria are needed for qualitative studies. For instance, since many qualitative studies use only a small number of participants, it has been suggested that the traditional criterion of generalis-ability be replaced with one of transferability (Lincoln & Guba, 1985). Several authors have already suggested sets of criteria for assessing qualita-tive research (see e.g. Yardley, 2000; Elliot, Fischer, & Rennie, 1999). While the suggestion of criteria is to be welcomed, there has also been a debate about whether or not they provide unnecessary constraints for qualitative researchers. See the chapter by Henwood (this volume) for further consider-ation of this and related issues.

If we are to apply separate criteria to quantitative and qualitative research, then we need to consider which criteria we will apply to mixed method studies. Yin's (1994) excellent volume on case studies already provides some ideas, and the field has also been advanced by Tashakkori and Teddlie's work (1998) which contains many useful suggestions. Indeed, Tashakkori & Teddlie's logically exhaustive categorisation of mixed model designs provides a frame-work within which criteria for mixed method studies could be developed.

Re-assessing and mixing qualitative methods

When deciding to use qualitative methods alongside a quantitative study, which method do you pick? One issue affecting the decision will clearly be expertise, since it is important to have knowledge of the methods you are going to use. However, this is also a potential problem, as people will pick the method they find easiest to use, without considering whether it is the best for the research question. The research question will of course always shape the method of qualitative analysis – as to whether you are interested in the con-versational structure, the rhetoric used to present ideas, or the content of what people have said.

The increased – and welcome – use of data depositories makes qualitative data (as well as quantitative data) available for re-analysis by other researchers, possibly many years after the original point of data collection, and with potentially quite different research questions in mind. The re-use of data in this way will inevitably lead to the possibility of comparing different qualitative methods of analysis with each other, even without this being a primary aim of the re-analysis. Thus, would you expect to achieve triangula-tion using different methods of qualitative data analysis? Quite possibly not, and depending on the epistemological standpoint it might not even be seen as desirable. The practice of different groups using different methods to analyse the same data set may already be an occasional way of teaching research students about qualitative methods, and a helpful way of illustrating differences among them, but to our knowledge this has not been carried out systematically on data sets as a way of comparing them. One study that has looked empirically at this question is Madill, Jordan and Shirley (2000), in which two separate grounded theory analyses were applied to the same data set.

Analysis of large-scale qualitative databases

One area in which qualitative and quantitative methods are likely to be used in combination is in the analysis of large-scale qualitative databases, such as studies in which many participants were interviewed. Qualitative analysis is time-consuming, and even with the use of computers to assist data analysis, a full qualitative analysis might ultimately be prohibitive. One likely outcome is that qualitative analysis will be merged with quantitative analysis, hopefully providing a richer understanding of participants' views and experiences whilst also encapsulating something important about the whole data set. It is already the case that some researchers use a quantitative or partly quantitative analysis of qualitative data. For example, Cornah, Sonuga-Barke, Stevenson and Thompson (2003) conducted a quantitative analysis of maternal attributions from unstructured interview data. From a set of 142 interviews (part of a wider study), they selected 70 for analysis, on the basis of attributes of the mother and child. The data were coded for attributions by raters who were blind to prior information about the mother and child. These data were then available for quantitative analysis, and also used as the basis for categorisation under which further analyses of standardised questionnaires was conducted. In this case, unstructured interview data have been converted into quantitative data on the topic in question.

Another approach to a large corpus of qualitative data, as already mentioned, is to combine a qualitative analysis with some quantitative information. This is the approach taken by Trix and Psenka (2003) in their analysis of letters of recommendation for faculty. Their analysis of 312 letters used both critical discourse analysis and corpus analytic methods. The quantitative analysis found that letters of recommendation written for women faculty were shorter, more likely to be what they term "letters of minimal assurance", were more likely to include doubt raisers, and more likely to include grindstone adjectives. The quantitative analysis is presented within an important critical framework. Thus, for example, whilst letters for both genders were equally likely to mention research, letters for men were much more likely to mention it more than once; and there were more lines using scientific terminology. Research ability is essential for faculty, and the use of terminology demonstrates that the author has knowledge of the research area, making the candidate seem more serious, whilst repetition also strengthens the case for research ability. Thus, in this study, the items of analysis that were used for the quantitative study were derived from a critical discourse analytic perspective.

Another approach to using quantitative methods in a qualitative analysis was used by Kuiken and Miall (2001) in their numerically aided phenomenology. After using phenomenology to identify constituents from qualitative data, they calculated similarity co-efficients and carried out a cluster analysis. In turn, this enabled the identification of which constituents belonged in which category, and participants could be classified according to the kind of response they had given. They argue that:

numerically aided phenomenology integrates some of the sources of precision available through quantitative methods with some of the sources of precision promised by qualitative methods. Their integration provides both rigor and subtlety. Their rigor derives from the contribution that numeric algorithms make to judgements of "extent"; their subtlety derives from careful comparisons of the meanings that are expressed in numerous experiential narratives.

(Kuiken & Miall, 2001: Section 5)

In this case, the quantitative measures are used to give clarity and structure to the qualitative results. Harré and Crystal (this volume) and Vann and Cole (this volume) consider similar issues: the use of statistics within a discursive approach, and of quantitative methods within the interpretive tradition, respectively.

These are three very different approaches to the use of quantitative methods in the analysis of qualitative data: wholly quantitative analysis of qualitative data, quantitative analysis guided by qualitative analysis, and qualitative analysis developed further by quantitative analysis. The difference is not just one of degree but also of philosophical underpinnings. The increasing use and availability of large qualitative data sets, and advances in corpus analytic techniques, mean that such approaches will develop further in the years to come.

Research reviews

Quite apart from whether or not researchers within a particular field of research choose to adopt a mixed method approach, it is highly likely that some researchers within the field will sometimes use quantitative research, and others will sometimes use qualitative. This gives rise to two related potential problems: considering what extent to make use of the "alternative" approach when conducting background literature reviews for a particular study, and considering how to successfully incorporate the findings from both approaches into a literature review.

There are two main approaches to conducting research reviews. Statistical meta-analyses allow researchers to combine findings from many different experimental or quasi-experimental studies, and have been useful in many fields. The problem here is that it is apparently impossible to include qualitative studies that deal with words and meanings rather than numbers and frequencies. There is a danger that qualitative research will not contribute fully to the development of a field if it is left out of such summaries. One group that is currently investigating solutions to this problem is the Qual-Quan Evidence Synthesis Group at the University of Leicester. An approach they are testing is the use of Bayesian meta-analysis techniques for the inclusion of qualitative research in a systematic review (Dixon-Woods, Fitzpatrick, & Roberts, 2001).

Another approach to research reviews is the use of content analysis. This looks at which words and phrases are used, how frequently, and perhaps how that has changed over time, in order to build up a picture of a research field. Since such an approach directly involves words, it is obvious that qualitative studies are not neglected by this approach. Since qualitative researchers are often interested in different aspects of a topic than quantitative researchers, it would be interesting to know if the results of such content analyses might reveal chasms within a discipline.

This brings us to another important point. Qualitative research has often worked to try to change the discipline, and to persuade (some) psychologists to reconceptualise the way they think about particular topics. One example of this is the approach taken to attitudes by social psychologists. Quantitative social psychologists, working with attitude scales within the theory of planned behaviour (Ajzen, 1991) have been investigating how to predict people's behaviour based on their attitudes, beliefs and expectations. On the other hand discursive social psychologists such as Potter and Wetherell (1987) have argued for an approach that looks at talk and text in interaction, instead of locating attitudes within individuals. Wiggins and Potter (in press), for example, argue that a discursive approach to food evaluations in mealtime conversations highlights distinctions that have been missed by traditional attitude researchers. Another area in which discursive psychology has tried to challenge experimental approaches is the area of cognitive psychology (see Edwards, 1997).

All of this means that even if we take a pragmatic approach to integrating both qualitative and quantitative work within a research overview, we will still come up against philosophical and epistemological issues. Inclusion of such contrasting approaches within research reviews will be important, but another question will be to consider the extent to which each method can bring a useful approach to the research topics and the extent to which the shape of the discipline should be changed. While one approach directly challenges the other, it is questionable to say that both contribute equally.

Conclusions

In this volume, we have explored various issues around the use of mixed method research in psychology. In this chapter, we have identified potentially useful areas of future research. We predict that mixed method research will increase in importance, and as it does so it is necessary to develop appropriate guidelines and criteria, and to ensure that researchers have the necessary expertise and training. We argued that both qualitative and quantitative approaches have an important role to play in the discipline, and that it is therefore important to develop ways of conducting research reviews that will take account of work conducted using both approaches. Since qualitative psychology has tended, historically, to be less valued within psychology as a discipline, we particularly make the case that ways of incorporating results from qualitative studies into research reviews must be developed that do not undermine the qualitative nature of the studies and their stress on participants' meanings. We advocate a pragmatic approach, whereby it makes sense to adopt the research method(s) most appropriate for the research question. At the same time, however, we recognise that different approaches have different epistemological underpinnings, and further investigation of the (in)compatibilities within methods will lead to a better understanding of the position of the subject in psychology.

References

Ajzen, I. (1991). The theory of planned behaviour. *Organizational Behaviour and Human Decision Processes, 50*, 179–211.

Cornah, D., Sonuga-Barke, E., Stevenson, J., & Thompson, M. (2003). The impact of maternal mental health and child's behavioural difficulties on attributions about child behaviours. *British Journal of Clinical Psychology, 42*, 69–79.

Dixon-Woods, M., Fitzpatrick, R., & Roberts, K. (2001). Including qualitative research in systematic reviews: Problems and opportunities. *Journal of Evaluation in Clinical Practice, 7*, 125–133.

Edwards, D. (1997). *Discourse and Cognition*. London: Sage.

Elliot, R., Fischer, C., & Rennie, D. (1999). Evolving guidelines for publication of qualitative research studies in psychology and related fields. *British Journal of Clinical Psychology, 38*, 215–229.

Gough, B., Lawton, R., Madill, A., & Stratton, P. (2003). *Guidelines for the supervision of undergraduate qualitative research in psychology*. York: Learning and Teaching Support Network.

Kuiken, D., & Miall, D. S. (2001, February). Numerically aided phenomenology: Procedures for investigating categories of experience [68 paragraphs]. *Forum Qualitative Sozialforschung / Forum: Qualitative Social Research* [Online journal] 2(1). Available at http://qualitative-research.net/fqs/fqs-eng.htm [date of access: 15 October 2002].

Lincoln, Y. S., & Guba, E. G. (1985). *Naturalistic enquiry*. Beverly Hills, CA: Sage.

Madill, A., Jordan, A., & Shirley, C. (2000). Objectivity and reliability in qualitative analysis: Realist, contextualist and social constructionist epistemologies. *British Journal of Psychology, 91*, 1–20.

Tashakkori, A., & Teddlie, C. (1998). *Mixed methodology: Combining qualitative and quantitative approaches*. Applied Social Research Methods Series, Volume 46. London: Sage.

Trix, F., & Psenka, C. (2003). Exploring the color of glass: Letters of recommendation for female and male medical faculty. *Discourse and Society, 14*, 191–220.

Wiggins, S., & Potter, J. (in press). Attitudes and evaluative practices: Category vs item and subjective vs objective constructions in everyday food assessments. *British Journal of Social Psychology*.

Yardley, L. (2000). Dilemmas of qualitative research. *Psychology and Health, 15*, 215–228.

Yin, R. K. (1993). *Case study research: Design and methods* (2nd ed.). Applied Social Reseach Methods Series, Volume 5. London: Sage.

Further reading

Part I

Brannen, J. (Ed.) (1992). *Mixing methods: Qualitative and quantitative research*. Aldershot: Avebury.

Bryman, A. (1988). *Quantity and quality in social research*. London: Unwin.

Henwood, K., & Pidgeon, N. (1995). Beyond the qualitative paradigm: A framework for introducing diversity in to qualitative psychology. *Journal of Community and Applied Social Psychology*, *4*(4), 225–238.

Henwood, K. L., Griffin, C., & Phoenix, A. (Eds.) (1998). *Standpoints and differences: Essays in the practice of feminist psychology*. London: Sage.

Danziger, K. (1990). *Constructing the subject. Historical origins of psychological research*. Cambridge: Cambridge University Press.

Part II

Armstrong, J. S. (Ed.) (2001). *Principles of forecasting: A handbook for researchers and practitioners*. Norwell, MA: Kluwer.

Clarke, D. D., & Blake, H. (1997). The inverse forecast effect. *Journal of Social Behavior and Personality*, *12*(4), 999–1018.

Clarke, D. D., & Letchford, A. N. (1998). Action rules extracted by machine induction from feature-coded self-reports. *Journal of Social Behavior and Personality*, *13*(1), 33–50.

Harré, R. (2002). *Cognitive science: A philosophical introduction*. London: Sage.

Harré, R., & Gillett, G. (1994). *The discursive mind*. London: Sage.

Smith, J., Harré, R., & van Langenhove, L. (Eds.) (1995). *Rethinking methods in psychology*. London: Sage.

Stainton Rogers, W. (1991). *Explaining health and illness: an exploration in diversity*. Hemel Hempstead: Harvester Wheatsheaf.

Stainton Rogers, R. (1995). Q Methodology. In J. Smith, R. Harré, & L. van Langengrove (Eds.), *Rethinking methods in psychology*. London: Sage (pp. 178–192).

Stenner, P., Dancey, C., & Watts, S. (2000). The understanding of their illness amongst people with irritable bowel syndrome: A Q methodological study. *Social Science and Medicine*, *51*, 439–452.

Part III

Baron, J. (1997). Biases in the quantitative measurement of values for public decisions. *Psychological Bulletin, 122*, 72–88.

Billig, M., Condor, S., Edwards, D., Gane, M., Middleton, D., & Radley, A. (1988). *Ideological dilemmas: A social psychology of everyday thinking*. London: Sage.

Cole, M. (1996). *Cultural psychology: A once and future discipline*. Cambridge, MA: The Belknap Press of Harvard University Press.

Henwood, K. L., & Pidgeon, N. F. (1992). Qualitative research and psychological theorizing. *British Journal of Psychology, 83*, 97–111.

Kaplowitz, M. D. (2000). Statistical analysis of sensitive topics in group and individual interviews. *Quality and Quantity, 34*, 419–431.

Kidd, P. S., & Parshall, M. B. (2000). Getting the focus and getting the group: Enhancing analytical rigor in focus group research. *Qualitative Health Research, 10*, 293–308.

Massé, R. (2000). Qualitative and quantitative analyses of psychological distress: Methodological complementarity and ontological incommensurability. *Qualitative Health Research, 10*, 411–423.

Ratner, C. (1997). *Cultural psychology and qualitative methodology: Theoretical and empirical considerations*. New York: Plenum.

Scribner, S., & Cole, M. (1981). *The psychology of literacy*. Cambridge, MA: Harvard University Press.

Part IV

Bem, S. L. (1993). *The lenses of gender*. London: Yale University Press.

Dixon-Woods, M., Fitzpatrick, R., & Roberts, K. (2001). Including qualitative research in systematic reviews: Problems and opportunities. *Journal of Evaluation in Clinical Practice, 7*, 125–133.

Gilligan, C. (1993). *In a different voice: Psychological theory and women's development*. Cambridge, MA: Harvard University Press.

Miller, A. (1995). Building grounded theory within educational psychology practice. *Educational and Child Psychology, 12*, 5–14.

Miller, A. (1996). *Pupil behaviour and teacher culture*. London: Cassell.

Nicolson, P. (1998). *Postnatal depression: Psychology, science and the transition to motherhood*. London: Routledge.

Tashakkori, A., & Teddlie, C. (1998). *Mixed methodology: combining qualitative and quantitative approaches*. Applied Social Research Methods Series, Volume 46. London: Sage.

Wilkinson, S. J. (Ed.) (1996). *Feminist social psychologies*, Milton Keynes: Open University Press.

Yardley, L. (2000). Dilemmas of qualitative research. *Psychology and Health, 15*, 215–228.

Author index

Subject index